D1222679

Picture-Perfect
Science
Lessons

Picture-Perfect
Science
Lessons

Using Children's Books to Guide Inquiry

Grades 3–6

By Karen Rohrich Ansberry
and Emily Morgan

NSTApress
National Science Teachers Association

Arlington, Virginia

National Science Teachers Association

Claire Reinburg, Director
Judy Cusick, Senior Editor
Andrew Cocke, Associate Editor
Betty Smith, Associate Editor

ART AND DESIGN, Linda Olliver, Director
   Linda Olliver, Cover art and interior illustration
PRINTING AND PRODUCTION, Catherine Lorrain, Director
   Nguyet Tran, Assistant Production Manager
   Jack Parker, Electronic Prepress Technician

NATIONAL SCIENCE TEACHERS ASSOCIATION
Gerald F. Wheeler, Executive Director
David Beacom, Publisher

Library of Congress Cataloging-in-Publication Data
Ansberry, Karen Rohrich, 1966-
  Picture perfect science lessons : using children's books to guide inquiry / by Karen Rohrich Ansberry and Emily Morgan.
     p. cm.
  Includes bibliographical references and index.
         ISBN   978-0-87355-243-1
  1. Science—Study and teaching (Elementary) 2. Children's books. I. Morgan, Emily R. (Emily Rachel), 1973- II. Title.
  Q181.A66 2004
  372.3'5044—dc22

                              2004018033

NSTA is committed to publishing quality material that promotes the best in inquiry-based science education. However, conditions of actual use may vary and the safety procedures and practices described in this book are intended to serve only as a guide. Additional precautionary measures may be required. NSTA and the authors do not warrant or represent that the procedures and practices in this book meet any safety code or standard of federal, state, or local regulations. NSTA and the authors disclaim any liability for personal injury or damage to property arising out of or relating to the use of this book including any of the recommendations, instructions, or materials contained therein.

Contents

Foreword

I had the good fortune to meet the authors of *Picture-Perfect Science Lessons*, Karen Rohrich Ansberry and Emily Morgan, in the fall of 2003 at a workshop I facilitated on inquiry-based science. At that event, we had a lively discussion about the nature of science and how the teachers in attendance might impart their love of science to elementary-age children. The authors then took me aside and told me of their plans to write a book for teachers (and parents, too) using children's literature to engage children in scientific inquiry. I have always believed that children in the elementary grades would experience more science if elementary teachers were provided better ways to integrate literacy and science. So, of course, I was intrigued.

As I reviewed this manuscript, I was reminded of one of my favorite "picture books" as an adult—*The Sense of Wonder* by Rachel Carson. In that book, Ms. Carson expresses her love of learning and how she helped her young nephew discover the wonders of nature. As she expressed,

> I sincerely believe that for the child, and for the parent seeking to guide him, it is not half so important to know as to feel. If facts are the seeds that later produce knowledge and wisdom, then the emotions and the impressions of the senses are the fertile soil in which the seeds must grow. The years of early childhood are the time to prepare the soil. Once the emotions have been aroused—a sense of the beautiful, the excitement of the new and the unknown, a feeling of sympathy, pity, admiration or love—then we wish for knowledge about the object of our emotional response. Once found, it has lasting meaning. It is more important to pave the way for the child to want to know than to put him on a diet of facts he is not ready to assimilate. (Carson 1956)

Rachel Carson used the natural environment to instill in her nephew the wonders of nature and scientific inquiry, but I believe, along with the authors, that picture books can have a similar emotional effect on children and inspire their wonder and their curiosity. Then, when teachers and parents couple scientific inquiry experiences with the content of the picture books, science really comes to life for children. *Picture-Perfect Science Lessons* provides an ideal framework that encourages children to read first; explore objects, organisms, and events related to what they've read; discern relationships, patterns, and explanations in the world around them; and then read more to gather more information which will lead to new questions worth investigating.

In addition, *Picture-Perfect Science Lessons* is the perfect antidote to leaving science behind in the elementary classroom. As elementary teachers struggle to increase the basic literacy of all students, they often cannot find the time to include science in the curriculum, or they are discouraged from teaching science when literacy scores decline. Teachers need resources such as *Picture-Perfect Science Lessons* to genuinely integrate science and literacy.

There is no doubt that inquiry-based science experiences motivate children to learn. Through this book, teachers have the best of both worlds—they will have the resources to motivate children to read and to "do science." What could be better?

As one of the developers of the BSCS 5E Instructional Model, I was gratified to learn that the authors intended to use the "5Es" to structure their learning experiences for children and teachers. These authors, as with many teachers across the country, had become acquainted with the 5Es and used the model extensively to promote learning in their own classrooms; however, they did not know the origin of the model until we had a conversation about BSCS and the 5Es. This book helps to set the record straight—the 5E Instructional Model was indeed developed at BSCS in the late 1980s in conjunction with an elementary curriculum project and thus is appropriately titled "The BSCS 5E Instructional Model" in this book. The authors' iterative use of the BSCS 5Es is appropriate because the model is meant to be fluid where one exploration leads to a partial explanation that invites further exploration before a child has a grasp of a complete scientific explanation for a phenomenon. As the authors mention, the final E—evaluate—is applied more formally at the end of a unit of study, but the BSCS 5E model by no means implies that teachers and students do not evaluate, or assess, student learning as the students progress through the model. Ongoing assessment is an integral part of the philosophy of the BSCS 5Es and the authors appropriately weave formative assessment into each lesson.

Once you place your toe into the waters of this book, I guarantee that you will dive right in! Whether you are a teacher, a parent, or both, you will enjoy this inviting approach to inquiry-based science. If you follow the methods outlined in *Picture-Perfect Science Lessons*, you and the children with whom you interact will have no choice but to learn science concepts through reading and scientific inquiry.

I don't know about you, but I'm rather curious about those sheep in a jeep. Enjoy!

Nancy M. Landes
Director
Center for Professional Development
Biological Sciences Curriculum Study

Reference

Carson, R. 1956. *The sense of wonder.* Berkeley, CA: The Nature Company. (Copyright renewed 1984 by Roger Christie. Text copyright 1956 by Rachel Carson.)

Preface

A class of fifth-grade students laughs as their teacher reads Jeanne Willis's *Dr. Xargle's Book of Earthlets.* Students are listening to the alien professor, Dr. Xargle, teaching his pupils about Earthlets (human babies): "Earthlets are born without fangs. At first, they drink only milk, through a hole in their faces called a mouth. When they finish the milk, they are patted and squeezed so they won't explode." The fifth grade class giggles at his outrageous lesson as Dr. Xargle continues to lecture. Students then begin sorting cards containing some of the alien professor's "observations" of Earthlets. The teacher asks her students, "Which of Dr. Xargle's comments are truly observations?" Students review their cards and realize that many of his comments are not observations but rather hilariously incorrect inferences. They re-sort their cards into two groups: observations and inferences. This amusing picture book and word sorting activity guide students into a hands-on inquiry where they make observations about sealed mystery samples Dr. Xargle collected from Earth. Eventually students develop inferences about what the mystery samples might be. Through this exciting lesson, students construct their own understandings of the difference between an observation and an inference, how scientists use observations and inferences, and how to make good observations and inferences.

What Is Picture-Perfect Science?

This scenario describes how a children's picture book can help guide students through an engaging, hands-on inquiry lesson. *Picture-Perfect Science Lessons* contains 15 science lessons for students in grades three through six, with embedded reading comprehension strategies to help them learn to read and read to learn while engaged in inquiry-based science. To help you teach according to the National Science Education Standards, the lessons are written in an easy-to-follow format for teaching inquiry-based science: the Biological Sciences Curriculum Study 5E Instructional Model (Bybee 1997, used with permission from BSCS). This learning cycle model allows students to construct their own understanding of scientific concepts as they cycle through the following phases: Engage, Explore, Explain, Elaborate, and Evaluate. Although *Picture-Perfect Science Lessons* is primarily a book for teaching science, reading comprehension strategies are embedded in each lesson. These essential strategies can be modeled throughout while keeping the focus of the lessons on science.

Use This Book Within Your Science Curriculum

We wrote *Picture-Perfect Science Lessons* to supplement, not replace, an existing science program. Although each lesson stands alone as a carefully planned learning cycle based on clearly defined science objectives, the lessons are intended to be integrated into a more complete unit of instruction in which concepts can be more fully developed. The lessons are not designed to be taught sequentially. We want you to use *Picture-Perfect Science Lessons* where appropriate within your school's current science curriculum to support, enrich, and extend it. And we want you to adapt the lessons to fit your school's curriculum, the needs of your students, and your own teaching style.

Special Features

1. Ready-to-Use Lessons with Assessments

Each lesson contains engagement activities, hands-on explorations, student pages, suggestions for student and teacher explanations, opportunities for elaboration, assessment suggestions, and annotated bibliographies of more books to read on the topic. Assessments range from poster sessions with rubrics to teacher checkpoint labs to formal multiple choice and extended response quizzes.

2. Reading Comprehension Strategies

Reading comprehension strategies based on the book *Strategies that Work* (Harvey and Goudvis 2000) and specific activities to enhance comprehension are embedded throughout the lessons and clearly marked with an icon 📖. Chapter 2 describes how to model these strategies while reading aloud to students.

3. Standards-Based Objectives

All lesson objectives were adapted from *National Science Education Standards* (NRC 1996) and are clearly identified at the beginning of each lesson. Because we wrote *Picture-Perfect Science Lessons* for students in grades three though six, we used two grade ranges of the Standards: K–4 and 5–8. Chapter 5 outlines the National Science Education Standards for those grade ranges and shows the correlation between the lessons and the Standards.

4. Science as Inquiry

As we said, the lessons in *Picture-Perfect Science Lessons* are structured as guided inquiries following the 5E model. Guiding questions are embedded throughout each lesson and marked with an icon ?. The questioning process is the cornerstone of good teaching. A teacher who asks thoughtful questions arouses students' curiosity, promotes critical thinking skills, creates links between ideas, provides challenges, gets immediate feedback on student learning, and helps guide students through the inquiry process. Each lesson includes an "Inquiry Place," a section at the end of the lesson that suggests ideas for developing open inquiries. Chapters 3 and 4 explore science as inquiry and the BSCS 5E instructional model.

References

Bybee, R. W. 1997. *Achieving scientific literacy: From purposes to practices.* Portsmouth, NH: Heinemann.

Harvey, S., and A. Goudvis. 2000. *Strategies that work: Teaching comprehension to enhance understanding.* York, ME: Stenhouse Publishers.

National Research Council. 1996. *National science education standards.* Washington, DC: National Academy Press.

Children's Book Cited

Willis, J. 2003. *Dr. Xargle's book of earthlets.* London, UK: Anderson Press Ltd.

Editors' Note: *Picture-Perfect Science Lessons* builds upon the texts of 27 children's picture books to teach science. Some of these books feature animals that have been anthropomorphized—sheep crash a jeep, a hermit crab builds his house. While we recognize that many scientists and educators believe that personification, teleology, animism, and anthropomorphism promote misconceptions among young children, others believe that removing these elements would leave children's literature severely under-populated. Further, backers of these techniques not only see little harm in their use but also argue that they facilitate learning.

Because *Picture-Perfect Science Lessons* specifically and carefully supports scientific inquiry—"The Changing Moon" lesson, for instance, teaches students how to weed out misconceptions by asking them to point out inaccurate depictions of the Moon—we, like our authors, feel the question remains open.

Acknowledgments

We would like to give special thanks to science consultant Carol Collins for sharing her expertise in teaching inquiry-based science, for giving us many wonderful opportunities to share *Picture-Perfect Science Lessons* with teachers, and for continuing to support and encourage our efforts.

We would also like to express our gratitude to language arts consultant Susan Livingston for opening our eyes to the power of modeling reading strategies in the content areas and for teaching us that every teacher is a reading teacher.

We appreciate the care and attention to detail given to this project by Claire Reinburg, Betty Smith, and Linda Olliver at NSTA Press. And these thank you's as well:

- To the Ohio Department of Education for funding our very first teacher workshop.
- To NSTA and Toyota Motor Corporation for giving us a jump start with the Toyota Tapestry Grant in 2002.
- To all the wonderful teachers and students of Mason City Schools for trying our lessons and giving us feedback for improvement.
- To the administration of Mason City Schools for supporting our efforts.
- To Nancy Landes at BSCS for helping us to better understand the 5Es and guiding us with her advice.
- To Diana Hunn and Katie Kinnucan-Welsh for their help with our research study.
- To Patricia Quill and her students at Western Row Elementary for piloting our lessons in their classroom.
- To Krissy Hufnagel for sharing her expertise in teaching reading.
- To Jean Muetzel and Sil Bobinski, wonderful librarians at Western Row Elementary, for going to the ends of the Earth to find picture books for us.
- To Ray Bollhauer and John Odell for their legal and business advice.
- To Christopher Canyon for inspiring us with his beautiful artwork and for encouraging us with kind words.
- To Jeff Alt for advising us to keep calling, keep calling, keep calling …
- To Jenni Davis for the opportunities to share Picture-Perfect Science with teachers.
- To Jodee Seibert with Heinemann Library for supplying us with books to preview.
- To John R. Meyer at North Carolina State University Department of Entomology and Don Koller and Mike Wright at Mi-

ami University of Ohio for having the "gall" to review our Close Encounters dichotomous key.

- To Linda Sutphin for reviewing Close Encounters.

- To Chris Lucas for proofreading sections of the book.

- To Amy Bleimund for sharing *Seven Blind Mice* with us.

- To Shirley Hudspeth and her class at Mason Intermediate School for trying out the turtle fortune-tellers.

- To Kim Rader and her class at Mason Intermediate School for their popcorn investigations.

- To Julie Wellbaum for her "instrumental help" with the Sounds of Science lesson.

- To Sheri Hill, John Hutton, Sandra Gross, and all the good people at the Blue Manatee Children's Bookstore in Cincinnati for helping us in our search for fabulous picture books.

- To Michelle Gallite and Erica Poulton for help in "cleaning up" our Oil Spill! lesson.

- To Theresa Gould and the research staff at RiceTec for their advice on growing rice in the classroom.

- To Gerald Skoog for reviewing material in Chapter 11.

- To our husbands, families, and friends for their moral support.

- And to our parents, who were our very first teachers.

The contributions of the following reviewers are also gratefully acknowledged: Mariam Jean Dreher, Nancy Landes, Christine Anne Royce, Carol Collins, Lisa Nyberg, and Chris Pappas.

About the Authors

Karen Rohrich Ansberry is the elementary science curriculum leader and a former fifth- and sixth-grade science teacher at Mason City Schools, in Mason, Ohio. She has a Bachelor of Science in Biology from Xavier University and a Master of Arts in Teaching from Miami University. Karen lives in historic Lebanon, Ohio, with her husband, Kevin, and their two dogs and two cats.

Emily Morgan is a Science Consultant at the Hamilton County Educational Service Center in Cincinnati, Ohio. She is a former elementary science lab teacher at Mason City Schools in Mason, Ohio, and a seventh-grade science teacher at Northridge Local Schools in Dayton, Ohio. She has a Bachelor of Science in Elementary Education from Wright State University and a Master of Science in Education from the University of Dayton. Emily lives in West Chester, Ohio, with her husband, Jeff, and their dog and two cats.

Karen and Emily, along with language arts consultant Susan Livingston, received a Toyota Tapestry grant for their Picture-Perfect Science grant proposal in 2002.

They share a passion for science, nature, animals, travel, food, and children's literature. They enjoy working together to facilitate Picture-Perfect Science teacher workshops.

KAREN ROHRICH ANSBERRY, RIGHT, AND EMILY MORGAN, DEVELOPED *PICTURE-PERFECT SCIENCE LESSONS* BASED ON THEIR WORKSHOPS SUPPORTED BY A TOYOTA TAPESTRY GRANT.

About the Picture-Perfect Science Program

The Picture-Perfect Science program originated from Emily Morgan's and Karen Ansberry's shared interest in using children's literature to make science more engaging. In Emily's 2001 master's thesis study involving 350 of her third-grade science lab students at Western Row Elementary, she found that students who used science trade books instead of the textbook scored significantly higher on district science performance assessments than students who used the textbook only. Convinced of the benefits of using picture books to engage students in science inquiry and to increase science understanding, Karen and Emily began collaborating with Susan Livingston, the elementary language arts curriculum leader for the Mason, Ohio, City Schools, in an effort to integrate literacy strategies into inquiry-based science lessons. They received grants from the Ohio Department of Education (2001) and Toyota Tapestry (2002) in order to train all third-grade through sixth-grade science teachers, and in 2003 also trained seventh- and eighth-grade science teachers with district support. The program has been presented both locally and nationally, including at the National Science Teachers Association national conventions in San Diego and Philadelphia.

For more information on Picture-Perfect Science teacher workshops, go to: *www.pictureperfectscience.com*

How to Find the Picture Books

Almost all of the picture books used in the lessons were recently available at *www.powells.com*. The great majority can also be found in libraries, both public and school, at bookstores, or at other online booksellers. Here are ways, listed by chapter, in which you can find the three books that might not be available through those sources.

Chapter 6, "Earthlets"

Dr. Xargle's Book of Earthlets can be ordered at *www.powells.com*.

Chapter 15, "Sound"

Perfection Learning publishers (*www. perfectionlearning.com*) will make single copies of *Sound*, normally available in packages of six, available to readers of *Picture-Perfect Science Lessons*. The price at press time was $7.00 plus shipping costs.

Send the following e-mail to Customer Service Supervisor Shannon Troshynski at *stroshynski@plconline.com*:

Please send me a single copy, number 38658, of *Sound* by Jenny Karpelenia for use with *Picture-Perfect Science Lessons: Using Children's Books to Guide Inquiry* published by NSTA Press. *Sound* is part of Perfection Learning's *Energy Works!* series in Physical Science, Reading Essentials in Science.

Chapter 19, "Erosion"

Perfection Learning publishers (*www. perfectionlearning.com*) will make single copies of *Erosion,* normally available only in packages of six, available to readers of *Picture-Perfect Science Lessons*. The price at press time was $7.00.

Send the following e-mail to Customer Service Supervisor Shannon Troshynski at *stroshynski@plconline.com*:

Please send me a single copy, number 39595, of *Erosion* by Virginia Castleman for use with *Picture-Perfect Science Lessons: Using Children's Books to Guide Inquiry* published by NSTA Press. *Erosion* is part of Perfection Learning's *The Weather Report* series in Earth/ Space Science, Reading Essentials in Science.

Lessons by Grade

Why Read Picture Books in Science Class?

Think about a book you loved as a child. Maybe you remember the zany characters and rhyming text of Dr. Seuss classics like *Green Eggs and Ham* or *The Lorax*. Perhaps you enjoyed the page-turning suspense of *The Monster at the End of This Book* or the fascinating facts found in Joanna Cole's *Dinosaur Story*. You may have seen a little of yourself in *Where the Wild Things Are, Curious George,* or *Madeline*. Maybe your imagination was stirred by the detailed illustrations in *Jumanji* or the stunning photographs in Seymour Simon's *The Moon*. You probably remember the warm, cozy feeling of having a treasured book like *The Snowy Day* or *Goodnight Moon* being read to you by a parent or grandparent. But chances are your favorite book as a child was *not* your fourth-grade science textbook! The format of picture books offers certain unique advantages over textbooks and chapter books for engaging students in a science lesson. More often than other books, fiction and nonfiction picture books stimulate students on both the emotional and intellectual levels. They are appealing and memorable because children readily connect with the imaginative illustrations, vivid photographs, experiences and adventures of characters, engaging storylines, the fascinating information that supports them in their quest for knowledge, and the warm emotions that surround the reading experience.

What characterizes a picture book? We like what *Beginning Reading and Writing* says, "Picture books are unique to children's literature as they are defined by format rather than content. That is, they are books in which the illustrations are of equal importance as or more important than the text in the creation of meaning" (Strickland and Morrow 2000). Because picture books are more likely to hold children's attention, they lend themselves to reading comprehension strategy instruction and to engaging students within an inquiry-based cycle of science instruction. "Picture books, both fiction and nonfiction, are more likely to hold our attention and engage us than reading dry, formulaic text. ... engagement leads to remembering what is read, acquiring knowledge and enhancing understanding" (Harvey and Goudvis 2000). We wrote *Picture-Perfect Science Lessons* so teachers can take advantage of the positive features of children's picture books by supplementing the traditional science textbook with a wide variety of high-quality fiction and nonfiction science-related picture books.

The Research

1. Context for Concepts

Literature gives students a context for the concepts they are exploring in the science classroom. Children's picture books, a branch of literature, have interesting storylines that can help students understand and remember concepts better than they would by using textbooks alone, which tend to present science as lists of facts to be memorized (Butzow and Butzow 2000). In addition, the colorful pictures and graphics in picture books are superior to many texts for explaining abstract ideas (Kralina 1993). As more and more content is packed into the school day, and higher expectations are placed on student performance, it is critical for teachers to teach more in the same amount of time. Integrating curriculum can help accomplish this. The wide array of high-quality children's literature available today can help you model reading comprehension strategies while teaching science content in a meaningful context.

2. More Depth of Coverage

Science textbooks can be overwhelming for many children, especially those who have reading problems. They often contain unfamiliar vocabulary and tend to cover a broad range of topics (Casteel and Isom 1994; Short and Armstrong 1993; Tyson and Woodward 1989). However, fiction and nonfiction picture books tend to focus on fewer topics and give more in-depth coverage of the concepts. It can be useful to pair an engaging fiction book with a nonfiction book to round out the science content being presented.

For example, "Oil Spill!" the Chapter 13 lesson, features both *Prince William*, a fictionalized account of a young girl's experience rescuing an oil-covered baby seal, and *Oil Spill!*, a nonfiction book detailing causes and effects of oil spills. The emotion-engaging storyline and the realistic characters in *Prince William* hook the reader, and the book, *Oil Spill!*, presents facts and background information. Together they offer a balanced, in-depth look at how oil spills affect the environment.

3. Improved Reading and Science Skills

Research by Morrow, Pressley, Smith, and Smith (1997) on using children's literature and literacy instruction in the science program indicated gains in science as well as literacy. Romance and Vitale (1992) found significant improvement in both science and reading scores of fourth graders when the regular basal reading program was replaced with reading in science that correlated with the science curriculum. They also found an improvement in students' attitudes toward the study of science.

4. Opportunities to Correct Science Misconceptions

Students often have strongly held misconceptions about science that can interfere with their learning. "Misconceptions, in the field of science education, are preconceived ideas that differ from those currently accepted by the scientific community" (Colburn 2003). Children's picture books, reinforced with hands-on inquiries, can help students correct their misconceptions. Repetition of the correct concept by reading several books, doing a number of experiments, and inviting scientists to the classroom can facilitate a conceptual change in children (Miller, Steiner, and Larson 1996).

But teachers must be aware that scientific misconceptions can be inherent in the picture books. Although many errors are explicit, some of the misinformation is more implicit or may be inferred from text and illustrations (Rice 2002). This problem is more likely to occur within fictionalized material. Mayer's (1995) study demonstrated that when both inaccuracies and science facts are presented in the same book, children do not necessarily remember the correct information.

Scientific inaccuracies in picture books can be useful for teaching. Research shows that errors in picture books, whether identified by the teacher or the students, can be used to help children learn to question the accuracy of what they read by comparing their own observations to the science presented in the books (Martin 1997). Scientifically inaccurate children's books can be helpful when students analyze inaccurate text or pictures after they have gained understanding of the correct scientific concepts through inquiry experiences.

For example, in "The Changing Moon" lesson, Chapter 17, students analyze the inaccurate moon phases in Eric Carle's *Papa, Please Get the Moon for Me* and then correct them through their own illustrations of the story. This process takes students to a higher level of thinking as they use their knowledge to evaluate and correct the misinformation in the picture book.

Use with Upper Elementary Students

Picture-Perfect Science Lessons is designed for students in grades three through six. Although picture books are more commonly used with younger children, we have good reasons to recommend using them with upper elementary students. In *Strategies that Work* (2000), reading experts Harvey and Goudvis maintain that "the power of well-written picture books cannot be overestimated ... picture books lend themselves to comprehension strategy instruction at every grade level." The benefits of using picture books to teach science and reading strategies are not reserved for younger children. We have found them effective for engaging students, for guiding scientific inquiry, and for teaching comprehension strategies to students in kindergarten through eighth grade. We believe that the wide range of topics, ideas, and genres found in picture books reaches all readers, regardless of their ages, grades, reading levels, or prior experiences.

Selection of Books

Each lesson in *Picture-Perfect Science Lessons* focuses on one or more of the National Science Education Standards. We selected one to three fiction and/or nonfiction children's picture books that closely relate to the Standards. An annotated "More Books to Read" section is provided at the end of each lesson. If you would like to select more children's literature to use in your science classroom, try *The Outstanding Science Trade Books for Students K-12* listing, a cooperative project between the National Science Teachers Association (NSTA) and the Children's Book Council (CBC). The books are selected by a book review panel appointed by the NSTA and assembled in cooperation

with the CBC. Each year a new list is featured in the March issue of NSTA's elementary school teacher journal, *Science and Children.* See *www.nsta.org/ostbc* for archived lists.

When you select children's picture books for science instruction, you should consult with a knowledgeable colleague who can help you check them for errors or misinformation. You might talk with a high school science teacher, a retired science teacher, or a university professor. To make sure that the books are developmentally appropriate or lend themselves to a particular reading strategy you want to model, you could consult with a language arts specialist.

Finding Out-of-Print Books

We have included the most up-to-date information we have, but children's picture books go in and out of print frequently. Check your school library, public library, or a used-book store for copies of out-of-print books. In addition, the following Web sites may be helpful:

- *www.abebooks.com*—abebooks.com is a large online marketplace for books that can locate new, used, rare, or out-of-print books through a community of more than 12,000 independent booksellers from around the world.

- *www.alibris.com*—Alibris connects people with books, music, and movies from thousands of independent sellers around the world. They offer more than 35 million used, new, and hard-to-find titles to consumers, libraries, and retailers.

- *www.bibliofind.com*—Bibliofind has combined with Amazon.com to provide millions of rare, used, and out-of-print books.

- *www.powells.com*—Powell's has an extensive list of both new and used books.

Considering Genre

Considering genre when you determine how to use a particular picture book within a science lesson is important. Donovan and Smolkin (2002) identify four different genres frequently recommended for teachers to use in their science instruction: story, non-narrative information, narrative information, and dual purpose. *Picture-Perfect Science Lessons* identifies the genre of each featured book at the beginning of each lesson. Summaries of the four genres, a representative picture book for each genre, and suggestions for using each genre within the BSCS 5E learning cycle we use follow. (The science learning cycle known as the BSCS 5E Model is described in detail in Chapter 4.)

Storybooks

Storybooks center on specific characters who work to resolve a conflict or problem. The major purpose of stories is to entertain, not to present factual information. The vocabulary is typically commonsense, everyday language. An engaging storybook can spark interest in a science topic and move students toward informational texts to answer questions inspired by the story. For example, "Earthlets," Chapter 6, uses the storybook *Dr. Xargle's Book of Earthlets* to hook the learners and engage them in an inquiry about mystery samples from Planet Earth.

Scientific concepts in stories are often implicit, so teachers must make the concepts explicit to students. As we mentioned, be aware that storybooks often contain scientific errors, either explicit or implied by text or illustrations. Storybooks with scientific errors should not be used in the introduction of a topic, but may be used later in the lesson to teach students how to identify and correct the misconceptions. For example, "The Changing Moon," Chapter 17, features Eric Carle's *Papa, Please Get the Moon for Me*, a storybook that contains many scientific inaccuracies. This book would not be appropriate for introducing how the Moon seems to change shape, but it can be a powerful vehicle for assessing the ability of learners to analyze the scientific accuracy of a text.

Non-narrative Information Books

Non-narrative information books are factual texts that introduce a topic, describe the attributes of the topic, or describe typical events that occur. The focus of these texts is on the subject matter, not specific characters. The vocabulary is typically technical. Readers can enter the text at any point in the book. Many contain features found in nonfiction such as a table of contents, bold-print vocabulary words, a glossary, and an index. Young children tend to be less familiar with this genre and need many opportunities to experience this type of text. Using non-narrative information books will help students become familiar with the structure of textbooks, as well as "real-world" reading, which is primarily expository. Teachers may want to read only those sections that provide the concepts and facts needed to meet particular science objectives.

We wrote the articles included in some of the lessons (see chapters 8, 11, 14, and 16) in non-narrative information style to give students more opportunity to practice reading this type of text. For example, "Close Encounters of the Symbiotic Kind," Chapter 11, includes an article written in an expository style that shows key words in bold print. Another example of non-narrative information writing is the book *Rice*, which contains nonfiction text features such as a table of contents, bold-print words, diagrams, a glossary, and an index. *Rice* is featured in "Rice Is Life," Chapter 8. The appropriate placement of non-narrative information text in a science learning cycle is after students have had the opportunity to explore concepts through hands-on activities. At that point, students are engaged in the topic and are moti-

vated to read the non-narrative informational text to learn more.

Narrative Information Books

Narrative information books, sometimes referred to as "hybrid books," provide an engaging format for factual information. They communicate a sequence of factual events over time and sometimes recount the events of a specific case to generalize to all cases. When using these books within science instruction, establish a purpose for reading so that students focus on the science content rather than the storyline. In some cases, teachers may want to read the book one time through for the aesthetic components of the book and a second time for specific science content. *Animal Lives: The Barn Owl*, an example of a narrative information text, is used in "Mystery Pellets," Chapter 10. This narrative chronicles a year in the life of a barn owl and contains factual information about barn owls. The narrative information genre can be used at any point within a science learning cycle. This genre can be both engaging and informative.

Dual-Purpose Books

Dual-purpose books are intended to serve two purposes: present a story and provide facts. They employ a format that allows readers to use the book like a storybook or to use it like a non-narrative information book. Sometimes information can be found in the running text, but more frequently it appears in insets and diagrams. Readers can enter on any page to access specific facts, or they can read it through as a story. You can use the story component of a dual-purpose book to engage the reader at the beginning of the science learning cycle. For example, Chapter 8 features the book, *Rice Is Life*, which is used to engage the students in an investigation about rice.

Dual-purpose books typically have little science content within the story. Most of the

informational ideas are found in the insets and diagrams. If the insets and diagrams are read, discussed, explained, and related to the story, these books can be very useful in helping students refine concepts and acquire scientific vocabulary *after* they have had opportunities for hands-on exploration. *One Tiny Turtle* is a dual-purpose book listed in the "More Books to Read" section of Chapter 12, "Turtle Hurdles." Although the story part is a lyrical depiction of one turtle's journey, the insets can be read to give students factual information about the characteristics and life cycles of sea turtles.

Using Fiction and Nonfiction Texts

As we mentioned previously, pairing fiction and nonfiction books in read alouds to round out the science content being presented is effective. Because fiction books tend to be very engaging for students, they can be used to hook students at the beginning of a science lesson. But most of the reading people do in everyday life is nonfiction. We are immersed in informational text every day, and we must be able to comprehend it in order to be successful in school, at work, and in society. Nonfiction books and other informational text such as articles should be used frequently in the elementary classroom. They often include text structures that differ from stories, and the opportunity to experience these structures in read alouds can strengthen students' abilities to read and understand informational text. Duke (2004) recommends four strategies to help teachers improve students' comprehension of informational text. Teachers should

- increase students' access to informational text.

- increase the time they spend working with informational text.

- teach comprehension strategies through direct instruction.

- create opportunities for students to use informational text for authentic purposes.

Picture-Perfect Science Lessons addresses these recommendations in several ways. The lessons expose students to a variety of nonfiction picture books and articles on science topics, thereby increasing access to informational text. The lessons explain how word sorts, anticipation guides, pairs reading, and using nonfiction features all help improve students' comprehension of the informational text by increasing the time they spend working with it. Each lesson also includes instructions for explicitly teaching comprehension strategies within the learning cycle. The inquiry-based lessons provide an authentic purpose for reading informational text, as students are motivated to read or listen in order to find the answers to questions generated within the inquiry activities.

References

Butzow, J., and C. Butzow. 2000. *Science through children's literature: An integrated approach.* Portsmouth, NH: Teacher Ideas Press.

Casteel, C. P., and B. A. Isom. 1994. Reciprocal processes in science and literacy learning. *The Reading Teacher* 47: 538–544.

Colburn, A. 2003. *The lingo of learning: 88 education terms every science teacher should know.* Arlington, VA: NSTA Press.

Donovan, C., and L. Smolkin. 2002. Considering genre, content, and visual features in the selection of trade books for science instruction. *The Reading Teacher* 55: 502–520.

Duke, N.K. 2004. The case for informational text. *Educational Leadership* 61: 40–44.

Harvey, S., and A. Goudvis. 2000. *Strategies that work: Teaching comprehension to enhance understanding.* York, ME: Stenhouse Publishers.

Kralina, L. 1993. Tricks of the trades: Supplementing your science texts. *The Science Teacher* 60(9): 33–37.

Martin, D. J. 1997. *Elementary science methods: A constructivist approach.* Albany, NY: Delmar.

Mayer, D. A. 1995. How can we best use children's literature in teaching science concepts? *Science and Children* 32(6): 16–19, 43.

Miller, K. W., S. F. Steiner, and C. D. Larson. 1996. Strategies for science learning. *Science and Children* 33(6): 24–27.

Morrow, L. M., M. Pressley, J. K. Smith, and M. Smith. 1997. The effect of a literature-based program integrated into literacy and science instruction with children from diverse backgrounds. *Reading Research Quarterly*, 32: 54–76.

National Research Council. 1996. *National science education standards.* Washington, DC: National Academy Press. Available online at *books.nap.edu/books/0309053269/html/index.html*

Rice, D. C. 2002. Using trade books in teaching elementary science: Facts and fallacies. *The Reading Teacher* 55(6): 552–565.

Romance, N. R., and M. R. Vitale. 1992. A curriculum strategy that expands time for in-depth elementary science instruction by using science-based reading strategies: Effects of a year-long study in grade four. *Journal of Research in Science Teaching* 29: 545–554.

Short, K. G., and J. Armstrong. 1993. Moving toward inquiry: Integrating literature into the science curriculum. *New Advocate* 6(3): 183–200.

Strickland, D. S., and L. M. Morrow, eds. 2000. *Beginning reading and writing.* New York, NY: Teachers College Press.

Tyson, H., and A. Woodward. 1989. Why aren't students learning very much from textbooks? *Educational Leadership* 47(3): 14–17.

Children's Books Cited

Bemelmans, L. 1958. *Madeline.* New York, NY: Viking Press.

Berger, M. 1994. *Oil spill!* New York, NY: HarperTrophy.

Brown, M. W. 1976. *Goodnight moon.* New York, NY: HarperCollins.

Carle, E. 1986. *Papa, please get the moon for me.* New York, NY: Simon & Schuster.

Cole, J. 1974. *Dinosaur story.* New York, NY: William Morrow.

Davis, N. 2001. *One tiny turtle.* Cambridge, MA: Candlewick Press.

Gelman, R. G. 2000. *Rice is life.* New York, NY: Henry Holt.

Keats, E. J. 1963. *The snowy day.* New York, NY: Viking Press.

Rand, G. 1992. *Prince William.* New York, NY: Henry Holt.

Rey, H. A. 1973. *Curious George.* Boston, MA: Houghton Mifflin.

Sendak, M. 1988. *Where the wild things are.* New York, NY: HarperCollins.

Seuss, Dr. 1960. *Green eggs and ham.* New York, NY: Random House Books for Young Readers.

Seuss, Dr. 1971. *The lorax.* New York, NY: Random House Books for Young Readers.

Simon, S. 1984. *The Moon.* Salem, OR: Four Winds.

Spilsbury, L. 2001. *Rice.* Chicago, IL: Heinemann Library.

Stone, J. 2003. *The monster at the end of this book.* New York, NY: Golden Books.

Tagholm, S. 1999. *Animal lives: The barn owl.* New York, NY: Kingfisher.

Van Allsburg, C. 1981. *Jumanji.* Boston, MA: Houghton Mifflin.

Willis, J. 2003. *Dr. Xargle's book of earthlets.* London, UK: Anderson Press.

Reading Aloud

This chapter addresses some of the research supporting the importance of reading aloud, tips to make your read-aloud time more valuable, descriptions of Harvey and Goudvis's six key reading strategies (2000), and tools you can use to enhance students' comprehension during read-aloud time.

Why Read Aloud?

Being read to is the most influential activity for building the knowledge required for eventual success in reading (Anderson et al. 1985). It improves reading skills, increases interest in reading and literature, and can even improve overall academic achievement. A good reader demonstrates fluent, expressive reading and models the thinking strategies of proficient readers, helping to build background knowledge and fine-tune students' listening skills. When a teacher does the reading, children's minds are free to anticipate, infer, connect, question, and comprehend (Calkins

READ-ALOUD TIME IS A SPECIAL PART OF MRS. WILSON'S CLASS.

2000). In addition, being read to is risk-free. In *Yellow Brick Roads: Shared and Guided Paths to Independent Reading 4–12* (2000), Allen says, "For students who struggle with word-by-word reading, experiencing the whole story can finally give them a sense of the wonder and magic of a book."

Reading aloud is appropriate in all grade levels and for all subjects. It is important not only when children can't read on their own but also even after they have become proficient readers (Anderson et al. 1985). Allen supports this view: "Given the body of research supporting the importance of read-aloud for modeling fluency, building background knowledge, and developing language acquisition, we should remind ourselves that those same benefits occur when we extend read-aloud beyond the early years. You may have to convince your students of the importance of this practice, but after several engaging read-alouds they will be sold on the idea" (2000). Just as students of all ages enjoy a good picture book, none of them is too old to enjoy read-aloud time.

Ten Tips for Reading Aloud

We have provided a list of tips to help you get the most from your read-aloud time. Using these suggestions can help set the stage for learning, improve comprehension of science material, and make the read-aloud experience richer and more meaningful for both you and your students.

1 Preview the Book

Select a book that meets your science objectives *and* lends itself to reading aloud. Preview it carefully before sharing it with the students. Are there any errors in scientific concepts or misinformation that could be inferred from the text or illustrations? If the book is not in story form, is there any nonessential information you could omit to make the read-aloud experience better? If you are not going to read the whole book, choose appropriate starting and stopping points before reading.

2 Set the Stage

Because reading aloud is a performance, you should pay attention to the atmosphere and physical setting of the session. Gather the students in a special reading area, such as on a carpet or in a semicircle of chairs. Seat yourself slightly above them. Do not sit in front of a bright window where the glare will keep students from seeing you well or in an area where students can be easily distracted. You may want to turn off the overhead lights and read by the light of a lamp or use soft music as a way to draw students into the mood of the text. Establish expectations for appropriate behavior during read-aloud time, and, before reading, give the students an opportunity to settle down and focus their attention on the book.

3 Celebrate the Author and Illustrator

Always announce the title of the book, the author, and the illustrator before reading. Build connections by asking students if they have read other books by the author or illustrator. Increase interest by sharing facts about the author or illustrator from the book's dust jacket or from library or Internet research. This could be done either before or after the reading. The following resources are useful for finding information on authors and illustrators:

Books
- Kovacs, D., and J. Preller. 1991. *Meet the authors and illustrators: Volume one.* New York, NY: Scholastic.
- Kovacs, D., and J. Preller. 1993. *Meet the authors and illustrators: Volume two.* New York, NY: Scholastic.
- Peacock, S. 2003. *Something about the author: Facts and pictures about authors and illustrators of books for young people.* Farmington Hills, MI: Gale Group.

- Preller, J. 2001. *The big book of picture-book authors and illustrators.* New York, NY: Scholastic.

Web Sites

- *www.teachingbooks.net*—Teaching Books continually identifies, catalogs, and maintains reliable links to children's books' author and illustrator Web sites and organizes them into categories relevant to teachers' needs.

- *www.cbcbooks.org*—The Children's Book Council (CBC) is a nonprofit trade organization encouraging literacy and the use and enjoyment of children's books. Its Web site has a feature titled "About Authors and Illustrators" with links to author and illustrator Web sites.

4 Read with Expression

Practice reading aloud to improve your performance. Try listening to yourself read on a tape recorder. (One of the *Picture-Perfect Science Lessons* authors practices reading aloud to her dog!) Can you read with more expression to more fully engage your audience? Try louder or softer speech, funny voices, facial expressions, or gestures. Make eye contact with your students every now and then as you read. This strengthens the bond between reader and listener, helps you gauge your audience's response, and cuts down on off-task behaviors. Read slowly enough that your students have time to build mental images of what you are reading, but not so slowly that they lose interest. When reading a nonfiction book aloud, you may want to pause after reading about a key concept to let it sink in, and then re-read that part. At suspenseful parts in a storybook, use dramatic pauses or slow down and read softly. This can move the audience to the edge of their seats!

5 Share the Pictures

Don't forget the power of visual images to help students connect with and comprehend what you are reading. Make sure that you hold the book in a way such that students can see the pictures on each page. Read captions if appropriate. In some cases, you may want to hide certain pictures so students can infer from the reading before you reveal the illustrator's interpretation of the text.

6 Encourage Interaction

Keep chart paper and markers nearby in case you want to record questions or new information. Try providing students with "think pads" in the form of sticky notes to write on as you read aloud. Not only does this help extremely active children keep their hands busy while listening, but it also encourages students to interact with the text as they jot down questions or comments. After the read aloud, have students share their questions and comments. You may want students to place their sticky notes on a class chart whose subject is the topic being studied. Another way to encourage interaction without taking the time for each student to ask questions or comment is to do an occasional "Think-Pair-Share" during the read-aloud. Stop reading, ask a question, allow thinking time, and then have each student share answers or comments with a partner.

7 Keep the Flow

Although you want to encourage interaction during a read aloud, avoid excessive interruptions that may disrupt fluent, expressive reading. Aim for a balance between allowing students to hear the language of the book uninterrupted and providing them with opportunities to make comments, ask questions, and share connections to the reading. As we have suggested, you may want to read the book all the way through one time so students can enjoy the aesthetic components of the story. Then go back and read the book for the purpose of meeting the science objectives.

8 Model Reading Strategies

Use read-aloud time as an opportunity to model questioning, making connections, visualizing, inferring, determining importance, and synthesizing. Modeling these reading comprehension strategies when appropriate before, during, and/or after reading helps students internalize the strategies and begin to use them in their own reading. These six key strategies are described in detail later in this chapter.

9 Don't Put It Away

Keep the read-aloud book accessible to students after you read it. They will want to get a close-up look at the pictures and will enjoy reading the book independently. Don't be afraid of reading the same book more than once. Younger children benefit especially from the repetition.

10 Have Fun

Let your passion for books show. It is contagious! Read nonfiction books with interest and wonder. Share your thoughts and questions about the topic and your own connections to the text. When reading a story, let your emotions show—laugh at the funny parts and cry at the sad parts. Seeing an authentic response from the reader is important for students. If you read with enthusiasm, read-aloud time will become special and enjoyable for everyone involved.

Reading Comprehension Strategies

A common misconception about reading is that students are fully capable of reading to learn in the content areas by the time they reach the upper elementary grades. But becoming a proficient reader is an ongoing, complex process, and people of all ages must develop strategies to improve their reading skills. In *Strategies that Work,* Harvey and Goudvis identify six key reading strategies that are essential for achieving full understanding when we read. These strategies are used where appropriate in each lesson and are seamlessly embedded into the 5E model. The strategies should be modeled as you read aloud to students from both fiction and nonfiction texts. Research shows that explicit teaching of reading comprehension strategies can foster comprehension development (Duke and Pearson 2002). Explicit teaching of the strategies is the initial step in the gradual-release-of-responsibility approach to delivering reading instruction (Fielding and Pearson 1994). During this first phase of the gradual-release method, the teacher *explains* the strategy, demonstrates *how* and *when* to use the strategy, explains *why* it is worth using, and *thinks aloud* in order to model the mental processes used by good readers. Duke (2004) describes this process: "I often discuss the strategies in terms of good readers, as in 'Good readers think about what might be coming next.' I also model the uses of comprehension strategies by thinking aloud as I read. For example, to model the importance of monitoring understanding, I make comments such as, 'That doesn't make sense to me because ...' or 'I didn't understand that last part —I'd better go back.'" Using the teacher modeling phase within a science learning cycle will reinforce what students do during reading instruction, when the gradual-release-of-responsibility model can be continued. After teacher modeling, students should be given opportunities in the reading classroom for both guided and independent practice until they are ready to apply the strategy in their own reading.

Descriptions of the six key reading comprehension strategies featured in *Strategies that Work* follow. The ☠ icon highlights these strategies here and within the lessons.

Making Connections

Making meaningful connections during reading can improve comprehension and engagement by helping learners better relate to what they read. Comprehension breakdown that occurs when reading or listening to expository text can come from a lack of prior information. These three techniques can help readers build background knowledge where little exists.

- *Text-to-Self* connections occur when readers link the text to their past experiences or background knowledge.
- *Text-to-Text* connections occur when readers recognize connections from one book to another.
- *Text-to-World* connections occur when readers connect the text to events or issues in the real world.

Questioning

Proficient readers ask themselves questions before, during, and after reading. Questioning allows readers to construct meaning, find answers, solve problems, and eliminate confusion as they read. It motivates readers to move forward in the text. Asking questions is not only a critical reading skill but is also at the heart of scientific inquiry and can lead students into meaningful investigations.

Visualizing

Visualizing is the creation of mental images while reading or listening to text. Mental images are created from the learner's emotions and senses, making the text more concrete and memorable. Imagining the sensory qualities of things described in a text can help engage learners and stimulate their interest in the reading. When readers form pictures in their minds, they are also more likely to stick with a challenging text. During a reading, you can stop and ask students to visualize the scene. What sights, sounds, smells, colors are they imagining?

Inferring

Reading between the lines, or inferring, involves a learner's merging clues from the reading with prior knowledge to draw conclusions and interpret the text. Good readers make inferences before, during, and after reading. Inferential thinking is also an important science skill and can be reinforced during reading instruction.

Determining Importance

Reading to learn requires readers to identify essential information by distinguishing it from nonessential details. Deciding what is important in the text depends upon the purpose for reading. In *Picture-Perfect Science Lessons,* the lesson's science objectives determine importance. Learners read or listen to the text to find answers to specific questions, to gain understanding of science concepts, and to identify science misconceptions.

Synthesizing

In synthesizing, readers combine information gained through reading with prior knowledge and experience to form new ideas. In order to synthesize, readers must stop, think about what they have read, and contemplate its meaning before continuing on through the text.

Tools to Enhance Comprehension

We have identified several activities and organizers that can enhance students' science understanding and reading comprehension in the lessons. These tools, which support the Harvey and Goudvis reading comprehension strategies, are briefly described on the following pages and in more detail within the lessons.

Anticipation Guides

Anticipation guides (Herber 1978) are sets of questions that serve as a pre- or post-reading activity for a text. They can be used to activate and assess prior knowledge, determine misconceptions, focus thinking on the reading, and motivate reluctant readers by stimulating interest in the topic. An anticipation guide should revolve around four to six key concepts from the reading that learners respond to before reading. They will be motivated to read or listen carefully in order to find the evidence that supports their predictions. After reading, learners revisit their anticipation guide to check their responses. In a revised extended anticipation guide (Duffelmeyer and Baum 1992), learners are required to justify their responses and explain why their choices were correct or incorrect.

 ## Chunking

Chunking is dividing the text into manageable sections and reading only a section at any one time. This gives learners time to digest the information in a section before moving on. Chunking is also a useful technique for weeding out essential from nonessential information when reading nonfiction books. Reading only those parts of the text that meet your learning objectives focuses the learning on what is important.

 ## Visual Representations

Organizers such as T-charts; K-W-L charts ("What I **K**now, What I **W**ant to Know, What I **L**earned") (Ogle 1986); O-W-L charts ("**O**bservations, **W**onderings, **L**earnings"); the Frayer Model (Frayer, Frederick, and Klausmeier 1969); semantic maps (Billmeyer and Barton 1998); and personal vocabulary lists (Beers and Howell 2004) can help learners activate prior knowledge, organize their thinking, understand the essential characteristics of con-

cepts, or see relationships among concepts. They can be used for prereading, for assessment, or for summarizing or reviewing material. Visual representations are effective because they help learners perceive abstract ideas in more concrete form. Examples of these visual representations, with instructions for using them within the lesson, can be found throughout the book. (See Chapters 6, 8, 12, and 14 for examples of T-charts. See Chapter 9 for an example of a K-W-L chart. See Chapters 6 and 16 for examples of the Frayer Model. See Chapters 7, 10, and 11 for examples of O-W-L charts. See Chapter 8 for an example of a semantic map. See Chapter 19 for a variation of a personal vocabulary list.)

 ## Pairs Read

Pairs read (Billmeyer and Barton 1998) requires the learners to work cooperatively as they read and make sense of a text. While one learner reads aloud, the other listens and then summarizes the main idea. Encourage students to ask their partners to reread if clarification is needed. Benefits of pairs read include increased reader involvement, attention, and collaboration. In addition, students become more independent, less reliant on the teacher.

 ## Rereading

Nonfiction text is often full of unfamiliar ideas and difficult vocabulary. Rereading content for clarification is an essential skill of proficient readers, and you should model this frequently. Rereading content for a different purpose can aid comprehension. For example, you might read aloud a text for enjoyment and then revisit the text to focus on specific science content.

 ## Sketch to Stretch

During sketch to stretch (Seigel 1984), learners pause to reflect on the text and do a comprehension self-assessment by drawing on paper the images they visualize in their heads during reading. They might illustrate an important event from the text, sketch the characters in a story, or make a labeled diagram. Have students use pencils so they understand the focus should be on collecting their thoughts rather than creating a piece of art. You may want to use a timer so students understand that sketch to stretch is a brief pause to reflect quickly on the reading. Students can share and explain their drawings in small groups after sketching.

 ## Stop and Jot

Learners stop and think about the reading and then jot down a thought. They may write about something they've just learned, something they are wondering about, or what they expect to learn next. If they use sticky notes for this, the notes can be added to a whole-class chart to connect past and future learning.

 ## Think-Pair-Share

Learners pair up with a partner to share their ideas, explain concepts in their own words, or tell about a connection they have to the book. This method allows each child to respond so that everyone in the group is involved as either a talker or a listener. Saying "Take a few minutes to share your thoughts with someone" gives students an opportunity to satisfy their needs to express their own thoughts about the reading.

 ## Word Sorts

Word sorts (Gillett and Temple 1983) help learners understand the relationships among key concepts and help teach classification. They can also reveal misconceptions if you use them as a prereading activity. Ask learners to sort vocabulary terms, written on cards, into different categories. In an *open sort*, learners sort the words into categories of their own mak-

ing. They can classify and reclassify to help refine their understanding of concepts. In a *closed sort*, you give them the categories for sorting. Learners can also use the vocabulary words to build sentences about specific concepts before and after reading. (See Chapters 10, 11, and 14 for examples of word sorts.)

 ## Using Features of Nonfiction

Many nonfiction books include a table of contents, index, glossary, bold-print words, picture captions, diagrams, and charts that provide valuable information. Because children are generally more used to narrative text, they often skip over these text structures. It is important to model how to interpret the information these features provide the reader. To begin, show the cover of a nonfiction book and read the title and table of contents. Ask students to predict what they'll find in the book. Show students how to use the index in the back of the book to find specific information. Point out other nonfiction text structures as you read and note that these features are unique to nonfiction. Model how nonfiction books can be entered at any point in the text, because they generally don't follow a storyline.

Why Do Picture Books Enhance Comprehension?

Students should be encouraged to read a wide range of print materials, but picture books offer many advantages when teaching reading comprehension strategies. Harvey and Goudvis not only believe that interest is essential to comprehension, but they also maintain that, because picture books are extremely effective for building background knowledge and teaching content, instruction in reading comprehension strategies during picture book read alouds allows students to better access that content. In summary, picture books are invaluable for teaching reading comprehension strategies because they are extraordinarily effective at keeping readers engaged and thinking.

References

Allen, J. 2000. *Yellow brick roads: Shared and guided paths to independent reading 4-12*. Portland, ME: Stenhouse Publishers.

Anderson, R. C., E. H. Heibert, J. Scott, and I. A. G. Wilkinson. 1985. *Becoming a nation of readers: The report of the commission on reading*. Champaign, IL: Center for the Study of Reading; Washington, DC: National Institute of Education.

Beers, S., and L. Howell. 2004. *Reading strategies for the content areas: An action tool kit, volume 2*. Alexandria, VA: Association for Supervision and Curriculum Development.

Billmeyer, R., and M. L. Barton. 1998. *Teaching reading in the content areas: If not me, then who?* Aurora, CO: Mid-continent Regional Educational Leadership Laboratory.

Calkins, L. M. 2000. *The art of teaching reading*. Boston, MA: Pearson Allyn & Bacon.

Duffelmeyer, F. A., and D. D. Baum. 1992. The extended anticipation guide revisited. *Journal of Reading* 35: 654–656.

Duke, N. K. 2004. The case for informational text. *Educational Leadership* 61: 40–44.

Duke, N. K., and P. D. Pearson. 2002. Effective practices for developing reading comprehension. In *What research has to say about reading instruction*, edited by A. E. Farstrup and S. J. Samuels. Newark, DE: International Reading Association.

Fielding, L., and P. D. Pearson. 1994. Reading comprehension: What works? *Educational Leadership* 51(5): 62–67.

Frayer, D. A., W. E. Frederick, and H. J. Klausmeier. 1969. *A schema for testing the level of concept mastery*. Madison, WI: University of Wisconsin Research and Development Center for Cognitive Learning.

Gillett, J. W., and C. Temple. 1983. *Understanding reading problems: Assessment and instruction*. Boston, MA: Little, Brown.

Harvey, S., and A. Goudvis. 2000. *Strategies that work: Teaching comprehension to enhance understanding*. York, ME: Stenhouse Publishers.

Herber, H. 1978. *Teaching reading in the content areas*. Englewood Cliffs, NJ: Prentice Hall.

Ogle, D. 1986. The K-W-L: A teaching model that develops active reading of expository text. *The Reading Teacher* 39: 564–570.

Seigel, M. 1984. Sketch to stretch. In *Reading, writing, and caring*, edited by O. Cochran. New York, NY: Richard C. Owen.

Teaching Science Through Inquiry

The word *inquiry* brings many different ideas to mind. For some teachers, it may evoke fears of giving up control in the classroom or spending countless hours preparing lessons. For others, it may imply losing the focus of instructional objectives while students pursue answers to their own questions. And for many, teaching science through inquiry is perceived as intriguing but unrealistic. But inquiry doesn't have to cause anxiety for teachers. Simply stated, inquiry is an approach to learning that involves exploring the world and that leads to asking questions, testing ideas, and making discoveries in the search for understanding. There are many degrees of inquiry, and it may be helpful to start with a variation that emphasizes a teacher-directed approach and then gradually builds to a more student-directed approach. As a basic guide, the National Research Council (2000) identifies five essential features for classroom inquiry, shown in Table 3.1.

Table 3.1 Five Essential Features of Classroom Inquiry

1 Learners are engaged by scientifically oriented **questions**.

2 Learners give priority to **evidence**, which allows them to develop and evaluate explanations that address scientifically oriented questions.

3 Learners formulate **explanations** from evidence to address scientifically oriented questions.

4 Learners **evaluate** their explanations in light of alternative explanations, particularly those reflecting scientific understanding.

5 Learners **communicate** and justify their proposed explanations.

From *Inquiry and the National Science Education Standards: A Guide for Teaching and Learning* (NRC 2000).

Essential Features of Classroom Inquiry

The following descriptions illustrate each of the five essential features of classroom inquiry using Chapter 11, "Close Encounters." Any classroom activity that includes all five of these features is considered to be inquiry.

1. *Learners are engaged by scientifically oriented questions.* In "Close Encounters," students are given "mystery objects" (plant galls) that engage them in the initial question, "What are these objects?" In this case, the mystery objects pique students' curiosity, stimulating additional questions.

2. *Learners give priority to evidence, which allows them to develop and evaluate explanations that address scientifically oriented questions.* Students use measuring tools and hand lenses to make quantitative and qualitative observations about the mystery objects and use the observations as evidence to develop answers to questions.

3. *Learners formulate explanations from evidence to address scientifically oriented questions.* Students develop explanations about the mystery objects based on their observations.

4. *Learners evaluate their explanations in light of alternative explanations, particularly those reflecting scientific understanding.* After using a dichotomous key to identify their objects and reading an article about plant galls, students evaluate, and possibly eliminate or revise, their explanations.

5. *Learners communicate and justify their proposed explanations.* Students show their mystery objects to the rest of the class, share their explanations, and justify the explanations with evidence. This provides other students the opportunity to ask questions, examine the evidence, identify faulty reasoning, and suggest alternative explanations.

Benefits of Inquiry

Developing an inquiry-based science program is a central tenet of the *National Science Education Standards* (NRC 1996). So what makes inquiry-based teaching such a valuable method of instruction? Many studies state that it is equal or superior to other instructional modes and results in higher scores on content achievement tests. *Inquiry and the National Science Education Standards* (NRC 2000) summarizes the findings of *How People Learn* (Bransford, Brown, and Cocking 1999), which support the use of inquiry-based teaching. Those findings include the following points:

- Understanding science is more than knowing facts. Most important is that students understand the major concepts. Inquiry-based teaching focuses on the major concepts, helps students build a strong base of factual information to support the concepts, and gives them opportunities to apply their knowledge effectively.

- Students build new knowledge and understanding on what they already know and believe. Students often hold preconceptions that are either reasonable in only a limited context or scientifically incorrect. These preconceptions can be resistant to change, particularly when teachers use conventional teaching strategies (Wandersee, Mintzes, and Novak 1994). Inquiry-based teaching uncovers students' prior knowledge and, through concrete explorations, helps them correct misconceptions.

- Students formulate new knowledge by modifying and refining their current concepts and by adding new concepts to what they already know. In an inquiry-based model, students give priority to evidence when they prove or disprove their preconceptions. Their preconceptions are challenged by their observations or the explanations of other students.

- Learning is mediated by the social environment in which learners interact with others. Inquiry provides students with opportunities to interact with others. They explain their ideas to other students and listen critically to the ideas of their classmates. These social interactions require that students clarify their ideas and consider alternative explanations.

- Effective learning requires that students take control of their own learning. When teachers use inquiry, students assume much of the responsibility for their own learning. Students formulate questions, design procedures, develop explanations, and devise ways to share their findings. This makes learning unique and more valuable to each student.

- The ability to apply knowledge to novel situations, that is, transfer of learning, is affected by the degree to which students learn with understanding. Inquiry provides students a variety of opportunities to practice what they have learned, connect to what they already know, and therefore moves them toward application, a sophisticated level of thinking that requires them to solve problems in new situations.

Inquiry learning not only contributes to better understanding of scientific concepts and skills, but, because science inquiry in school is carried out in a social context, it also contributes to children's social and intellectual development (Dyasi 1999). Within an inquiry-based lesson, students work collaboratively to brainstorm questions, design procedures for testing their predictions, carry out investigations, and ask thoughtful questions about other students' conclusions. This mirrors the social context in which "real science" takes place.

What Makes a Good Question?

Questioning lies at the heart of inquiry and is a habit of mind that should be encouraged in any learning setting. According to *Inquiry and the National Science Education Standards* (NRC 2000), "Fruitful inquiries evolve from questions that are meaningful and relevant to students, but they also must be able to be answered by students' observations and scientific knowledge they obtain from reliable sources." One of the most important skills students can develop in science is to understand which questions can be answered by investigation and which cannot. The teacher plays a critical role in guiding the kinds of questions the students pose. Students often ask *why* questions which cannot be addressed by scientific investigations. For example, "Why does gravity make things fall toward Earth?" is a question that would be impossible to answer in the school setting.

"Investigatable," or testable, questions, on the other hand, generally begin with *how can, does, what if,* or *which* and can be investigated using controlled procedures. For example, encouraging students to ask questions such as "How can you slow the fall of an object?," "Which object falls faster, a marble or a basketball?," or "What materials work best for constructing a toy parachute?" guides them toward investigations which can be done in the classroom.

Helping students select developmentally appropriate questions is also important. For example, "What will the surface of the Moon look like in a hundred years?" is a question that is scientific but much too complex for elementary students to investigate. A more developmentally appropriate question might be "How does the size of a meteorite affect the size of the crater it makes?" This question can be tested by dropping different-sized marbles into a pan of sand, simulating how meteors hit the Moon's surface. It is essential to help students formulate age-appropriate and testable questions to ensure that their investigations are both engaging and productive.

Variations within Classroom Inquiry

Inquiry-based teaching can vary widely in the amount of guidance and structure you choose to provide. Table 3.2 describes these variations for each of the five essential features of inquiry.

The most open form of inquiry takes place in the variations on the right-hand column of the Inquiry Continuum. Most often, students do not have the abilities to begin at that point. For example, students must first learn what makes a question scientifically oriented and testable before they can begin posing such questions themselves. The extent to which you structure what students do determines whether the inquiry is *guided* or *open* inquiry. The more responsibility you take, the more guided the inquiry. The more responsibility the students have, the more open the inquiry. Guided inquiry experiences, such as those on the left-hand side of the inquiry continuum, can be effective in focusing learning on the development of particular science concepts. Students, however, must have open inquiry experiences, such as those in the right column of the Inquiry Continuum, to develop the fundamental abilities necessary to do scientific inquiry.

One common misconception about inquiry is that all science subject matter should be taught through inquiry. It is not possible or practical to teach all science subject matter through inquiry (NRC 2000). For example, you would not want to teach lab safety through inquiry. Good science teaching requires a variety of approaches and models. *Picture-Perfect Science Lessons* combines a guided inquiry investigation with an open inquiry investigation. Dunkhase (2000) refers to this approach as "coupled inquiry." In *Picture-Perfect Science Lessons*, the guided inquiries are the lessons presented in each chapter. The lessons generally fall on the left-hand (teacher-guided) side of the inquiry continuum. The Inquiry Place suggestion box (discussed in depth later in this chapter) at the end of each lesson will produce experiences falling more toward the right-hand, or student self-directed, side of the inquiry continuum.

Checkpoint Labs in Guided Inquiry

One way to manage a guided inquiry is to use a "checkpoint lab." This type of lab is divided into sections, with a small box located at the end of each section for a teacher check mark or stamp. Five lessons in this book contain checkpoint labs to guide teams of students through an inquiry (Chapters 9, 13, 14, 19, and 20). In a checkpoint lab, each team works at its own pace. A red cup and a green cup taped together at their openings are used to signal the teacher. When teams are working, they keep the green cup on top. When teams have a question or when they reach a checkpoint, they signal the teacher by flipping their cups so that red is on top.

Tips for Managing a Checkpoint Lab:

- Give students task cards (like those provided in "Sheep in a Jeep," Chapter 14) to assign each student a job.

- Tell students that every member of the team is responsible for recording data and writing responses. All team members must be at the same checkpoint in order to get the stamp or check mark and continue on to the next section.

- Explain how to use the red-green cup. Tell students that when the green cup is on top, it is a signal to you that the team is progressing with no problems or questions.

Table 3.2 Inquiry Continuum

Teacher Guided ◀———▶ **Learner Self-Directed**

ESSENTIAL FEATURE	VARIATIONS			
1. Learners are engaged in scientifically oriented questions.	Learner engages in question provided by teacher or materials	Learner sharpens or clarifies the question provided	Learner selects among questions, poses new questions	Learner poses a question
2. Learners give priority to evidence, which allows them to develop and evaluate explanations that address scientifically oriented questions.	Learner given data and told how to analyze	Learner given data and asked how to analyze	Learner directed to collect certain data	Learner determines what constitutes evidence and collects it
3. Learners formulate explanations from evidence to address scientifically oriented questions.	Learner provided with evidence	Learner given possible ways to use evidence to formulate explanations	Learner guided in process of formulating explanations from evidence	Learner formulates explanation after summarizing evidence
4. Learners evaluate their explanations in light of alternative explanations, particularly those reflecting scientific understanding.	Learner told connections	Learner given possible connections	Learner directed toward areas and sources of scientific knowledge	Learner independently examines other resources and forms the links to explanations
5. Learners communicate and justify their proposed explanations.	Learner given steps and procedures for communication	Learner provided broad guidelines to sharpen communication	Learner coached in development of communication	Learner communicates and justifies explanations

Teacher Guided ◀———▶ **Learner Self-Directed**

Adapted from *Inquiry and the National Science Education Standards: A Guide for Teaching and Learning* (NRC 2000).

SIGNALING THE TEACHER WITH A "RED-GREEN CUP"

When the red cup is on top, it is a signal that the team needs you.

- Explain that there are only two situations in which students should flip the red cup on top:
  - ✦ Everyone on the team is at a checkpoint, or
  - ✦ The team has a question.

- Tell students that, before they flip the cup to red for a question, they must first ask everyone else on the team the question ("Ask three, then me"). Most of the time, the team will be able to answer the question without asking you.

- When a team reaches a checkpoint and signals you, make sure every member of the team has completed all of the work in that section. Then ask each member a probing question about that part of the lab. Asking each student a question holds each one accountable and allows you to informally assess each student's learning. Examples of probing questions are

  - ? How do you know?
  - ? What is your evidence?
  - ? What do you think will happen next?

Inquiry Place

As we mentioned earlier, a box called Inquiry Place is provided at the end of each lesson to help you move your students toward more open inquiries. The Inquiry Place lists questions related to the lesson that students may select to investigate. Students may also use them as sample questions for writing their own scientifically oriented and testable questions. After selecting one of the questions in the box or formulating their own questions, students can make predictions, design investigations to test their predictions, collect evidence, devise explanations, examine related resources, and communicate their findings.

The Inquiry Place boxes suggest that students share the results of their investigations with each other through a poster session. Scientists, engineers, and researchers routinely hold poster sessions to communicate their findings. Here are some suggestions for poster sessions:

- Posters should include a title, the researchers' names, a brief description of the investigation, and a summary of the main findings.

- Observations, data tables, and/or graphs should be included as evidence to justify conclusions.

- The printing should be large enough that people can read it from a distance.

- Students should have the opportunity to present their posters to the class.

- The audience in a poster session should examine the evidence, ask thoughtful questions, identify faulty reasoning, and suggest alternative explanations to presenters in a polite, respectful manner.

Not only do poster sessions mirror the work of real scientists, but they also provide you with excellent opportunities for authentic assessment.

Implementing the guided inquiries in this book along with the Inquiry Place suggestions at the end of each lesson provides a framework for moving from teacher guided to learner self-directed inquiry. The Inquiry Place Think Sheet on page 25 (Table 3.3) can help students organize their own inquiries.

An example of how the Inquiry Place can be used to give students the opportunity to engage in an open inquiry follows. This particular example is from "The Changing Moon," Chapter 17. In that lesson, students learn about the Moon's phases by observing them for a month, modeling the phases with a foam ball and lamp, and reading about the Moon. This is how one teacher chose to use the Inquiry Place following a guided inquiry lesson:

After "The Changing Moon" lesson, Mrs. Bell begins a discussion about the Moon's surface. She and her students talk about the craters on the Moon and the fact that they are caused by meteorites.

Mrs. Bell: *There are so many different-sized craters on the Moon. I wonder, does the speed of the meteorite affect the size of the crater it makes? I have some supplies we can use as a model: a pan of sand to represent the surface of the Moon and marbles to represent the meteorites. How can we use these supplies to find the answer to the question?*

Mrs. Bell writes the question on the board: "Does the speed of a meteorite affect the size of the crater it makes?"

Pedro: *We can drop the marbles in the pan at different speeds and measure the craters.*

Mrs. Bell: *How can we get the marbles to hit at different speeds?*

Hannah: *We can drop one from high and one from low and measure the craters.*

Mrs. Bell: *Is there a way we can measure the height of the drop?*

Rudy: *We can use a meter stick. We'll drop one from 50 cm and the other from 1 meter.*

Mrs. Bell: *Good. Is there a way we can collect even more data than just two drops?*

Julia: *We can drop it from 25 cm, 50 cm, 75 cm, and 100 cm.*

Mrs. Bell: *How can we record our data?*

Eva: *We can make a table with the height on one side and the size of the crater on the other side.*

Mrs. Bell: *Great idea! Let's make a data table on the board. Now, what do we need to keep the same to make this a fair experiment? (Silence.)*

Mrs. Bell: *For example, should we use four different-sized marbles?*

Jeff: *No, we should use the same marble each time to keep it fair.*

Mrs. Bell: *Good. Is there anything else we need to do to keep it fair?*

Mikayla: *We should use the same pan of sand each time.*

Mrs. Bell: *Yes! I think we are ready to begin the experiment. Let's make some predictions first.*

Mrs. Bell and her class make predictions and then perform the experiment together and record their data on the board. They use their data as evidence to answer the question and reach the conclusion that faster-moving meteorites make larger craters than slower-moving meteorites.

Mrs. Bell: *Now that we have answered my question, I wonder if you have any questions about meteorites and craters that we could investigate using the pan and marble model.*

Mrs. Bell passes out the Inquiry Place Think Sheet to each student. She instructs them to answer number 1: "My questions about moon craters." After providing students time to write down some questions, Mrs. Bell asks them to share some of their questions.

Rudy: *Where do meteorites come from?*

Mrs. Bell: *That's a good question, Rudy. Can we use this model to find the answer?*

Rudy: *No.*

Mrs. Bell: *How could we find the answer to that question?*

Rudy: *Maybe at the library or on the computer.*

Mrs. Bell: *Yes. Maybe we can look for that answer next time we are in the library. Let's try to think of questions that we can answer using the sand and marble model.*

Yushi: *We could find out if bigger meteorites make bigger craters.*

Marcus: *Do square meteorites make square craters?*

Hannah: *Do heavier meteorites make bigger craters?*

Julia: *Does it matter what kind of moon dirt it hits?*

Mrs. Bell rephrases the questions and writes them on the board.

- ? Does the size of a meteorite affect the size of the crater?´
- ? Does the shape of a meteorite affect the shape of the crater?
- ? Does the mass of the meteorite affect the size of the crater?´
- ? Does the type of surface the meteorite lands on affect the size of the crater?

Mrs. Bell: *Excellent! These four questions can be answered by investigating with the marble and pan model. Choose one of the questions that you would like to investigate and write it down for number 2.*

Mrs. Bell provides time for students to think about which question they want to investigate and to write it down. She then forms teams of students who have chosen the same question.

Mrs. Bell: *Now that you have formed your teams, complete the rest of the Inquiry Place Think Sheet together. When your experiment is planned and you are ready for the teacher checkpoint, signal by placing the green cup on top.*

Mrs. Bell circulates to ask questions and check progress as teams complete the Inquiry Place Think Sheet. Students finish planning the investigations and look forward to completing them the next day. They will share their findings during a poster session later in the week.

Table 3.3 Inquiry Place Think Sheet

Name: _____

Inquiry Place Think Sheet

1 My questions about: _____

_____

_____

2 My "investigatable" question:

_____

3 My prediction:

_____

4 Steps I will follow to investigate my question:

_____

_____

_____

_____

_____

5 Materials I will need:

_____

6 How I will share my findings:

_____

_____

_____

CHECKPOINT ☐

PERFORMING THE INVESTIGATION DESIGNED ON THE INQUIRY PLACE THINK SHEET

References

Bransford, J. D., A. L. Brown, and R. Cocking, eds. 1999. *How people learn: Brain, mind, experience, and school.* Washington, DC: National Academy Press.

Dunkhase, J. 2000. *Coupled inquiry: An effective strategy for student investigations.* Des Moines, IA: Paper presented at the Iowa Science Teachers Section Conference.

Dyasi, H. 1999. What children gain by learning through inquiry. In *Foundations Volume II: Inquiry—thoughts, views, and strategies for the K-5 classroom.* Arlington, VA: Division of Elementary, Secondary, and Informal Education in conjunction with the Division of Research, Evaluation, and Communication, National Science Foundation.

National Research Council. 1996. *National science education standards.* Washington, DC: National Academy Press. Available online at books.nap.edu/books/0309053269/html/index.html

National Research Council. 2000. *Inquiry and the national science education standards: A guide for teaching and learning.* Washington, DC: National Academy Press. Available online at www.nap.edu/books/0309064767/html

Wandersee, J. H., J. J. Mintzes, and J. D. Novak. 1994. Research on alternative conceptions in science. In *Handbook of research on science teaching and learning,* ed. D. L. Gable, 177–210. New York, NY: Macmillan.

BSCS 5E Instructional Model

The guided inquiries in this book are designed using the BSCS 5E Instructional Model, commonly referred to as the 5E model (or the 5Es). Developed by the Biological Sciences Curriculum Study (BSCS), the 5E model is a learning cycle based on a constructivist view of learning. Constructivism embraces the idea that learners bring with them preconceived ideas about how the world works. According to the constructivist view, "learners test new ideas against that which they already believe to be true. If the new ideas seem to fit in with their pictures of the world, they have little difficulty learning the ideas ... if the new ideas don't seem to fit the learners' picture of reality then they won't seem to make sense. Learners may dismiss them ... or eventually accommodate the new ideas and change the way they understand the world" (Colburn 2003). The objective of a constructivist model, therefore, is to provide students with experiences that make them reconsider their conceptions. Then, students "redefine, reorganize, elaborate, and change their initial concepts through self-reflection and interaction with their peers and their environment" (Bybee 1997). The 5E model provides a planned sequence of instruction that places students at the center of their learning experiences, encouraging them to explore, construct their own understanding of scientific concepts, and relate those understandings to other concepts. An explanation of each phase of the BSCS 5E model—Engage, Explore, Explain, Elaborate, and Evaluate—follows.

engage

The purpose of this introductory stage, *engage*, is to capture students' interest. Here you can uncover what students know and think about

a topic as well as determine their misconceptions. Engagement activities might include a reading, a demonstration, or other activity that piques students' curiosity.

ENGAGE: MRS. RADER GAVE EACH OF HER STUDENTS A BOWL OF POPCORN TO EAT WHILE SHE WROTE WHAT THEY KNOW AND WHAT THEY ARE WONDERING ABOUT POPCORN ("WHAT'S POPPIN'?," CHAPTER 9).

explore

In the *explore* stage, you provide students with cooperative exploration activities, giving them

common, concrete experiences that help them begin constructing concepts and developing skills. Students can build models, collect data, make and test predictions, or form new predictions. The purpose is to provide hands-on experiences you can use later to formally introduce a concept, process, or skill.

EXPLORE: BEFORE FORMALLY INTRODUCING THE TERM *PITCH*, MISS SCHULTZ HAD HER STUDENTS TEST THEIR IDEAS AFTER BRAINSTORMING WAYS TO MAKE THEIR STRAW INSTRUMENTS PRODUCE HIGH AND LOW SOUNDS ("SOUNDS OF SCIENCE," CHAPTER 15).

explain

In the *explain* stage, learners articulate their ideas in their own words and listen critically to one another. You clarify their concepts, correct misconceptions, and introduce scientific terminology. It is important that you clearly connect the students' explanations to experiences they had in the engage and explore phases.

EXPLAIN: STUDENTS IN MR. MICHALAK'S CLASS ARE JUSTIFYING HOW THEY SORTED THEIR CARDS IN THE CLOSE ENCOUNTER WORD SORT ("CLOSE ENCOUNTERS OF THE SYMBIOTIC KIND," CHAPTER 11).

elaborate

At the *elaborate* point in the model, some students may still have misconceptions, or they may understand the concepts only in the context of the previous exploration. Elaboration activities can help students correct their remaining misconceptions and generalize the concepts in a broader context. These activities also challenge students to apply, extend, or elaborate upon concepts and skills in a new situation, resulting in deeper understanding.

ELABORATE: A STUDENT IN MRS. HUDSPETH'S CLASS ELABORATES ON WHAT HE HAS LEARNED ABOUT MOTION BY DESIGNING A PARACHUTE FOR A TOY ANIMAL ("SHEEP IN A JEEP," CHAPTER 14).

evaluate

At the *evaluate* phase, you evaluate students' understanding of concepts and their proficiency with various skills. You can use a variety of formal and informal procedures to assess conceptual understanding and progress toward learning outcomes. The evaluation phase also provides an opportunity for students to test their own understanding and skills.

Although the fifth phase is devoted to evaluation, a skillful teacher evaluates throughout the 5E model, continually checking to see if students need more time or instruction to learn the key points in a lesson. Ways to do this include informal questioning, teacher checkpoints, and class discussions. Each lesson in *Picture-Perfect Science Lessons* also includes a formal evaluation such as a written

quiz or poster session. These formal evaluations take place at the end of the lesson.

Cycle of Learning

The 5Es are listed above in linear order—engage, explore, explain, elaborate, and evaluate—but the model is most effective when you use it as a cycle of learning as in Figure 4.1.

Each lesson begins with an engagement activity, but students can reenter the 5E model at other points in the cycle. For example, in "Name That Shell!," Chapter 7, students *explore* the characteristics of shells and sort them. Then they *explain* the characteristics they used to sort the shells and the teacher introduces the scientific terms "bivalve" and "univalve." Next, the students reenter the *explore* phase by sorting the shells into bivalves and univalves. Moving from the *explain* phase back into the *explore* phase gives students the opportunity to add to the knowledge they have constructed so far in the lesson by participating in additional hands-on explorations.

The traditional roles of the teacher and student are virtually reversed in the 5E model. Students take on much of the responsibility

EVALUATE: A STUDENT IN MRS. MANN'S CLASS HAS DESIGNED AN EXPERIMENT TO TEST THE EFFECTIVENESS OF AN INVENTION. MRS. MANN WILL EVALUATE THE STUDENT'S SKILLS IN DESIGNING AND CARRYING OUT AN EXPERIMENT ("BRAINSTORMS," CHAPTER 20).

Table 4.1 The BSCS 5Es Teacher

What the teacher does

	CONSISTENT with the BSCS 5E model	INCONSISTENT with the BSCS 5E model
engage	• Generates interest and curiosity • Raises questions • Assesses current knowledge, including misconceptions	• Explains concepts • Provides definitions and conclusions • Lectures
explore	• Provides time for students to work together • Observes and listens to students as they interact • Asks probing questions to redirect students' investigations when necessary	• Explains how to work through the problem or provides answers • Tells students they are wrong • Gives information or facts that solve the problem
explain	• Asks for evidence and clarification from students • Uses students' previous experiences as a basis for explaining concepts • Encourages students to explain concepts and definitions in their own words, then provides scientific explanations and vocabulary	• Does not solicit the students' explanations • Accepts explanations that have no justification • Introduces unrelated concepts or skills
elaborate	• Expects students to apply scientific concepts, skills, and vocabulary to new situations • Reminds students of alternative explanations • Refers students to alternative explanations	• Provides definite answers • Leads students to step-by-step solutions to new problems • Lectures
evaluate	• Observes and assesses students as they apply new concepts and skills • Allows students to assess their own learning and group process skills • Asks open-ended questions	• Tests vocabulary words and isolated facts • Introduces new ideas or concepts • Promotes open-ended discussion unrelated to the concept

Adapted from *Achieving Scientific Literacy: From Purposes to Practices* (Bybee 1997).

Table 4.2 The BSCS 5Es Student

What the student does

	CONSISTENT with the BSCS 5E model	**INCONSISTENT** with the BSCS 5E model
engage	• Asks questions such as, "Why did this happen? What do I already know about this? What can I find out about this?" • Shows interest in the topic	• Asks for the "right" answer • Offers the "right" answer • Insists on answers and explanations
explore	• Thinks creatively, but within the limits of the activity • Tests predictions and hypotheses • Records observations and ideas	• Passively allows others to do the thinking and exploring • "Plays around" indiscriminately with no goal in mind • Stops with one solution
explain	• Explains possible solutions to others • Listens critically to explanations of other students and the teacher • Uses recorded observations in explanations	• Proposes explanations from "thin air" with no relationship to previous experiences • Brings up irrelevant experiences and examples • Accepts explanations without justification
elaborate	• Applies new labels, definitions, explanations, and skills in new but similar situations • Uses previous information to ask questions, propose solutions, make decisions, design experiments • Records observations and explanations	• "Plays around" with no goal in mind • Ignores previous information or evidence • Neglects to record data
evaluate	• Demonstrates an understanding of the concept or skill • Answers open-ended questions by using observations, evidence, and previously accepted explanations • Evaluates his/her own progress and knowledge	• Draws conclusions, not using evidence or previously accepted explanations • Offers only yes-or-no answers and memorized definitions or explanations • Fails to express satisfactory explanations in his/her own words

Adapted from *Achieving Scientific Literacy: From Purposes to Practices* (Bybee 1997).

Figure 4.1 The BSCS 5Es as a Cycle of Learning

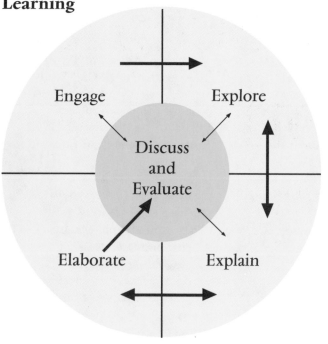

Adapted from Barman, C.R. 1997. *The Learning Cycle Revised: A Modification of an Effective Teaching Model.* Arlington, VA: Council for Elementary Science International.

for learning as they construct knowledge through discovery, whereas in traditional models the teacher is responsible for dispensing information to be learned by the students. Table 4.1 shows actions of the teacher that are consistent with the 5E model and actions that are inconsistent with the model.

In the 5E model, the teacher acts as a guide: raising questions, providing opportunities for exploration, asking for evidence to support student explanations, referring students to existing explanations, correcting misconceptions, and coaching students as they apply new concepts. This model differs greatly from the traditional format of lecturing, leading students step-by-step to a solution, providing definite answers, and testing isolated facts. The 5E model requires the students to take on much of the responsibility for their own learning. Table 4.2 shows the actions of the student that are consistent with the 5E model and those that are inconsistent with the model.

References

Bybee, R. W. 1997. *Achieving scientific literacy: From purposes to practices.* Portsmouth, NH: Heinemann.

Colburn, A. 2003. *The lingo of learning: 88 education terms every science teacher should know.* Arlington, VA: NSTA Press.

National Science Education Standards

The National Science Education Standards were published in 1996, with the intent of helping our nation's students achieve science literacy. They outline what students at different grade ranges need to know, understand, and be able to do in order to be considered scientifically literate. The book, *National Science Education Standards*, defines scientific literacy as "the knowledge and understanding of scientific concepts and processes required for personal decision making, participation in civic and cultural affairs, and economic productivity" (NRC 1996). The Standards are designed to be achievable by all students, regardless of their backgrounds or characteristics, and are based on the premise that science is an active process. "Learning science is something that students do, not something that is done to them. 'Hands-on' activities, while essential, are not enough. Students must have 'minds-on' experiences as well" (NRC

1996). *Picture-Perfect Science Lessons* embraces this philosophy by engaging students in meaningful, hands-on science experiences that require them to construct their own knowledge.

The lesson objectives in *Picture-Perfect Science Lessons* have been adapted from the Standards. Because the content standards themselves are not very specific, we consulted the bulleted lists of fundamental concepts and principles that underlie each standard when developing lesson objectives. We refer to these as "fundamental understandings" and have included them at the beginning of each lesson in the box titled "Lesson Objectives: Connecting to the Standards." For example, in "Earthlets," Chapter 6, one of the content standards for K–4 that the lesson addresses is "Content Standard B: Physical Science." The fundamental understanding from K–4 Content Standard B that we selected for this particular lesson is "Understand that objects have many observable properties, including size, weight,

shape, color, temperature, and the ability to react with other substances. Those properties can be measured using tools, such as rulers, balances, and thermometers."

The fundamental understandings used to develop the lesson objectives in *Picture-Perfect Science Lessons* were adapted from the "Guide to the Content Standard" sections of the *National Science Education Standards,* which describe the fundamental ideas that underlie the Standard.

Because *Picture-Perfect Science Lessons* focuses on student learning of specific science content objectives in grades three through six, this chapter outlines only the National Science Education Content Standards. The content standards for kindergarten through grade four are listed in Table 5.1. The content standards for grade five through grade eight are listed in Table 5.2.

Table 5.3 shows the correlation between the lessons presented in this book and the National Science Education Standards for grades K–4 and 5–8.

Reference

National Research Council. 1996. *National science education standards.* Washington, DC: National Academy Press.

Table 5.1

National Science Content Standards K–4

Unifying Concepts and Processes
- Systems, order, and organization
- Evidence, models, and explanation
- Change, constancy, and measurement
- Evolution and equilibrium
- Form and function

Content Standard A: Science as Inquiry
- Abilities necessary to do science inquiry
- Understandings about science inquiry

Content Standard B: Physical Science
- Properties of objects and materials
- Position and motion of objects
- Light, heat, electricity, and magnetism

Content Standard C: Life Science
- The characteristics of organisms
- Life cycles of organisms
- Organisms and environments

Content Standard D: Earth and Space Science
- Properties of Earth materials
- Objects in the sky
- Changes in Earth and sky

Content Standard E: Science and Technology
- Abilities of technological design
- Understanding about science and technology
- Abilities to distinguish between natural objects and objects made by humans

Content Standard F: Science in Personal and Social Perspectives
- Personal health
- Characteristics and changes in populations
- Types of resources
- Changes in environments
- Science and technology in local challenges

Content Standard G: History and Nature of Science
- Science as a human endeavor

National Science Education Standards. (NRC 1996).

Table 5.2

National Science Content Standards 5–8

Unifying Concepts and Processes
- Systems, order, and organization
- Evidence, models, and explanation
- Change, constancy, and measurement
- Evolution and equilibrium
- Form and function

Content Standard A: Science as Inquiry
- Abilities necessary to do science inquiry
- Understandings about science inquiry

Content Standard B: Physical Science
- Properties and changes in properties of matter
- Motions and forces
- Transfer of energy

Content Standard C: Life Science
- Structure and function in living systems
- Reproduction and heredity
- Regulation and behavior
- Populations and ecosystems
- Diversity and adaptations of organisms

Content Standard D: Earth and Space Science
- Structure of the Earth system
- Earth's history
- Earth in the solar system

Content Standard E: Science and Technology
- Abilities of technological design
- Understandings about science and technology

Content Standard F: Science in Personal and Social Perspectives
- Personal health
- Populations, resources, and environments
- Natural hazards
- Risks and benefits
- Science and technology in society

Content Standard G: History and Nature of Science
- Science as a human endeavor
- Nature of science
- History of science

National Science Education Standards. (NRC 1996).

Table 5.3 Connecting to the National Science Education Standards

	Content Standard A Science as Inquiry	Content Standard B Physical Science	Content Standard C Life Science	Content Standard D Earth and Space Science	Content Standard E Science and Technology	Content Standard F Science in Personal and Social Perspectives	Content Standard G History and Nature of Science
Chapter 6: Earthlets	K–4, 5–8	K–4					
Chapter 7: Name That Shell!	K–4, 5–8		K–4				
Chapter 8: Rice Is Life	K–4, 5–8		K–4				
Chapter 9: What's Poppin'?	5–8						
Chapter 10: Mystery Pellets	K–4, 5–8		K–4, 5–8				
Chapter 11: Close Encounters of the Symbiotic Kind	K–4, 5–8		K–4, 5–8				
Chapter 12: Turtle Hurdles			K–4			K–4	
Chapter 13: Oil Spill!	K–4, 5–8					K–4, 5–8	
Chapter 14: Sheep in a Jeep	K–4	K–4			K–4		
Chapter 15: Sounds of Science		K–4			K–4		
Chapter 16: Chemical Change Café	K–4, 5–8	K–4, 5–8					
Chapter 17: The Changing Moon	K–4, 5–8			K–4, 5–8			
Chapter 18: Day and Night	K–4, 5–8			K–4, 5–8			
Chapter 19: Grand Canyon	K–4, 5–8			K–4, 5–8			
Chapter 20: Brainstorms: From Idea to Invention	5–8				5–8	5–8	5–8

Earthlets

Description

Learners develop understandings of the differences between observations and inferences by analyzing Dr. Xargle's comical, yet misguided, attempts to teach his students about human babies. Learners then make observations and inferences of "mystery samples" collected from Earth by Dr. Xargle.

Suggested Grade Levels: 3–6

Lesson Objectives Connecting to the Standards

Content Standard A:
Science as Inquiry
K–4: Employ simple equipment and tools to gather data and extend the senses.

5–8: Develop descriptions, explanations, predictions, and models using evidence.

Content Standard B:
Physical Science
K–4: Understand that objects have many observable properties, including size, weight, shape, color, temperature, and the ability to react with other substances. Those properties can be measured using tools, such as rulers, balances, and thermometers.

Featured Picture Books

Title **Dr. Xargle's Book of Earthlets**

Author **Jeanne Willis**
Illustrator **Tony Ross**
Publisher **Andersen Press**
Year **2003**
Genre **Story**
Summary **Dr. Xargle, a green, five-eyed alien, teaches a lesson about that most mysterious of creatures: the human baby.**

Title **Seven Blind Mice**

Author **Ed Young**
Illustrator **Ed Young**
Publisher **Penguin Putnam Books for Young Readers**
Year **2002**
Genre **Story**
Summary **Retells the fable of the blind men discovering the different parts of an elephant and arguing about its appearance**

Or a U.S. edition of the same book

Title **Earthlets as Explained by Professor Xargle**
Publisher **Dutton Children's Books**
Year **1988 (reprinted 1994 by Puffin)**

Time Needed

This lesson will take several class periods. Suggested scheduling is as follows:

Day 1: **Engage** with read aloud of *Dr. Xargle's Book of Earthlets*, **Explore** with word sorts, and **Explain** with observation versus inference and Inference Frayer Model

Day 2: **Explore** and **Explain** with mystery samples from Planet Earth

Day 3: **Elaborate** with *Seven Blind Mice*, **Evaluate** with Observation and Inference Practice

Day 4: **Evaluate** with review and Observation and Inference Quiz

Materials

- Black film canisters with lids (1 per student) to make mystery samples: Before the mystery sample from Planet Earth activity, prepare one film canister for each student. Put in items that make distinctive sounds, such as water, a paper clip, rice, a marble, or a penny. Make the mystery samples in pairs so you can randomly distribute two of each kind: two canisters with rice in them, two with marbles in them, and so forth. (Make sure you put in equal amounts, such as 1 tsp. rice in each and one of the same-sized marble in each.) Number the canisters, and make a key so you can determine whether students have found a matching sample.

- Magnets for testing magnetic properties

- Balances for measuring mass

Student Pages

- Earthlets Word Sort Cards
- Inference Frayer Model
- Mystery Sample from Planet Earth Data Sheet
- Observation and Inference Practice
- Observation and Inference Quiz

engage

Read Aloud

Introduce the author and illustrator of *Dr. Xargle's Book of Earthlets*. If you are using the version published under the title *Earthlets as Explained by Professor Xargle,* refer to the alien teacher as *professor* rather than *doctor*. All other information in the book is the same.

Making Inferences

Show students the cover of the book, and ask the following questions:

? Who do you think Dr. Xargle is?

? What do you think Earthlets are?

Then read *Dr. Xargle's Book of Earthlets* to the class.

explore

Ask students the following questions after reading the book:

? Who is Dr. Xargle? (a teacher or professor from another planet)

? What are Earthlets? (human babies)

? What observations did Dr. Xargle make about human babies? (responses will vary)

? What is an observation? (information taken in directly through the senses)

Word Sorts

Word sorts help learners understand the relationships among key concepts and help teach classification.

Open Sort: Pass out the Earthlets Word Sort Cards student page to each pair of students. Have them cut out the cards containing several statements made by Dr. Xargle about Earthlets. Then ask them to sort the cards any way they wish. At this point, it should be an open sort, in which students group the cards into categories of their choice and then

create their own labels for each category. As you move from pair to pair, ask students to explain how they categorized the cards. Then ask

? Do you notice any differences among the kinds of statements Dr. Xargle makes on the cards?

? Which statements are truly observations: information Dr. Xargle got directly through his eyes or ears?

Closed Sort: Tell students that now you want them to classify the cards into only two groups: statements that are *observations* and those that aren't. Give them time to sort the cards.

Next, make a T-chart on the board. Don't label it yet. Discuss the statements the students have identified as observations. As students give answers, write them on the left side of the T-chart if they are truly observations with the corresponding (incorrect) inferences on the right. Then ask

? Does anyone know what the statements on the right-hand side of the T-chart are called? (inferences)

Next, label the T-chart with "Observations" on the left and "Inferences" on the right.

Sample T-Chart

Observations	Inferences
Earthlets are patted and squeezed.	Earthlets are patted and squeezed so they won't explode.
The parent Earthling mashes food.	Earthlets are fed through the mouth, nose, and ears.
The parent Earthling dries the Earthlets.	Earthlets are dried so they won't shrink.
Earthlets are sprinkled with dust.	Earthlets are sprinkled with dust so they won't stick to things.

explain

Observation versus Inference

Discuss the differences between observations and inferences using the following explanation: "Making an *observation* involves using one or more of the senses to find out about objects or events. Making an *inference* involves logical reasoning—drawing a conclusion using prior knowledge to explain our observations. A problem Dr. Xargle has is that he makes incorrect inferences to explain his observations. Dr. Xargle observes people patting their babies. Dr. Xargle infers that people pat babies so the babies won't explode."

? Why do people really pat babies? How do you know? (People pat babies so they will burp or to calm them. We know this from our past experiences with babies.)

Use the following example to further illustrate the concept of inference:
"Inferences are always based on observations. When you make an inference, you use your observations combined with your past experiences to draw a conclusion. Think about this example: You are walking on the grass barefoot. It is a warm, sunny day. You reach the end of the grass and have a choice between walking barefoot on blacktop or on a sidewalk. You notice heat waves rising from the blacktop. You choose to walk on the sidewalk, because you *infer* from the heat waves and your prior knowledge about dark surfaces that the blacktop is too hot. This is an inference because you did not directly observe the temperature of the blacktop by stepping on it, but your observations, combined with past experience, lead you to the conclusion that the blacktop is hotter than the sidewalk.

"Dr. Xargle, being from another planet, doesn't have any past experiences with human babies. So, he makes inferences that are incorrect. For example, Dr. Xargle makes an incorrect inference about the babies exploding if they are not patted. He does not base his inference on past experience with Earthlets (perhaps babies from his planet explode if not patted!). Sometimes scientists have to reject their first inferences when observations later disprove them. If Dr. Xargle went back to Earth to make more observations, he would be able to revise his incorrect inferences."

Lead students to more examples of inferences by asking the following questions:

? Your dog comes in from outside and you observe its fur is wet. What inferences could you make from your observation? (It is raining outside, your dog jumped in a creek, someone gave it a bath.)

? You walk into your backyard and you observe feathers all over the ground. What inferences could you make from your observation? (An animal caught a bird, someone had a pillow fight, birds were fighting.)

? A paleontologist observes a fossil of a fish in the desert. What inferences could she make from her observation? (The desert was covered with water at one time, someone dropped the fossil there.)

explain

Inference Frayer Model

The Frayer Model is a tool used to help students develop their vocabularies. Students write a particular word in the middle of a box and proceed to list characteristics, examples, nonexamples, and a definition in other quadrants of the box.

Give each student an Inference Frayer Model student page. Explain that the Frayer Model is a way to help them understand the meaning of concepts like *inference*. Have students formulate a definition for inference in their own words in

Sample Frayer Model for "Inference"

Definition	Characteristics
Conclusion you draw to explain your observations	• Uses your past experiences • Always based on observations

Inference

Examples	Nonexamples
• I inferred that it was raining outside because people came in carrying wet umbrellas	• I saw an umbrella

the top left box of the Inference Frayer Model student page. Then have students write some characteristics of inferences in the top right box. Have students work in pairs to come up with examples and nonexamples from their own lives. Encourage them to use their previous experiences as a basis for their inference examples. Refer back to the blacktop example and encourage them to think of similar experiences from their lives. For nonexamples, encourage students to think of direct observations they have made using their senses. Students can then present and explain their models to other groups. As they present to each other, informally assess their understanding of the concept and clarify as necessary.

explore

Mystery Samples from Planet Earth

Tell students that they are scientists from Dr. Xargle's planet and that he has asked for their help in identifying certain samples that have been collected from Planet Earth. The problem is that students cannot look

directly at the samples to make observations. The samples must be kept sealed in small black containers because Dr. Xargle believes they could contain radiation or harmful microorganisms. Tell students that under no circumstances can they open the containers. Discuss the properties of the objects that they might be able to observe without looking at them (sound, mass, and magnetic properties). Then pass out the Mystery Sample from Planet Earth Data Sheet and the sealed mystery samples.

Procedure for Mystery Samples from Planet Earth Activity

1. Before the lesson, prepare one film canister for each student. Put in items that make distinctive sounds, such as water, a paper clip, rice, a marble, or a penny. Make pairs of canisters so that you can randomly distribute two of each kind: two canisters with rice in them, two with marbles in them, and so forth. Make sure you put equal amounts of materials in each pair of canisters, such as 1 teaspoon rice in each, and one of the same-sized marble in each. Number the canisters and make a key so you will know whether students have found a matching sample.

2. Students can calculate the mass of the samples in their canisters by subtracting the mass of an empty canister from the mass of their full canisters.

3. Ask students to make observations of the sounds the samples make. Walk around and check their descriptions. Are they making observations or inferences? They may find it difficult to make an observation of sound without inferring based on past experience. Accept observations such as "swishy," but do not accept inferences such as "It is water" at this point. Students should be using their senses to describe

what they hear without making inferences as to the identities of the samples.

4 Students can slide a magnet against the side of the film canister to observe whether the contents move with the magnet.

5 Have students make an inference about the contents of their canisters. "I think the mystery sample is _____ because_____."

FINDING THE MASS OF A "MYSTERY SAMPLE"

explain

After they have finished the Mystery Sample from Planet Earth student page, and before they open their containers, discuss how scientists use observations from their data to make inferences. For example, biologists collect evidence from scat (animal droppings) to make inferences about the diet and habits of animals they are studying. Forensic scientists examine evidence from crime scenes to infer what happened during a crime. Archaeologists make observations of artifacts to infer how people lived long ago. Paleontologists study fossils to make inferences about ancient life forms. And very often, scientists have to make inferences without ever knowing for sure if those inferences are correct.

Students will want to open their samples to see if their inferences were correct, but don't let them yet. Instead, have them take turns quickly sharing the unseen, but observable, properties of their objects, such as

● "My object has a mass of 18 grams."

● "My object makes a rattling sound."

● "My object is magnetic."

Then, have each student get up and sit next to the person he or she thinks has the same sample based on the mass, sound, and magnetic properties of the sample. Use the key to check whether or not each student located his or her matching sample.

Have students explain what properties their objects may have that can't be observed, such as:

● shape

● color

● temperature

● ability to react with other substances

Discuss the following: "Think about some things in the world that cannot be directly observed using the senses. For example, atoms, which are the building blocks of all matter, are much too small to be seen, even with the most powerful microscopes. How, then, do scientists learn about the structure of atoms? Just about everything known about atoms has been learned from indirect evidence. This evidence is gathered by studying how matter behaves in all kinds of chemical reactions. Scientists have to make inferences about the structure of atoms based on this indirect evidence rather than by directly observing them. These inferences help develop various models of atoms. Does anyone know for sure what an atom looks like? No. Just as you can't be sure about what is inside your containers."

Let students open their containers now, or make them wait until the next class period—or the end of the year. Or, if you really want to make your point, never let your students open them!

Elaborate

Seven Blind Mice

 Questioning

Introduce the author and illustrator of the book, *Seven Blind Mice*. Show students the cover of the book.

? What do you think this book might be about?

Then read the book aloud. Ask the following questions:

? What did the first mouse observe? (He felt the elephant's foot.)

? What did he infer from his observation? (He thought it was a pillar.)

? What did the seventh mouse do before making an inference? (She ran from one end of the elephant to the other and made observations of each part.)

? Why is it a good idea to make multiple observations before making an inference? (When you base your inference on more observations, you are less likely to make an incorrect inference.)

? The mouse moral is, "Knowing in part may make a fine tale, but wisdom comes from seeing the whole." How does this apply to making good observations and inferences? (Making only one observation may allow you to make an inference, but it is not likely to give you the big picture. Making multiple observations is more likely to give you the wisdom to draw an accurate conclusion about something.)

Making Connections: Text-to-Text

? What advice could White Mouse give Dr. Xargle about his study of Earthlets? (Dr. Xargle should go back to Earth to make more observations, reject his original ideas about Earthlets, and make new inferences.)

Evaluate

Observation and Inference Practice

Have students practice making observations and inferences using the Observation and Inference Practice. Check for understanding by having students explain their thinking.

Evaluate

Review and Observation and Inference Quiz

After reviewing the differences between observations and inferences, have students complete the Observation and Inference Quiz. Answers are below:

1 Answers will vary, but should be based on what can be directly observed in the picture. Responses may include the following: water or another liquid is dripping from the fish bowl, water or another liquid is on the floor, there is no fish in the bowl, the cat is "smiling."

2 Answers will vary, but should be based upon the observation in question number 1. Responses may include the following: the cat put its head in the fishbowl, the cat ate the fish, the cat is happy.

3 b.

4 b.

5 d.

6 c.

7 Answers will vary, but should indicate an understanding of the difference between an observation and an inference.

Inquiry Place

Have students investigate animal tracks in a natural area. A good time to do this is when the ground is wet or snow-covered. Students can place food in the area to attract animals. A cast of a track can be made by encircling it with a dam made of a strip of poster paper taped together at the ends, and then pouring plaster of paris into the track.

If a natural area is not available, you can construct a simulation by placing two or more different kinds of animal footprints made of paper on the floor of the classroom. Arrange them in a pattern that suggests how the animals interacted. For example, place rabbit and fox footprints in a pattern that implies there was a chase. When students enter the room, they can try to figure out what happened. As they work to solve the mystery, assess their ability to distinguish observations from inferences.

? What observations can you make about the footprints?

? What inferences can you make from your observations?

Students can present their findings in a poster session.

More Books to Read

Banyai, I. 1995. *Zoom*. New York, NY: Puffin Books.
Summary: This wordless picture book presents a series of scenes, each one from farther away, showing, for example, a girl playing with toys which is actually a picture on a magazine cover, which is then revealed to be part of a sign on a bus, and so on. Students will enjoy making observations about each page and then inferring what might really be happening in each scene.

Kramer, S. 2001. *Hidden worlds: Looking through a scientist's microscope*. Boston, MA: Houghton Mifflin Co.
Summary: This book for upper elementary students provides a wealth of information about how scientists study the world using powerful electron microscopes. The book features the work of microscopist Dennis Kunkel, who has examined and photographed objects ranging from a mosquito's foot to a crystal of sugar to the delicate hairs on a blade of grass. It describes how he became interested in microscopes as a boy, how he prepares specimens for study, and how different kinds of microscopes work. The description of how he worked on Mount St. Helens in 1980 in order to study the effect of volcanic ash on algae is an exciting example of how scientists do their jobs.

Pallotta, J. 2002. *The skull alphabet book*. Watertown, MA: Charlesbridge Publishing.
Summary: A detailed painting of an animal's skull represents each letter of the alphabet. The name of the animal isn't revealed, but visual tips to its identity are given in the background and through clues in the text. Readers will enjoy using their observational skills and prior knowledge to make inferences about the identity of the animals.

Selsam, M. E. 1998. *Big tracks, little tracks: Following animal prints*. New York, NY: HarperCollins Children's Books.
Summary: This picture book for lower elementary students leads readers through the process of identifying animals and animal activities by their tracks. Explaining that scientists use clues to investigate the natural world, the book tells readers to make observations of a set of tracks, collect information about the animals that left those tracks, and finally infer what happened based on information revealed by the tracks.

Earthlets

Word Sort Cards

The parent Earthling dries the Earthlets.	Earthlets are sprinkled with dust.
Earthlets are fed through the mouth, nose, and ears.	Earthlets are dried so they won't shrink.
The parent Earthling mashes food.	Earthlets are patted and squeezed.
Earthlets are patted and squeezed so they won't explode.	Earthlets are sprinkled with dust so they won't stick to things.

Name: _____

Inference
Frayer Model

Definition	Characteristics

Inference

Examples	Nonexamples

Name: _____

Mystery Sample From
Planet Earth
Data Sheet

Mass	Sample + Container = ——— g Empty Container = ——— g Sample = ——— g
Sound	Make an observation of the sound your sample makes when you shake the container: _____ _____
Magnetic Property	Use a magnet against the side of the container to determine if the sample is attracted to a magnet. _____ YES _____ NO
Inference	I think the mystery sample is _____ because_____ _____

Name: _____

Observation and Inference Practice

Look at the picture. List in the chart below three observations and three inferences that can be made from those observations. An example of each is given for you.

Observation	Inference
The man is sitting by a fireplace.	The man is warm.

NATIONAL SCIENCE TEACHERS ASSOCIATION

Name: _____

Observation
and Inference Quiz

Look at the picture above. Write one observation about the picture.
Then write one inference based upon that observation.

1 Observation: _____

2 Inference: _____

3 Scientists must be able to tell the difference between observations
and inferences. Which of the following is an **inference?**

   a The bird has blue feathers and a yellow beak that measures
3 cm long.

   b The rodent might be nocturnal, because it has large eyes and
long whiskers.

   c The snake is wrapping its body around its prey.

   d The leaf measures 12.4 cm long.

Name: _____

Observation and Inference Quiz cont.

Rainforest Journal 2/16/04

Today I found the body of an unusual frog. The frog might be poisonous because it is very brightly colored.

It has a mass of 22.4 grams. The frog is probably a tree climber because it has large, round toe pads. I think the frog is a species of poison dart frog because of its size and color.

4 A scientist discovers the body of an unknown species of frog in the rainforest of Brazil. She writes several statements in her journal about the animal shown above. Which of the following is an **observation** about the frog?

   a The frog might be poisonous because it is very brightly colored.

   b It has a mass of 22.4 grams.

   c The frog is probably a tree climber because it has large, round toe pads.

   d I think the frog is a species of poison dart frog because of its size and color.

Observation and Inference Quiz cont.

Trial	Number of mealworms under light	Number of mealworms in cardboard tube	Number of mealworms in water dish
1	12	37	1
2	6	44	0
3	7	43	0

5 A student placed 50 mealworms in the middle of an aquarium containing a light, a cardboard tube, and a water dish. He waited 5 minutes and then recorded the data in the table above. Analyze the data. Which of the following is the best **inference** that could be made from the data?

a One mealworm went to the water dish in Trial 1.

b 44 mealworms went to the cardboard tube in Trial 2.

c Mealworms seem to prefer light places.

d Mealworms seem to prefer dark places.

Name: _____

Observation and Inference Quiz cont.

6 A scientist finds the skeleton of an animal that lived long ago. He observes that the animal had broad, flat teeth and feet with hooves. What is the best **inference** he could make from his observations?

a The animal lived in an area with few trees.

b The animal was a good swimmer.

c The animal was probably a plant eater.

d The animal was probably a meat eater.

7 Write about a time you made an ***incorrect* inference**. What observations led to your incorrect inference? What observations made you realize your inference was incorrect? Use the back of this sheet if you need more space.

_____

_____

_____

_____

_____

_____

_____

_____

_____

Name That Shell!

Description

Learners make observations and inferences about seashells, generate questions about seashells, create and use categories to organize seashells, and use dichotomous keys to identify shells and other sea creatures by their characteristics.

Suggested Grade Levels: 3–6

Lesson Objectives Connecting to the Standards

Content Standard A:
Science as Inquiry

K–4: Ask a question about objects, organisms, and events in the environment.

5–8: Develop descriptions, explanations, predictions, and models using evidence.

Content Standard C:
Life Science

K–4: Understand that each plant or animal has different structures that serve different functions in growth, survival, and reproduction.

Featured Picture Books

Title	**Seashells by the Seashore**		Title	**A House for Hermit Crab**
Author	**Marianne Berkes**		Author	**Eric Carle**
Illustrator	**Robert Noreika**		Illustrator	**Eric Carle**
Publisher	**Dawn Publications**		Publisher	**Simon & Schuster**
Year	**2002**		Year	**2002**
Genre	**Story**		Genre	**Story**
Summary	**A counting book in which a girl and her companions collect a variety of seashells**		Summary	**A hermit crab who has outgrown his old shell moves into a new one, which he decorates with the sea creatures he meets in his travels.**

CHAPTER 7

Time Needed

This lesson will take several class periods. Suggested scheduling is as follows:

Day 1: **Engage** with read aloud of *Seashells by the Seashore*, **Explore** with Seashell O-W-L and Shell Sorting

Day 2: **Explain** with Let's Learn about Shells, **Explore** and **Explain** with Name That Shell! Dichotomous Key

Day 3: **Elaborate** with *A House for Hermit Crab*, **Evaluate** with Under the Sea Dichotomous Key and Seashell Poster

Materials

- Assorted seashells
- Rulers or tape measures
- Balances
- Hand lenses
- Zipper baggies containing six or seven different kinds of the numbered shells (one baggie per student pair)
- Poster board

Label the following shells A-G with a permanent marker (you will need one of each kind of shell per student pair):

- Cockle
- Whelk
- Olive
- Kitten's Paw
- Auger
- Scallop
- Jingle

> Collect empty seashells from a beach, or purchase assorted seashells from a craft store. Using real shells is better, but if you are unable to get them, you can use the drawings on the Shell Drawings student page.

Student Pages

- Seashell O-W-L
- Shell Sorting Sheet
- Let's Learn about Shells Anticipation Guide
- Name That Shell! Dichotomous Key
- Under the Sea Dichotomous Key
- Shell Drawings

engage

Read Aloud

Making Connections: Text-to-Self and Think-Pair-Share

Show students the cover of the book, *Seashells by the Seashore*. Introduce the author and illustrator. Ask students to think about a time they visited a seashore or lakeshore and to share their experiences with a partner. Then read *Seashells by the Seashore* to the students. Omit the information page that follows the story in some editions as you will be reading this to students during the Explain phase.

explore

Seashell O-W-L

Pass out one shell and a copy of the Seashell O-W-L (observations, wonderings, learnings) student page to each student. Provide rulers or tape measures, hand lenses, and balances. Ask students to draw and observe their shells carefully and write both quantitative observations (numbers) and qualitative observations (words) about the shells. Quantitative observations involve counting and measuring, such as "The shell is 6.2 cm long"; qualitative observations involve using the senses to describe the properties of the object, such as "The shell has grooves on one side." Then ask students to generate a list of wonderings about their shells.

When students are finished drawing, writing observations, and generating questions, collect all the shells and place them in a pile where all the students can see them. Ask a volunteer to come up and, using another student's Seashell O-W-L page, try to locate that student's shell from its drawing and description. Repeat with several other students. Then have students find their own shells using their observations and return to their seats. Discuss the following questions:

? How well does your description and drawing distinguish your shell from other shells?

? How could you describe your shell better?

? What are some characteristics that make your shell different from the rest?

? What are some questions you have about your shell?

Tell students they will be learning the answers to some of their questions about shells over the next few days. Encourage them to continue to add wonderings and learnings to their Seashell O-W-L page.

explore

Shell Sorting

Give pairs of students an assortment of seashells. Have them examine the characteristics of the shells—such as shape, size, texture, and structure—and make observations. Ask them to use the Shell Sorting Sheet to sort the shells into two groups using one characteristic. After the shells are sorted, pairs can switch places with other pairs and guess what characteristic the other pairs used to sort the shells.

STUDENTS SORTING SEASHELLS

explain

Let's Learn about Shells

First, have students explain to each other what characteristics they used to sort the shells and why.

 Anticipation Guide

Then, tell students they are going to revisit the book *Seashells by the Seashore* to learn more about shells. Have students complete the "before reading" column on the Let's Learn about Shells Anticipation Guide.

Next, take students to a reading corner—or have them stay at their seats but turn their anticipation guides over—and read only page 29 (the last page of text that provides information about seashells) of *Seashells by the Seashore*. Tell them to signal —"touch your ear"—when they hear answers to the questions on the anticipation guide.

Have students return to their seats and fill out the "after reading" column on the anticipation guide. Discuss each question as a class and ask students to cite evidence from the text that supports their answers. The correct answers to the anticipation guide are

1. True
2. True
3. False
4. True
5. False
6. False

Have students add any new information from the reading to the Learnings column of their Seashell O-W-L.

Then write the words *bivalve* and *univalve* on the board. Explain that scientists group mollusks into several classes, the two largest of which are bivalves (also called pelecypods, such as clams, oysters, and scallops) and univalves (also called gastropods, such as whelks, conchs, and snails). Ask the following questions:

? How many wheels are on a bicycle? (two)

? What do you think the prefix "bi" means? (two)

? How many pieces of shell make up a bivalve? (two)

? How many wheels are on a unicycle? (one)

? What do you think the prefix "uni" means? (one)

? How many pieces of shell make up a univalve? (one)

Show examples of bivalves, and point out the hinge. Shells that have a hinge had another shell connected at the hinge at one time. Place two bivalve shells of the same species together to show how they were once connected by a hinge.

HINGE

Explain that after the animal that lived in the shell died and decomposed, the two halves of the bivalve came apart.

If there is no hinge, the shell is a univalve. Show examples of univalves and point out that there is no hinge. Some univalves also have a spiral on them.

SPIRAL UNIVALVE

Then ask the following questions about shells:

? Why do mollusks need shells? (for protection; to aid in their survival)

? Do you think mollusks ever outgrow their shells? (Answers may vary; tell students that a mollusk's shell grows along with it.)

Again, have students add to the Learnings column of their Seashell O-W-L if they have learned any new information about shells.

explore & explain

Name That Shell! Dichotomous Key

The dichotomous key was designed to be used only with the set of shells used in the Materials section. It will not be helpful in identifying other shells.

Now students are ready to classify their shells as univalves and bivalves. They can use the Shell Sorting Sheet again for this—univalves in group A, bivalves in group B.

Introduce the Name That Shell! Dichotomous Key as a special tool that scientists can use to identify organisms. Explain that the word *dichtomous* means "dividing into two parts." A dichotomous key has two choices at every step. Direct students' attention to the pictures and labels at the top of the dichotomous key. Tell students that the first thing they should do when using a dichotomous key is look at the pictures and read the labels. This information will help them identify their objects. Discuss the different characteristics used in the key such as knobs, grooves, dome-shaped side view, and rounded hinge. Have students hold up a shell that has knobs on it, have them hold up a shell that has grooves, and so forth.

Read the directions for the dichotomous key together. Lead the students through the process of using the dichotomous key to find the name of shell A. Students should now try to identify each shell using the dichoto-

mous key and mark their answers on the answer sheet.

Have students explain their thought processes when they determined the correct name for each shell. Correct the answer sheets as a class. Use the pages that identify shells at the end of *Seashells by the Seashore* as a key.

If you use the Shell Drawings student page instead of real shells the answers are as follows: A. scallop; B. auger; C. whelk; D. cockle; E. jingle; F. kitten's paw, and G. olive.

elaborate

A House for Hermit Crab

 Inferring

Show students the cover of *A House for Hermit Crab* and read the title.

? What can you infer from the cover? (The book is about hermit crabs, hermit crabs live in a shell, and so forth.)

Discuss their inferences and ask them to explain their thinking. Then read the book aloud. After reading, discuss Hermit Crab's home.

? Why does Hermit Crab need a shell? (for protection)

? Does Hermit Crab choose a bivalve shell or a univalve shell to make his home? Why? (Univalve shells because he can hide inside them, univalves because they have a smaller opening, bivalves are only half of a shell after the animals inside them die, and so forth)

Then discuss some of the other ocean animals in the book:

? What are some of the animals that Hermit Crab encountered? (sea anemone, starfish, sea urchin, and others)

? What characteristics might scientists use to classify them? (number of body parts, how they move, type of body covering, and so forth)

? What tool could you use to identify the animals if you didn't know what they were called? (A key or a dichotomous key)

D. Sea anemone

E. Sea urchin

F. Sea cucumber

evaluate

Under the Sea Dichotomous Key

As a final evaluation, have students use the Under the Sea Dichotomous Key to identify a variety of sea creatures. The answers are listed below:

A. Octopus

B. Jellyfish

C. Nautilus

evaluate

Seashell Poster

Assign further research on seashells or the animals that make them. Students can research unanswered questions from their Seashell O-W-L or research questions you assign. Determine the criteria you would like students to meet, and then assign a poster project. Make sure students are aware of the criteria you will be using to assess their work.

Inquiry Place

Have students brainstorm "investigatable" questions about characteristics of mollusks such as:

? Which type of shell has the most space for the mollusk that lives inside? (How could you measure the capacity of a shell?)

? Do larger scallop shells have more grooves than smaller ones?

? Do snails prefer light or dark places? wet or dry places?

? What foods do snails prefer?

Students can select a question to investigate as a class, or groups of students can vote on the question they want to investigate as teams. After they make their predictions, students can design an investigation to test their predictions. They can present their findings at a poster session.

More Books to Read

Coldrey, J., and D. Bown. 1998. *Eyewitness explorers: Shells.* New York, NY: Dorling Kindersley Publishing.
Summary: Contains fascinating photographs and information about different kinds of shells.

Frasier, D. 1998. *Out of the ocean.* New York, NY: Voyager Books.
Summary: A young girl and her mother walk along the beach and marvel at the treasures cast up by the sea and the wonders of the world around them.

Lember, B. H. 1997. *The shell book.* Boston, MA: Houghton Mifflin.
Summary: Features fourteen shells commonly found along the shores of the United States. Includes a stunning hand-tinted photograph of each shell with a brief information-packed description.

Silver, D. M. 1997. *One small square series: Seashore.* New York, NY: McGraw-Hill.

Summary: This book examines the rich diversity of sea life from algae to manatees. Includes activities as well as journal keeping.

Zoehfeld, K. W. 1994. *What lives in a shell?* New York, NY: HarperTrophy.
Summary: Shows children in different settings observing various shelled creatures. Provides information about shell growth, locomotion, and the shells as protection for the animals that live in them.

References

Alvarado, A. E., and P. R. Herr. 2003. *Inquiry-based learning using everyday objects.* Thousand Oaks, CA: Corwin Press.

Ostlund, K., and S. Mercier. 1996. *Rising to the challenge of the National Science Education Standards.* Fresno, CA: S&K Associates.

Seashell O-W-L

Drawing

O-W-L Chart

O	W	L
Observations about My Seashell	**Wonderings** about My Seashell	**Learnings** about My Seashell

Name: _____

Shell
Sorting Sheet

Directions: Sort your shells into two groups based on one characteristic.

Group A	Group B

Name: _____

Let's Learn about
Shells
Anticipation Guide

Before Reading True or False		After Reading True or False

_____   **1** Seashells are made by animals.   _____

_____   **2** Sea creatures that make shells are called mollusks.   _____

_____   **3** Most shells found on the beach can be put into two groups: plants and animals.   _____

_____   **4** A bivalve is a shell with two parts.   _____

_____   **5** Oysters and scallops are types of fish.   _____

_____   **6** When you go to the beach it is okay to collect shells with live creatures in them.   _____

Name: _____

Name That Shell!
Dichotomous Key

Univalve

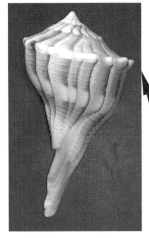

KNOBS

DOME-SHAPED
SIDE VIEW

Bivalve

GROOVES

ROUNDED
HINGE

Starting with one of the shells in your set, use the key below to identify the shell. Write the name of the shell on your answer sheet. Remember to go back to #1 on the key each time you start with a new shell!

1 Bivalve .... go to 2

  Univalve .... go to 5

2 Straight line across hinge .... SCALLOP

  Rounded hinge .... go to 3

3 Outer surface smooth and shiny .... JINGLE

  Outer surface rough with grooves .... go to 4

4 Fairly flat side view .... KITTEN'S PAW

  Dome-shaped side view .... COCKLE

5 Many knobs on closed end .... WHELK

  No knobs on closed end .... go to 6

6 Small opening on one end .... AUGER

  Long slit along length .... OLIVE

NATIONAL SCIENCE TEACHERS ASSOCIATION

Name: _____

Name That Shell!
Shell Drawings

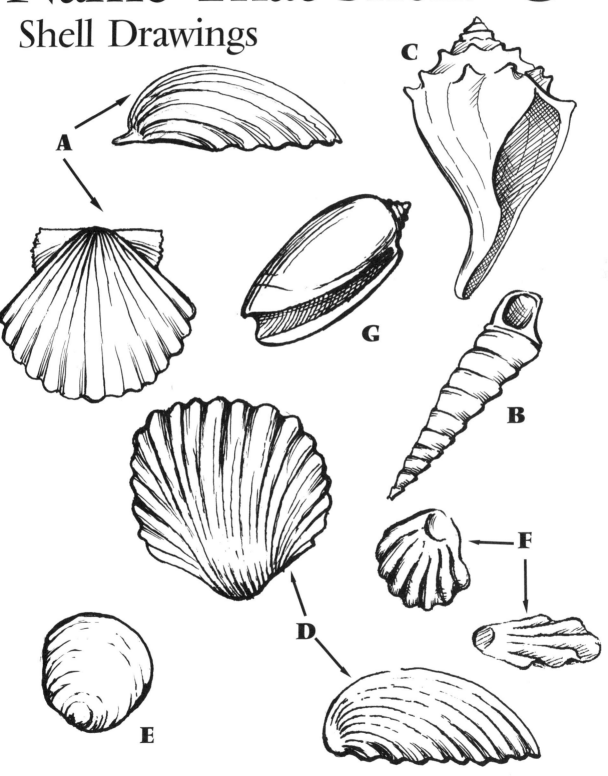

Name: _____

Name That Shell!

cont.

A _____

B _____

C _____

D _____

E _____

F _____

G _____

Under the Sea
Dichotomous Key

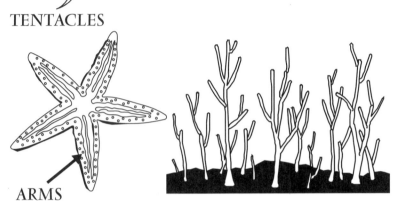

TENTACLES

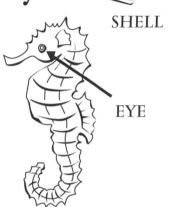

SHELL

EYE

ARMS

Starting with one of the animals on the next page, use the key below to identify the animal. Write the name of the animal on your answer sheet. Remember to go back to #1 on the key each time you start with a new animal!

1 Animal has eyes .... go to 2
Animal has no eyes .... go to 4

2 Outer shell present .... NAUTILUS
No outer shell .... go to 3

3 Rounded head and 8 arms .... OCTOPUS
Long narrow head and 10 arms .... SQUID

4 Animal is spherical with spikes .... SEA URCHIN
Not spherical .... go to 5

5 Animal has tentacles .... go to 6
Animal has no tentacles .... go to 7

6 Tentacles point upwards or outwards from tube-like body ....SEA ANEMONE
Tentacles dangle downwards from "umbrella"-shaped body .... JELLYFISH

7 Animal has 5 arms coming off center of body .... SEA STAR
Animal has no arms .... SEA CUCUMBER

Name: _____

Under the Sea

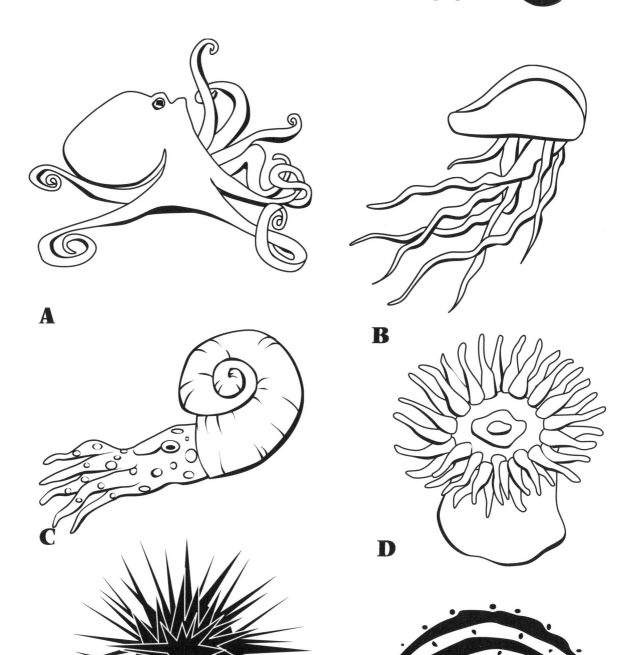

A

B

C

D

E

F

NATIONAL SCIENCE TEACHERS ASSOCIATION

Name: _____

Under the Sea cont.

A _____

B _____

C _____

D _____

E _____

F _____

Rice Is Life

Description

Learners explore the importance of rice as a food source, the differences among types of rice, the life cycle of rice, and rice production methods. Learners also explore controls, variables, and experimental design by investigating how rice grows and by designing their own plant growth experiments.

Suggested Grade Levels: 3–6

Lesson Objectives Connecting to the Standards

Content Standard A: Science as Inquiry

K–4: Plan and conduct a simple investigation.

K–4: Use data to construct a reasonable explanation.

5–8: Identify questions that can be answered through scientific investigations.

5–8: Design and conduct a scientific investigation.

5–8: Develop general abilities, such as systematic observation, making accurate measurements, and identifying and controlling variables.

Content Standard C: Life Science

K–4: Understand that plants have basic needs: air, water, nutrients, and light. Plants can survive only in environments in which their needs can be met.

Featured Picture Books

Title	*Rice Is Life*		Title	*Rice*
Author	**Rita Golden Gelman**		Author	**Louise Spilsbury**
Illustrator	**Yangsook Choi**		Illustrator	**Barry Atkinson**
Publisher	**Henry Holt & Company**		Publisher	**Heinemann Library**
Year	**2000**		Year	**2003**
Genre	**Dual Purpose**		Genre	**Non-narrative Information**
Summary	**Poetic text, factual information, and charming illustrations demonstrate the importance of rice to life on the island of Bali.**		Summary	**Describes how rice is grown and what happens to it on its way from the field to your table**

Time Needed

This lesson will take several class periods. Suggested scheduling is as follows:

Day 1:   **Engage** with Semantic Map and *Rice Is Life* read aloud, and **Explore** with observing rice grains

Day 2:   **Explain** with Let's Learn about Rice Article and Rice Journals

Day 3-7:   **Explore** with Rice Experiment and Rice Journals

Day 8:   **Explain** with *Rice* read aloud, and **Elaborate** with Journey through a Rice Mill

Day 9:   **Explain** with investigatable questions, and **Evaluate** with Design a Plant Experiment

Day 10:   **Evaluate** with Experimental Design Quiz

Materials

- Bowls of cooked rice (1 per student)
- Chart paper (2 sheets)
- Chopsticks (optional—1 pair per student)
- "Think pads" (1 pad of sticky notes per student)
- Hand lenses (1 per student)
- White rice
- Brown rice
- Rice in the husk
  (also called rice in the hull or unmilled rice seed)
- Clear plastic cups
- Water
- Sandpaper
- Bean plants (2 per student)
- Cups for growing bean plants
- Soil for growing bean plants

Rice seed in the husk is available from

Bountiful Gardens
18001 Shafer Ranch Road
Willits, CA 95490-9626
707-459-6410
www.bountifulgardens.org

Research & Technology
RiceTec, Inc.
P.O. Box 1305
Alvin, TX 77512
281-393-3502
research@ricetec.com

Student Pages

- Let's Learn about Rice Anticipation Guide
- Rice Article
- Rice Journal (Copy the cover on a separate sheet, and then copy page 1 back-to-back with 2 and 7; copy pages 6 and 3 back-to-back with 4 and 5. Fold and staple along spine.)
- Journey through a Rice Mill
- Design a Plant Experiment
- Experimental Design Quiz

Engage

Semantic Map and Read Aloud

Serve students some cooked rice (chopsticks optional) and begin creating a semantic map as they are eating. A semantic map is a tool that helps activate prior knowledge, determine misconceptions, and show relationships among concepts. Start by writing the word *rice* at the top of a sheet of chart paper. Ask students questions to get them thinking about rice, such as the following:

? What are some terms you think of when you hear the word *rice*?

? What do you know about rice?

List student responses on the chart paper. Then write the word *rice* in the center of another sheet of chart paper and circle it. Have students review the first list and begin to categorize the terms on the list. Discuss the categories and terms, and then have students determine how to display them in the form of a map or web. Discussion of the semantic map helps students become aware of new words, create new meanings for terms, and recognize the relationships among numerous words related to the lesson. Throughout the lesson that follows, display the semantic map for rice, adding new categories and terms as students learn more about rice.

Semantic Map Template

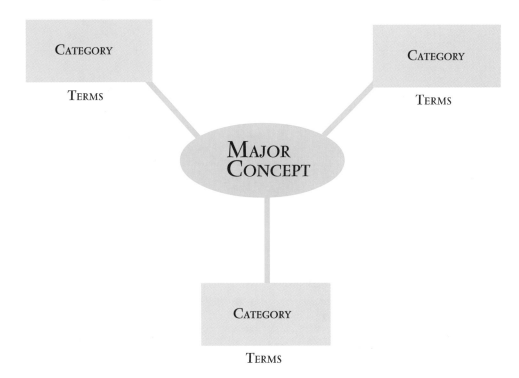

Sample Semantic Map for Rice

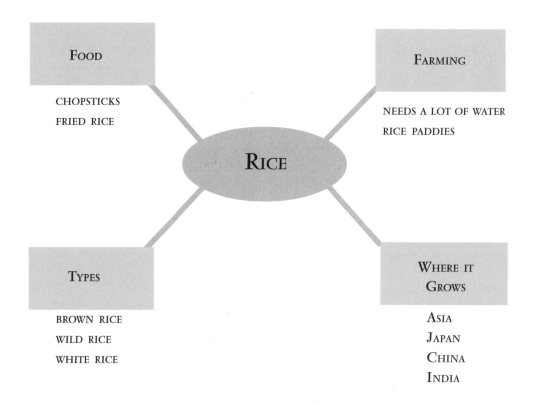

FOOD

CHOPSTICKS
FRIED RICE

FARMING

NEEDS A LOT OF WATER
RICE PADDIES

RICE

TYPES

BROWN RICE
WILD RICE
WHITE RICE

WHERE IT
GROWS

ASIA
JAPAN
CHINA
INDIA

 Inferring

Before you read *Rice Is Life* to students, write the comprehension activities suggested below on sticky notes and then insert them into the appropriate places in the text. This will help you avoid disrupting the flow of the poetic text.

Ask students to examine the cover of the book *Rice Is Life* and infer what the title might mean. Introduce the author and the illustrator. (You can find out more about this fascinating author at *www.ritagoldengelman.com*.) Then read *Rice Is Life* to the students.

 Inferring: Stop and Jot

On pages 6 and 7 (about the boys and girls "fishing" for dragonflies), read the verses and ask students to stop and jot on their sticky-

note "think pads" why they think the boys and girls are catching dragonflies.

 Visualizing: Sketch to Stretch

Don't show the picture (of the people scaring away the birds) on pages 14 and 15. Tell students to visualize as you read and draw a picture on their sticky-note "think pads" of what they think that scene might look like.

 Synthesizing

Ask students what they think the title, *Rice Is Life*, means after reading the book. Have them support their ideas with examples from the book. Then go back to the semantic map and add any new categories or terms they learned from the book. You can also have students correct any misconceptions that might have been written on the map. Continue adding to and revising the semantic map through-out the lesson to show relationships and correct misconceptions.

explore

Observing Rice Grains

Give each group of students a plate with a few grains each of brown rice, white rice, and rice in the husk, but don't tell them what they are at this point. Give them hand lenses and have them make observations. After students have had plenty of time to observe and infer what the samples are, point out the one that is white rice, the one that is brown rice, and the one that is rice in the *husk* (seed coat, also called hull). Ask students to predict which type of rice would *germinate* (sprout): rice in the husk, brown rice, or white rice.

explain

Let's Learn about Rice Article

 ### Anticipation Guide

Tell students that they are going to explore the question, "What does rice need to grow?" Pass out the Let's Learn about Rice Anticipation Guide. Have students fill in the "before reading" column.

 ### Pairs Read

Pass out the Rice Article. Put students in pairs and have them take turns reading aloud from the article. While one person reads a paragraph, the other listens and then summarizes. Have students read for the answers and mark the correct answers in the "after reading" column.

Answers to the Let's Learn about Rice Anticipation Guide are

1. T
2. T

3. F
4. F
5. T
6. F

explain

Rice Journals

Pass out the Rice Journals to students and tell them that they are going to be investigating to see which of the three types of rice (brown rice, white rice, and rice in the husk) will germinate. Have students fill in their predictions on page 1 of the journals.

The question at the bottom of page 1 asks what the experimental variable is in this experiment. Tell students that when scientists design an experiment, the first thing they do is determine what it is they want to test. The one thing in the experiment that is being tested is called the *experimental variable*.

? What is the experimental variable in our experiment? (the type of rice)

Have students record the experimental variable on page 1 of their journals.

Next, have students turn to page 2 in the journals. Read the instructions together. Tell students that scientists always make sure their experiments are fair tests by keeping everything but the experimental variable the same. The conditions kept the same are called *controlled variables*.

? What are the controlled variables in our experiment? (size of cups, color of cups, amount of water, amount of seeds per cup, amount of sunlight, temperature)

Have students record the controlled variables on page 2 of their journals.

explore

Rice Experiment and Rice Journals

Review the information about growing rice from the Rice Article by asking

? What conditions are necessary to grow rice? (a lot of water, temperature higher than 21°C, plenty of sunlight, and soil)

Then have students set up their experiments according to instructions 1 through 3 (for germinating rice) in the "How to Grow Rice" section of the Rice Article. Tell students to make sure to keep all variables controlled except the type of rice.

Setting Up the Rice Experiment:

- Sprinkle 10 white rice grains in the bottom of a clear plastic cup and label the cup "White Rice."
- Sprinkle 10 brown rice grains in another cup and label the cup "Brown Rice."

- Sprinkle 10 grains of rice in the husk in a third cup and label the cup "Rice in the Husk."
- Fill each cup to the 5 cm level with clean water.
- Keep the temperature above 21°C (70°F).
- Observe the rice every few days.

After students have set up their experiments, ask

? Why do you think the article suggests sprinkling 10 rice seeds in the bottom of each cup instead of just one? (It gives you a better chance of getting some rice to grow.)

? Why not put different numbers of rice grains in each cup? (We need to control that variable to make it a fair test; each cup should have the same number of rice grains.)

Students will use pages 3 and 4 of the Rice Journals to record observations of each type of rice every few days. Each day they should check to make sure the water level is at 5 cm and add more water as needed.

After four observations, students can fill in the "Results" section in the Rice Journal. Students should observe that only the rice in the husk actually germinates. Discuss the following questions:

? Why do you think the rice in the husk germinated and not the brown or white rice? What do you think might be missing from the brown and white rice?

MEASURING THE WATER LEVEL

explain

Read Aloud

Using Features of Nonfiction

Tell students that they will be learning about what's inside a grain of rice by looking at a nonfiction book called *Rice*. Introduce the nonfiction book *Rice* by Louise Spilsbury, and read pages 4 and 5, "What Is Rice?" Ask

? Is it necessary to finish reading the entire book to learn what's inside a grain of rice?

? What parts of a nonfiction book can help us look up specific information? (table of contents, index, or glossary)

Show students the table of contents. Ask them to raise their hands when they think they hear a chapter title that might help them find out what a rice grain looks like inside. Then read aloud the table of contents. (The chapter titled "Looking at Rice" has the information they need.)

Read pages 12 and 13 of *Rice,* and point out the labels on the photo and diagram. Sketch a rice grain on the board and label the parts. Include the embryo, which is not mentioned in the reading.

Then write the following words and definitions on the board:

● Embryo—the part of the seed that develops into a rice plant

● Husk—the hard outer covering, or seed coat, of the rice grain, which protects the embryo

● Bran layers—the thin brown layers between the husk and the rice grain

● Rice grain—the food for the embryo as it develops

Ask students

? What are the differences among rice in the husk, brown rice, and white rice? (Rice in the husk is the rice grain still in its seed

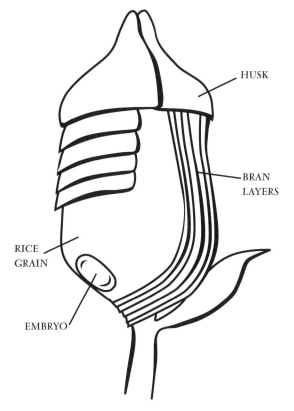

PARTS OF A RICE GRAIN

coat. Brown rice is the grain left after the outer husk has been removed. White rice is the same as brown rice, but with the outer bran layers removed.)

Show students the rice grain diagram again on page 13 of *Rice,* and refer to your diagram on the board. Then go back to the question generated by the rice experiment.

? Why do you think the rice in the husk germinated and not the brown or white rice? What do you think might be missing from the brown and white rice? (The milling process removes the husks as well as the embryos from the brown and white rice. They cannot germinate because the embryo is the part of the seed that develops into the plant.)

Students should now label the rice diagram on page 6 of their journals and fill in the explanation table on page 5. Then have them write their conclusions on the last page of their journals. Encourage them to use evidence from the experiment to write their conclusions.

elaborate

Journey through a Rice Mill

Ask students

? How do you think rice gets from the field to your table?

 ### *Determining Importance*

Tell students that the book *Rice* describes this process. As you read pages 14 through 21 in *Rice,* have students listen for the answers to the following questions:

? How are the rice grains removed from the stalks? (Farmers beat the stalks to shake off the grain. In some places they use a combine harvester to cut down the plants and separate the grain from the stalks.)

? How are the husks removed from the rice grains? (Some farmers crush the grains to loosen the hard husks, then toss the grains in the air to get the loose husks off. In some places, they use machines with big rollers to rub the grains off the husks. For white rice, the bran layer is also taken off by rubbing the grains together in a machine.)

Ask students to think about what happens to the rice after it is harvested. Pass out Journey through a Rice Mill, sandpaper, and a few grains each of rice in the husk and instant white rice to each student. Have students complete the student page and discuss their answers to the questions.

1 Describe the way your rice grains have changed. (Students should observe that the husk has been removed and the grain is lighter in color.)

2 Why do you think the husk and embryos are removed before rice is sold for food? (The husks are not edible, and removing the embryos keeps the seeds from germinating.)

3 In what ways are the rice in the husk and the instant rice different? (The instant white rice is very white, shriveled, and more brittle than the rice in the husk. The rice in the husk is darker, smoother, and harder.)

4 What might have been done to turn brown rice into instant white rice? Read the instant rice package for clues. (The bran layer has been removed, the rice has been enriched with vitamins and minerals, and it has been precooked.)

explain

"Investigatable" Questions

Pass out the Design a Plant Experiment student page. Allow time for students to complete number 1: "My questions about plant growth." Make a T-chart on the board labeled "investigatable" and "not investigatable." Tell students that some questions are investigatable questions that can be answered through experimentation. Then ask some of them to share a question from number 1 that might be investigatable. Write these questions on the left side of the T-chart.

Then explain that some questions can't be answered by experimentation. Often these questions can be answered through library or Internet research. Ask some students to share a question from number 1 that is not investigatable. Write these questions on the right side of the T-chart.

Sample T-Chart

Investigatable	Not Investigatable
How does sunlight affect plant growth?	Why do plants make their own food?
Does fertilizer really help plants grow?	What is the largest plant in the world?
Can plants grow in substances other than soil?	Why do plants have green leaves?

evaluate

Design a Plant Experiment

Tell students that they will receive two bean plants to use in their experiments. Have students write their own investigatable question for number 2. Then have them complete the rest of the Design a Plant Experiment student page. Use the following rubric to assess student work.

After you finish assessing the Design a Plant Experiment student page, pass them back to students. Allow students to correct any flaws in their experimental design and give them the materials to complete their experiment.

Scoring Rubric for Design a Plant Experiment

4 Point Response	The student selects an investigatable question, makes a prediction relating to the question, correctly identifies experimental and controlled variables, lists logical steps for performing the investigation, and lists materials needed for the investigation.
3 Point Response	The student demonstrates a flaw in understanding of the concepts of experimental design OR is missing one or two required elements.
2 Point Response	The student demonstrates a flaw in understanding of the concepts of experimental design AND is missing one or two required elements OR is missing three or four required elements.
1 Point Response	The student demonstrates a flaw in understanding of the concepts of experimental design AND is missing three or more required elements OR is missing four or more required elements.
0 Point Response	The student shows no understanding of the concepts of experimental design AND is missing all required elements.

evaluate

Experimental Design Quiz

Review experimental variables, controlled variables, and experimental design, and then administer the Experimental Design Quiz. The answers follow.

1. c

2. a

3. Responses may include any two of the following: type of bean, type of soil, amount of sunlight, size of containers, amount of soil, etc.

4. c

5. Brand of fertilizer

6. Responses may include any two of the following: the amount of water is different for each plant; the amount of sunlight is different for each plant; three different kinds of plants are used; three different sizes of container are used. Ashley could improve her experiment by making sure these variables are controlled.

Inquiry Place

Have students brainstorm investigatable questions such as

? How does the amount of light affect the germination of rice seeds?

? How does temperature affect the germination of rice seeds?

? How does the amount of water affect the germination of rice seeds?

? How do pollutants (bleach, salt, etc.) affect the germination of rice seeds?

? How does the type of soil affect the growth of rice plants?

Have students select a question to investigate as a class, or have groups of students vote on the question they want to investigate as teams. After they make their predictions, they can design an experiment to test their predictions. Students can present their findings at a poster session.

More Books to Read

Demi. 1997. *One grain of rice: A mathematical folktale.* New York, NY: Scholastic.
Summary: This beautifully illustrated Indian folktale tells the story of a resourceful girl who outsmarts a greedy raja and saves her village. When offered a reward for a good deed, clever Rani asks for only one grain of rice, doubled every day for thirty days. The result is enough rice to feed her village for a long, long time.

Gibbons, G. 1993. *From seed to plant.* New York, NY: Holiday House.
Summary: A simple introduction to plant reproduction, this picture book for lower elementary students discusses pollination, seed dispersal, parts of a seed, and growth from seed to plant. Includes a simple project with step-by-step directions for growing a bean plant.

Pascoe, E. 1996. *Seeds and seedlings: Nature close up.* Woodbridge, CT: Blackbirch Marketing.
Summary: This clearly written book of seed projects and experiments is enhanced by extraordinary close-up photographs.

Web Sites

California Rice Commission
www.calrice.org

USA Rice Federation
www.usarice.com

References

California Foundation for Agriculture in the Classroom. *Rice Activity Sheet.* 2003. Sacramento, CA: California Foundation for Agriculture in the Classroom.

Journey through a Rice Mill is adapted from an activity on this fact sheet.

Let's Learn about Rice
Anticipation Guide

Before reading the
article "Rice," guess
whether the following
statements about rice
are true (T) or false (F).
Mark your guess in
the left column. After
reading the article,
mark the statements
(T or F) in the right
column.

Before Reading	True or False	After Reading
_____	1 Rice is a type of grass.	_____
_____	2 The edible portion of a rice plant is part of the seed.	_____
_____	3 Rice plants do not need a lot of water to grow.	_____
_____	4 Rice plants should be grown in dark places.	_____
_____	5 Rice is the main food for over half the world.	_____
_____	6 Most of the world's rice is grown in the USA.	_____

Rice

The Rice Plant

Rice is a type of grass that germinates and grows in flooded fields. In fact, it takes 5,000 liters of water to produce 1 kilogram of rice. The edible portion of the rice plant is part of the seed.

How to Grow Rice

You can grow rice by following this procedure:

1. Sprinkle 10 rice seeds in the bottom of a clear plastic cup.
2. Fill the cup to the 5 cm level with clean water.
3. Keep the temperature above 21°C (70°F).
4. After the seeds germinate, put them in a large plastic tub filled to the 5 cm mark with soil.
5. Fill the tub with water until the water is 5 cm above the soil level.
6. Keep the water level at 5 cm throughout the growth cycle.
7. Provide growing plants with plenty of sunlight.

Rice Is Important

Rice is the primary food for over half of the world! Rice is packed with carbohydrates. This means it is a kind of food that gives you energy. In many countries, people eat rice for breakfast, lunch, and dinner. People in Asia have grown and eaten rice for over 5,000 years.

Rice around the World

About 90 percent of the world's rice is grown in Asia. China, India, and Indonesia are the top rice producers. There are a few states in the United States that grow rice, including California, Mississippi, Arkansas, Louisiana, and Texas.

Rice Journal

Scientist: _____

Dates: from _____ to _____

Prediction

Which of the following do you predict will **germinate** and eventually grow into a rice plant: white rice, brown rice, or rice in the hull? Why do you think so?

_____

_____

_____

Let's design an experiment to find out.

In this experiment, our **experimental** variable is

_____

1

Conclusions

What conclusions can you make from the results of this experiment?

What is your evidence?

7

Controlled Variables

Let's make a list of **controlled variables**, in other words, conditions we should keep the same for each type of seed.

2

Observations

Observation #1 Date:

Type of Rice	Observations
White Rice	
Brown Rice	
Rice in the Husk	

Observation #2 Date:

Type of Rice	Observations
White Rice	
Brown Rice	
Rice in the Husk	

3

Label the following parts on the diagram below: husk, embryo, bran layer, rice grain

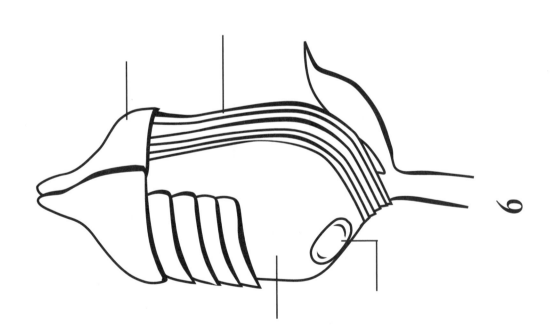

6

NATIONAL SCIENCE TEACHERS ASSOCIATION

Results

Type of Rice	Results (How many seeds germinated?)
White Rice	
Brown Rice	
Rice in the Husk	

Label the parts of the rice seed on the diagram on the next page. Then write the function of each of the seed parts in the table below.

Seed Part	Function
Husk	
Bran Layer	
Embryo	
Rice Grain	

5

Observation #3   Date:

Type of Rice	Observations
White Rice	
Brown Rice	
Rice in the Husk	

Observation #4   Date:

Type of Rice	Observations
White Rice	
Brown Rice	
Rice in the Husk	

4

Name: _____

Journey through a Rice Mill

The following activity is a simulation of part of the rice milling process:

- Observe some grains of rice in the husk.
- Place a piece of sandpaper on the desk.
- Place several grains of rice in the husk on the sandpaper and place another piece of sandpaper on top.
- Rub the two pieces gently back and forth until you see a change in the grains.

1 Describe the way your rice grains have changed.

_____

2 Why do you think the husk and embryos are removed before rice is sold for food?

_____

- Take the sanded rice grains and put them next to some instant white rice from the grocery store.
- Compare the rice grains to the instant white rice.

3 In what ways are the rice grains and the instant white rice different?

_____

4 What might have been done to turn brown rice into instant white rice? (Read the instant rice package for clues!)

_____

Design a Plant Experiment

1 My questions about plant growth:

_____

_____

2 My investigatable question:

_____

3 My prediction:

_____

4 My experimental variable:

_____

5 Variables I will control to keep the experiment fair:

_____

6 Steps I will follow to investigate my question:

_____

_____

7 Materials I will need:

_____

_____

Checkpoint ☐

Name: _____

Experimental Design
Quiz

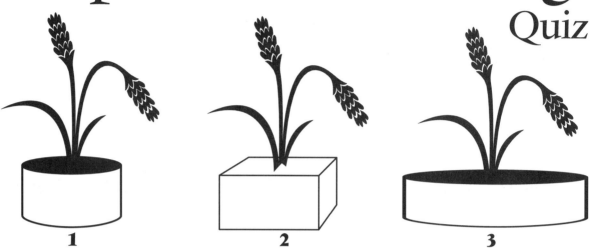

1   2   3

A researcher wants to learn which of three fields has the best soil for growing rice. The researcher fills each container with soil from a different field. The containers are placed next to each other in a sunny window. One rice plant is grown in each container, and each container receives the same amount of water.

1 What is wrong with the materials the researcher used in the experiment?

  a The rice plant in container 1 will receive the most sunlight.

  b The containers should each receive different amounts of water.

  c The containers hold different amounts of soil in different shapes.

2 Jeff wants to find out how the amount of water affects the growth of bean plants. What is Jeff's experimental variable?

  a amount of water

  b type of bean

  c type of soil

3 What are two things Jeff will need to control, or keep the same, to make his experiment fair?

_____ and_____

Name: _____

Experimental Design Quiz cont.

 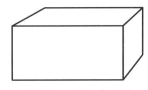 

BLUEGRASS   RYEGRASS   BENTGRASS

Rani wants to find out which type of grass grows the tallest. She is testing three types of grass seed as shown above. She puts equal amounts of soil in each container.

4 How many grass seeds should Rani plant in each container?

a Rani should plant only 1 grass seed in each container so that she will not have to measure as many grass plants.

b Rani should plant 1 grass seed in the first container, 2 grass seeds in the second container, and 3 in the third container.

c Rani should plant 10 grass seeds in each container in case some of them don't grow. She can measure all of the grass that grows in each container and average the measurements.

Experimental Design Quiz cont.

Ashley designed the experiment to find out which brand of fertilizer will make plants grow the tallest.

	Plant A	Plant B	Plant C
Brand of Fertilizer	Give Primo fertilizer.	Give K-Gro fertilizer.	Give Acme fertilizer.
Amount of Water	Water with 50 ml every day.	Water with 100 ml every day.	Water with 200 ml every day.
Amount of Sunlight	Place in bright sun.	Place in part sun.	Place in shade.
Data	Measure height daily.	Measure height daily.	Measure height daily.

5 What is Ashley's experimental variable?

_____

6 There are several things wrong with Ashley's experimental design. Describe two things that are wrong. Then explain how she could improve her experiment so that it is a fair test.

_____

_____

_____

_____

What's Poppin'?

Description

Learners explore the history of popcorn and investigate what makes popcorn pop. They design a safe, fair, and repeatable experiment to test various popcorn brands and share their findings in a poster session.

Suggested Grade Levels: 5–6

Lesson Objectives Connecting to the Standards

Content Standard A: Science as Inquiry

5-8: Develop descriptions, explanations, predictions, and models using evidence.

5-8: Think critically and logically to make the relationships between evidence and explanations.

5-8: Communicate scientific procedures and explanations.

5-8: Design and conduct a scientific investigation.

Featured Picture Book

Title	***The Popcorn Book***
Author	**Tomie de Paola**
Illustrator	**Tomie de Paola**
Publisher	**Holiday House**
Year	**1989**
Genre	**Dual Purpose**
Summary	**Full of information about poporn, including its history, varieties, and recipes**

Time Needed

This lesson will take several class periods. Suggested scheduling is as follows:

Day 1: **Engage** with *The Popcorn Book* read aloud, and **Explore** with What's Poppin'? Checkpoint Lab, Part A

Day 2: **Explore** with What's Poppin'? Checkpoint Lab, Parts B–D; **Explain** with reading and relating to the checkpoint lab

Day 3: **Elaborate** with Popcorn Brand Test Checkpoint Lab

Day 4: **Evaluate** with Popcorn Poster Session

Materials

For Engage Activity:

- Microwave popcorn (3 or 4 popped bags—enough for the whole class to eat)
- Bowls or napkins for popcorn (1 per student)
- Popcorn-shaped K-W-L chart

For the What's Poppin'? Checkpoint Lab:

Read safety note under "Explore"

- Fresh jar of popcorn
- Prepare ahead of time:
  - ✦ Write "A" on zipper baggies and divide 125 ml (about ½ cup) fresh popcorn kernels into the baggies (1 baggie per team).
  - ✦ Dry 125 ml (about ½ cup) of popcorn kernels by placing them in a single layer in a pan in an oven at 90° C (190° F) for at least five hours (or overnight). Write "B" on zipper baggies and divide the dried popcorn into the baggies (1 baggie per team).
- A red plastic cup and a green plastic cup with the openings taped together (1 per team)
- Hand lenses (1 per student)
- Safety goggles (1 per student)
- Glass test tubes (4 per team)
- Masking tape to label test tubes
- Wire test-tube holders (1 per team)
- Wooden test-tube racks (1 per team)
- Large sturdy candles attached to a base made of a chunk of clay (1 per team)
- Aluminum pie plates to hold candles (1 per team)
- Safety matches (for teacher use only)
- 3 cm x 3 cm aluminum foil squares (4 per team)
- Pipettes or eye droppers (1 per team)
- Small plastic cups containing about 5 ml of cooking oil (1 per team)
- Stopwatches (1 per team) or clock with second hand for entire class to use

For Demonstration:

- Brown paper bag
- White napkin or paper towel

For the Popcorn Brand Test Checkpoint Lab:

Read safety note under "Elaborate"

- Three different brands of microwave popcorn to test: same size, same flavor (Use 1 of each brand per team. You can have students bring them in.)
- Microwave ovens (about 1 per every three teams)
- A red plastic cup and a green plastic cup with the openings taped together (1 per team)
- Poster board (1 per team)

Student Pages

- What's Poppin'? Checkpoint Lab
- Popcorn Brand Test Checkpoint Lab
- Popcorn Poster Session

Engage

Read Aloud

 ### *K-W-L* Chart

Draw a large, whole-class K-W-L (know, wonder, learn) chart titled "Popcorn." Make some microwave popcorn. Give each student a bowl of hot popped popcorn to eat as you fill out the chart together. Ask students, "What do you know about popcorn?" Fill out the "K" column of the chart. Then ask, "What are you wondering about popcorn?" and add to the "W" column of the chart. If students do not volunteer the question, "What makes popcorn pop?," then add it to the chart as one of your own wonderings.

Tell students you are going to read about the history of popcorn. Have them listen for the answers to any of their wonderings or for any other important information they can add to the K-W-L chart. Introduce *The Popcorn Book,* by Tomie de Paola, by telling students that the author's favorite food is, of course—popcorn! (More information about the author can be found at *www.tomiedepaola.com*). Read aloud up to page 21, stopping before the explanation of what makes popcorn pop.

Have students add information they learned from the reading to the "L" column of the K-W-L chart, as well as any more wonderings they have about popcorn as new understandings develop.

Explore

What's Poppin'? Checkpoint Lab

In advance, prepare all of the materials necessary for the What's Poppin'? Checkpoint Lab. See "Teaching Science Through Inquiry," Chapter 3, for a list of tips for managing a checkpoint lab. Check your school policy for its rules on using an open flame in an elementary setting before using this activity.

Tell students that they are going to investigate what makes popcorn pop. Divide students into teams of four. Have the following materials available for each team:

- A red plastic cup and a green plastic cup with the openings taped together
- 4 unpopped popcorn kernels
- 4 pieces of popped popcorn
- 1 zipper baggie of fresh popcorn (marked "A")
- 1 zipper baggie of oven-dried popcorn (marked "B")
- 4 hand lenses
- 4 glass test tubes
- 1 wire test-tube holder

Sample K-W-L Chart

K	W	L
Popcorn comes from a popcorn plant.	Where does popcorn grow?	Popcorn is the oldest of the 3 types of corn: field corn, sweet corn, and popcorn.
Popcorn comes in many varieties.	What makes popcorn pop?	
Popcorn tastes good.	If you plant a popcorn kernel will it grow?	

- 1 large sturdy candle attached to a base made of a chunk of clay
- 1 aluminum pie plate to hold candles
- 1 wooden test-tube rack
- 4 safety goggles (Safety goggles should be chemical splash safety goggles conforming to the ANSI Z87.1 standard. These are also impact goggles.)
- Masking tape to label test tubes
- 4 small squares of aluminum foil (large enough to cover openings of test tubes)
- 1 pipette or eye dropper
- About 5 ml of cooking oil in a small plastic cup labeled "oil"

Popcorn Testing

Distribute the What's Poppin? Checkpoint Lab. Assign one person to be the reader for each team. Readers will read the directions out loud for their teams. They will put the green cup on top if their team is working. They will put the red cup on top if their team has a question or if they are ready for a check mark. Each member of the group is responsible for recording data and writing responses.

Let teams begin and work at their own paces. Before you give a team a check mark or stamp so that they can move ahead in the lab, informally evaluate them by asking probing questions of each member of the team, such as

SAFETY

Tell students that in this experiment they will be popping popcorn by heating it in a test tube over a flame. Because they are working with flame, tell them they must follow the following safety rules.

1. Roll up your sleeves and tie back long hair.
2. Wear safety goggles over your eyes.
3. Use a wire holder to hold the test tube over the flame, but not directly in the flame.
4. When you heat anything in a test tube, point the open end away from yourself and others.
5. Keep your work area clean and clear of flammable materials.

In *Safety in the Elementary (K-6) Science Classroom: Second Edition,* the American Chemical Society gives the following safety rules for working with fire and heat sources:

1. Teachers should never leave the room while any flame is lighted or other heat source is in use.
2. Never heat flammable liquids. Heat only water or water solutions.
3. Use only glassware made from borosilicate glass (Kimax or Pyrex) for heating.
4. When working around a heat source, tie back long hair and secure loose clothing.
5. The area surrounding a heat source should be clean and have no combustible materials nearby.
6. When using a hot plate, locate it so that a child cannot pull it off the worktop or trip over the power cord.

SAFETY

7. Never leave the room while the hot plate is plugged in, whether or not it is in use; never allow students near an in-use hot plate if the teacher is not immediately beside the students.

8. Be certain that hot plates have been unplugged and are cool before handling. Check for residual heat by placing a few drops of water on the hot plate surface.

9. Never use alcohol burners.

10. Students should use candles only under the strict supervision of the teacher. Candles should be placed in a "drip pan" such as an aluminum pie plate large enough to contain the candle if it is knocked over.

11. The teacher should wear safety goggles and use heat resistant mitts when working with hot materials. All students near hot liquids should wear safety goggles.*

12. The teacher should keep a fire extinguisher near the activity area and be trained in its use.

13. The teacher should know what to do in case of fire. If a school policy does not exist, check with local fire officials for information.

Before using this activity, check your school's policy on using an open flame. Some schools forbid it.

Tell students they should not eat popcorn from the test tubes.

*Investigating Safely: A Guide for High School Teachers recommends that chemical splash safety goggles conforming to the ANSI Z87.1 standard be used for all activities that require goggles. These chemical splash safety goggles are also impact goggles (Texley, Kwan, and Summers 2004).

? What is your evidence?

? What observations support your conclusion?

? Could there be another explanation?

Be sure to check students' experimental setups and review the safety rules with each team before you light their candles in Part C of the checkpoint lab.

explain

Reading and Relating to the Checkpoint Lab

When all teams have completed the checkpoint lab, have students share their observations and conclusions in their own words. Then discuss the following questions:

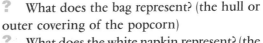
? What did you observe inside the test tubes as they were being heated? (Students should have observed water condensing on the sides of the test tubes and on the foil.)

? Where can you infer the water came from? (from inside the popcorn kernels)

? What do you know about how water molecules behave as they are heated? Think about a pot of water heating on the stove. (The water molecules move faster and spread out as the water begins boiling. Then they spread out so much they rise into the air as steam.)

 Determining Importance

Next, tell students you are going to read more of *The Popcorn Book*. Have them listen for an explanation of what makes popcorn pop. Read from page 22 to the end.

Sketch to Stretch

Ask students to imagine the water molecules inside a popcorn kernel just before it pops. Have them sketch what they think the water molecules might look like inside the kernel just as the kernel pops. Then do the following demonstration:

Place a white napkin or white paper towel inside a brown paper bag. Blow up the bag, and then pop it so that the napkin pops out. Ask students

? What does the bag represent? (the hull or outer covering of the popcorn)

? What does the white napkin represent? (the starchy stuff inside the popcorn)

? What makes the starch explode out of the hull in a real popcorn kernel? (The water inside boils and turns to steam. A little bit of water boils up into a lot of steam. There is much more steam than will fit inside the kernel. The steam builds up, and the kernel explodes.)

Finally, ask students what new information they have learned about popcorn and add it to the Popcorn K-W-L.

elaborate

Popcorn Brand Test Checkpoint Lab

In advance, set up one or more microwave ovens in your classroom. You can provide the popcorn for this activity, or, even better, have each student bring a bag from home, but make sure they bring in same-sized bags of the same flavor. See "Teaching Science Through Inquiry," Chapter 3, for a list of tips for managing a checkpoint lab.

Students can elaborate on what they have learned about popcorn by designing and carrying out their own experiments to find out which brand pops the most kernels. Ask the following questions to help students think

SAFETY Before using the Popcorn Brand Test Checkpoint Lab, check your school's policy on eating as part of a science lab activity. Some schools forbid it, and commercial labs can be fined for even the appearance of eating. Make sure your students know they should never taste anything in a lab activity. *Exploring Safely: A Guide for Elementary Teachers* recommends "Nothing should be tasted or eaten as part of science lab work" (Kwan and Texley 2002). The best way to do this activity is as an experiment that does not include eating the popped popcorn, but, if there is any chance your students will eat the popcorn, make sure your sanitary preparations have been adequate. Cleaning up a section of your room to do this activity in can be a teaching tool that helps students learn a way of doing science.

about controlling variables and good experimental design:

? What were we testing in the checkpoint lab? (We compared fresh popcorn to dried popcorn to see which one would pop. We wanted to find out what makes popcorn pop.)

? What was the *experimental variable*, or the thing that we changed, in our test? (the type of popcorn: fresh or oven-dried)

? What were the *controlled variables*, or the things we kept the same, in our popcorn test? (same-sized test tubes, same amount of oil, same number of kernels, same amount of heating time)

? Why did we keep all those things the same? (to keep the test "fair")

Pass out the Popcorn Brand Test student pages. Tell students they will be designing an experiment to find out which brand of popcorn pops the most kernels by counting the number of popped kernels. On these pages, students will determine that the experimental variable in this test is the brand of popcorn. They will also determine which of the following variables need to be controlled to make it a fair test, such as

● Size or weight of the popcorn bags
● Flavor of popcorn
● Microwave
● Power level of microwave
● Position of the bag in the microwave
● Amount of time in the microwave

Students will then write a procedure for their popcorn brand testing. Students should recognize the importance of formulating procedures and communicating data in a manner that allows others to understand and safely repeat an experiment. When each member of a team has completed "Part A: Designing a Popcorn Brand Test," that team can signal to you that they are ready to move on. Before signing off on their work, make sure their experimental design is safe, fair, and repeatable. Ask each member of the team a question about the experimental design as a quick assessment. Once each student gets a check mark, the team is ready to move ahead and perform the experiment.

Sample Procedure for Popcorn Brand Test:

● Remove plastic covering from popcorn bag.
● Place 3-ounce bag of Brand A popcorn in center of microwave with correct side up.
● Cook for exactly 2 minutes, 30 seconds, at highest power and remove bag.
● Allow bag to cool for 3 minutes.
● Open bag carefully, and count popped kernels.
● Record data and graph results in a bar graph.
● Repeat with Brand B and Brand C.
● Compare results, and draw conclusion.

Students will use "Part B: Popcorn Data" to record the results of their experiments. Discuss the type of graph that is appropriate for displaying the data.

? Which type of graph is the best for displaying the data? (bar graph)

? Why? (We are comparing totals, not parts of a whole or changes over time.)

If all teams are using the same three brands of popcorn, you may want to record their data on a whole-class table and average results. You can then graph the averages on a whole-class graph. Discuss reasons for variations in the results—for example, different controls, different procedures, freshness of popcorn, and experimental error.

Evaluate

Popcorn Poster Session

Students will present what they've learned about popcorn in a poster session. They will use the Popcorn Poster Session student page as a guide. Students should include the following in their poster presentations:

- Some important information they learned about popcorn
- A scientifically accurate diagram explaining how popcorn pops
- Their prediction for the popcorn brand testing
- The step-by-step procedure they followed in their experiment
- A graph showing the results of their experiment
- Their conclusion for the experiment
- An original advertisement, commercial, or jingle for the popcorn brand that popped the most kernels in their experiment

Use the following rubric to evaluate each team's work:

Scoring Rubric for Popcorn Poster Session

4 Point Response	The poster includes accurate facts about popcorn, a labeled and scientifically accurate diagram explaining how popcorn pops, a prediction, a logical and clearly communicated procedure, a labeled bar graph, an appropriate conclusion, and an original advertisement, commercial, or jingle for popcorn.
3 Point Response	The poster demonstrates a flaw in understanding of the concepts and procedures OR is missing one or two required elements.
2 Point Response	The poster demonstrates a flaw in understanding of the concepts and procedures AND is missing one or two required elements; OR the poster is missing three required elements.
1 Point Response	The poster demonstrates a flaw in understanding of the concepts and procedures AND is missing three required elements; OR the poster is missing more than three required elements.
0 Point Response	The poster shows no understanding of the concepts and procedures and is missing all required elements.

Inquiry Place

Have students brainstorm "investigatable" questions such as

? Does the color of the popcorn kernel affect the color of the popped corn?

? Which results in the most popped kernels: frozen, refrigerated, or room temperature kernels?

? Will other types of corn pop? Test field corn, sweet corn, and Indian corn.

Then have students select a question to investigate as a class, or groups of students can vote on the question they want to investigate as teams. After they make their predictions, they can design an experiment to test their predictions. Students can present their findings at a poster session.

More Books to Read

Kudlinski, K. 1998. *Popcorn plants*. Minneapolis, MN: Lerner Publications Company.
Summary: This fact-filled chapter book describes the life cycle of the popcorn plant from the time the farmer plants the seed until the kernel explodes. Includes color photographs, a glossary, and ideas for sharing the book with children.

References

American Chemical Society. 2001. *Safety in the elementary (K-6) science classroom: second edition.* Washington, DC: ACS.

Kwan, T., and J. Texley. 2002. *Exploring safely: A guide for elementary teachers.* Arlington, VA: NSTA Press.

Texley, J., T. Kwan, and J. Summers. 2004. *Investigating safely: A guide for high school teachers.* Arlington, VA: NSTA Press.

What's Poppin'?
Checkpoint Lab

Follow the directions below. If your team is working, put the green cup on top. If you have a question, put the red cup on top. If you are finished with a part and you are ready for a check from your teacher, put the red cup on top.

Part  Popcorn Observations

Unpopped Popcorn	Popped Popcorn
Use a hand lens to observe an unpopped popcorn kernel and draw it in this box.	Use a hand lens to observe a popped popcorn kernel and draw it in this box.

Name: _____

What's Poppin'?
Checkpoint Lab cont.

Part  Questions

1 What differences do you observe between unpopped and popped popcorn?

_____

_____

_____

_____

2 What do you think happened inside the popped popcorn kernel when it was heated?

_____

_____

_____

_____

Checkpoint A ☐

What's Poppin'?
Checkpoint Lab cont.

Part B Setting Up the Popcorn Investigation

☑ *Check the boxes as your team completes each step.*

☐ Attach the base of the candle firmly to the pie plate using a lump of clay.

☐ Place four test tubes in the test-tube holder.

☐ Put a small masking tape label near the top of each test tube. Use a pen or marker to label the test tubes A-1, A-2, B-1, and B-2.

☐ Use a pipette or eye dropper to place 2 drops of cooking oil into the bottom of each test tube. (The cooking oil will help the kernels heat evenly.)

☐ Place 4 kernels of **fresh** popcorn from the baggie marked "A" into test tube A-1.

☐ Place 4 kernels of **fresh** popcorn from the baggie marked "A" into test tube A-2.

☐ Place 4 kernels of **dried** popcorn from the baggie marked "B" into test tube B-1.

☐ Place 4 kernels of **dried** popcorn from the baggie marked "B" into test tube B-2.

☐ Cover each test tube with a square of aluminum foil and poke a tiny hole in the center of the foil with the tip of a pencil.

The popcorn in the test tubes labeled with an "A" is fresh popcorn straight from the jar. The popcorn in the test tubes labeled with a "B" has been dried in an oven overnight. Your task is to figure out what makes popcorn pop. You will make your conclusion based on evidence from this investigation. Before you begin, you will make some predictions.

Name: _____

What's Poppin'?

Checkpoint Lab cont.

Part B Questions

1 What do you predict will happen when you heat the test tubes marked with an "A" over a flame?

_____

_____

_____

_____

2 What do you predict will happen when you heat the test tubes marked with a "B" over a flame?

_____

_____

_____

_____

Checkpoint B ☐

Name: _____

What's Poppin'?
Checkpoint Lab cont.

Part **C** Setting Up the Investigation

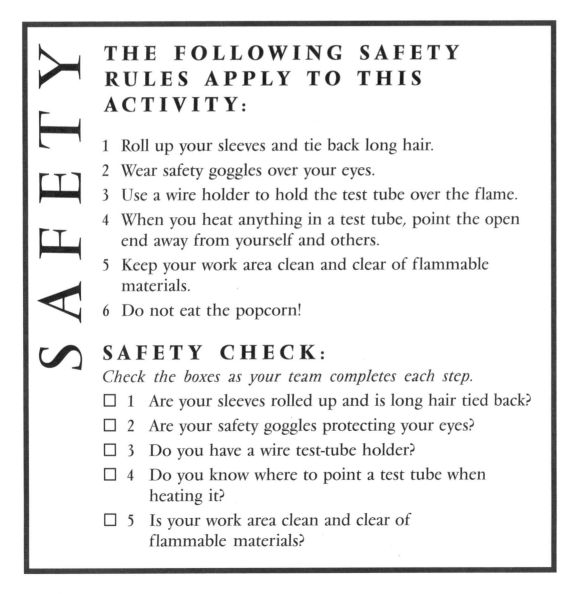

THE FOLLOWING SAFETY RULES APPLY TO THIS ACTIVITY:

1 Roll up your sleeves and tie back long hair.
2 Wear safety goggles over your eyes.
3 Use a wire holder to hold the test tube over the flame.
4 When you heat anything in a test tube, point the open end away from yourself and others.
5 Keep your work area clean and clear of flammable materials.
6 Do not eat the popcorn!

SAFETY CHECK:
Check the boxes as your team completes each step.
☐ 1 Are your sleeves rolled up and is long hair tied back?
☐ 2 Are your safety goggles protecting your eyes?
☐ 3 Do you have a wire test-tube holder?
☐ 4 Do you know where to point a test tube when heating it?
☐ 5 Is your work area clean and clear of flammable materials?

SAFETY

CHAPTER 9

What's Poppin'?
Checkpoint Lab cont.

SAFETY

When you are heating a test tube, do not put it directly in the flame. Hold it just above the flame, and move it in small circles as you are heating it. This will keep the popcorn and oil from burning, and keep the test tube from getting coated with black carbon (soot). Keep the top of the tube pointed away from everyone.

You will heat one test tube at a time. Each team member will heat a different test tube. Make careful observations as you are heating the test tube. Keep track of time: after *two minutes*, you will count the number of kernels popped and record your observations in the Popcorn Data Table.

Part **C** Questions

1 How will you heat the test tube safely?

_____

2 How long will you heat each test tube?

_____

When you are ready to begin, signal your teacher by putting your red cup up. Your teacher will light the candle for you.

Checkpoint C ☐

Name: _____

What's Poppin'?
Checkpoint Lab cont.

Part D What Makes Popcorn Pop?

POPCORN DATA TABLE		
Test Tube	# of Kernels Popped	Observations
A-1 Fresh Popcorn		
A-2 Fresh Popcorn		
B-1 Dried Popcorn		
B-2 Dried Popcorn		

Part D Questions

1 What did you observe on the sides and top of the test tubes as you heated them?

_____

2 Did you observe any differences between the A test tubes and the B test tubes as you heated them? If so, what was different?

_____

Name: _____

What's Poppin'?
Checkpoint Lab cont.

3 What was the average number of fresh popcorn kernels that popped? (To find the average, add the number of kernels popped in A-1 and A-2 and divide by 2.)

Average = _____ kernels of fresh popcorn popped

4 What was the average number of dried popcorn kernels that popped? (To find the average, add the number of kernels popped in B-1 and B-2 and divide by 2.)

Average = _____ kernels of dried popcorn popped

5 What differences did you observe between the A kernels that popped and the B kernels that popped?

_____

_____

6 What conclusion can you make from your data? What do you think makes popcorn pop? What is your evidence?

_____

_____

7 Why do you think one type of popcorn might pop more kernels than another type? What differences might there be between types?

_____

_____

Checkpoint D ☐

Popcorn Brand Test
Checkpoint Lab

Which brand of popcorn does your family buy? Do you buy it because of the taste, the price, the advertising, or because it pops more kernels? Your team will be designing a test to find out which brand of popcorn pops the most kernels. You will test three different brands of popcorn. Design your experiment on the following pages.

Part **A** Designing a Popcorn Brand Test

1 When scientists design an experiment, they must determine what it is they want to test. This is called the **experimental variable**. It is the one thing in the experiment that is being changed. In this experiment, what is the experimental variable?

_____

2 Scientists have to make sure their experiments are fair tests by keeping all other conditions the same. These conditions are called **controlled variables.** In this experiment, what variables should be controlled, or kept the same, in order to keep the test fair?

_____

_____

_____

_____

Name: _____

Popcorn Brand Test
Checkpoint Lab cont.

3 Scientists must follow careful procedures to make sure their experiments are safe, fair, and easily repeated by other scientists. What step-by-step procedures will you follow to make sure that your popcorn brand test is safe, fair, and repeatable?

SAFETY

SAFETY CAUTION TO INCLUDE IN YOUR PROCEDURE:

Allow popcorn to cool for three minutes before opening bags. Steam is hot!!!!

_____

_____

_____

_____

_____

_____

_____

_____

_____

_____

Checkpoint A ☐

Popcorn Brand Test
Checkpoint Lab cont.

Part **B** Popcorn Data

Write the names of the popcorn brands you are testing in the data table below. Then look at the advertising on the packages.

Prediction: I predict that _____ will have the most
popped kernels.　　　　　　　　　*Brand*

| POPCORN DATA TABLE ||
Brand of Popcorn	# of Popped Kernels

POPCORN BAR GRAPH

NUMBER OF POPPED KERNELS

BRANDS

Popcorn Brand Test
Checkpoint Lab cont.

Part **B** Questions

1 What conclusion can you make from your data? Which brand of popcorn had the most popped kernels?

_____

_____

_____

2 Was your prediction influenced by the advertising on the package? Was your prediction correct? How does advertising affect which brand of popcorn people buy?

_____

_____

_____

3 Were you satisfied with your experimental design? What changes would you make if you were going to repeat the experiment? Why?

_____

_____

_____

Checkpoint B ☐

Popcorn Poster Session

Make a poster with your team displaying what you have learned about popcorn. Be ready to share it with the class and answer any questions they might have. Include the following in your poster session:

1 Some important information you learned about popcorn.

2 A labeled diagram explaining how popcorn pops.

3 Your prediction for the popcorn brand testing.

4 The step-by-step procedure you followed in your experiment.

5 A graph showing the results of your experiment.

6 Your conclusion for the experiment.

8 An advertisement, commercial, or jingle for the popcorn brand that popped the most kernels in your experiment.

Decide who is going to explain each part of the poster. Everyone on your team should have a turn!

Posters will be presented on _____.
                              Date

Mystery Pellets

Description

Learners will explore food chains and webs by dissecting owl pellets, creating a food web poster, and describing the relationships among organisms in a pond food web.

Suggested Grade Levels: 3–6

Lesson Objectives Connecting to the Standards

Content Standard A: Science as Inquiry

K–4: Ask a question about objects, organisms, and events in the environment.

K–4: Employ simple equipment and tools to gather data and extend the senses.

5–8: Develop descriptions, explanations, predictions, and models using evidence.

Content Standard C: Life Science

K–4: Understand that all animals depend on plants, some animals eat plants for food, and other animals eat animals that eat the plants.

5–8: Understand that populations of organisms can be categorized by the function they serve in an ecosystem, e.g., producers, consumers, and decomposers; that food webs identify the relationships among producers, consumers, and decomposers in an ecosystem; and that the major source of energy in an ecosystem is sunlight.

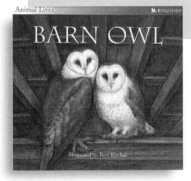

Featured Picture Books

Title	***Animal Lives: The Barn Owl***
Author	**Sally Tagholm**
Illustrator	**Bert Kitchen**
Publisher	**Kingfisher**
Year	**2000**
Genre	**Non-narrative Information**
Summary	**Describes physical characteristics, hunting, feeding, nesting, mating, and molting of the barn owl**

Title	***Butternut Hollow Pond***
Author	**Brian J. Heinz**
Illustrator	**Bob Marstall**
Publisher	**Millbrook Press**
Year	**2000**
Genre	**Narrative Information**
Summary	**Presents the dramatic dynamics of survival and competition on a North American pond**

Time Needed

This lesson will take several class periods. Suggested scheduling is as follows:

Day 1: **Engage** with mystery pellets and read aloud of *Animal Lives: The Barn Owl,* **Explore** with owl pellet dissection, and **Explain** with bone charts and bar graph

Day 2: **Explain** with food webs

Day 3: **Elaborate** with *Butternut Hollow Pond*

Day 4: **Evaluate** with Food Web Posters and Food Web Quiz

Materials

- Unwrapped owl pellets (1 for every 2 students)
- Owl Pellet Bone Chart (1 for every 2 students) from William K. Sheridan or elsewhere (bone charts are included with owl pellet orders)
- Toothpicks
- Centimeter rulers and tape measures
- Hand lenses
- White card stock
- Balances (optional)
- White glue
- Owl Pellet Bar Graph (copied onto an overhead transparency)
- (Optional) Several copies of *Butternut Hollow Pond* for the Elaborate activity

Owl pellets are available from
William K. Sheridan
1-800-433-6259
classroomgoodies.com
and from
Carolina Biological Supply Co.
1-800-334-5551
www.carolina.com

Student Pages

- O-W-L Chart
- Owl Pellet Bar Graph
- *Butternut Hollow Pond* Word Sort Cards
- *Butternut Hollow Pond* Food Web
- Food Web Quiz

engage

Mystery Pellets and Read Aloud

Do not tell students that the "mystery pellets" are owl pellets at this point. Unwrap owl pellets prior to the lesson. Put students in pairs. Tell students you have a mystery for them to solve. Your friend has a farm in the country, and he keeps finding these things in his barn. He wants to know if the class can help him figure out the mystery of their origin. Pass out the mystery pellets. Do not tell students what they are at this point, as they will be discovering this through their observations and the information in the book.

Give a copy of the O-W-L Chart to each student. Have balances and tape measures available for measuring mass, length, and circumference. Have hand lenses available for examining the objects. Tell students to record their observations of the pellets in the first column. Give them a few minutes to observe and measure the mystery pellets without taking them apart. Encourage students to write quantitative as well as qualitative observations. Quantitative observations (numbers) involve counting and measuring ("the mystery pellet is 6.2 cm long"); qualitative observations (words) involve using the senses to describe the properties of the object ("the mystery pellet is grayish"). Then ask students to write their wonderings about the mystery pellets in the second column.

 Chunking, Inferring

Now that the students are curious and engaged, tell them you are going to read a portion of a book that might give them some clues. Introduce the author and illustrator of *Animal Lives: The Barn*

Owl. Ask students to listen for any clues on what the mystery pellets might be, and then read pages 4 through 17. By merging clues from their mystery pellet observations and the text and illustrations on pages 16 and 17, students can infer that a mystery pellet is an owl pellet (the undigested fur, bones, and feathers from the animal[s] an owl ate).

explore

Owl Pellet Dissection

Tell students that today they are each going to be a special kind of scientist who studies birds, an ornithologist. Their task is to determine as much information as they can about the diet

EXPLORING THE "MYSTERY PELLETS"

of the owl that regurgitated that particular pellet. Students may now take the pellets apart using toothpicks, separating the fur from the bones. Tell students that the pellets have been sanitized by the vendor using high heat to kill germs, so they are safe to touch. Students should still wash hands with soap and water when they are finished with the pellet dissection.

explain

Bone Charts and Bar Graph

Tell students that an owl pellet forms 6 to 10 hours after the meal is eaten and is regurgitated 10 to 16 hours after the meal. This is necessary to keep the bird healthy. Explain to students that since owls can't digest fur and bones, they spit these parts out in a compressed pellet.

? What can scientists learn by studying owl pellets? (Scientists can learn a great deal by studying the remains in an owl pellet. They can tell what species of animal the owl ate and how much it ate. Sometimes scientists even find a bird band—a small metal ring that has been placed around a bird's leg—in a pellet, giving them information about the movement and fate of the banded bird.)

? Why is this a good method of study? (It is a good way to study owls without handling or harming them.)

Owl pellet bone charts are included when ordering owl pellets from most vendors. They contain labeled drawings of the animal bones generally found in owl pellets. Students can use the charts to determine what animals their owl ate. They can then try to arrange the bones to assemble the skeleton of the prey (in the same manner that paleontologists assemble dinosaur bones). Alternately, you may want to have them glue the bones on the paper in groups—all the skulls together, all the legs together, and so forth. Students can use white

glue on the end of a toothpick to attach the bones to a large piece of card stock and then label them with the name of the animal. Students can present these posters to other teams and share their findings.

Owl Pellet Bar Graph

After the students present their posters to other pairs, ask the following questions of the whole class:

? What bones would be the best to use to determine the different types of animals your owl ate? (The skulls would be best, because each type of animal the owl ate has a distinctly different skull. The other bones look similar from animal to animal, and are much smaller.)

? How many of each animal did your owl eat? How can you tell? (Answers will vary; we can tell by counting the number of each type of skull.)

Have the students count how many skulls of each kind of animal were in their pellets. On the x-axis of the Owl Pellet Bar Graph transparency, write the names of the most common species the students found, such as vole, shrew, mouse, and bird. Using the data from each pellet, make a whole-class bar graph. Then have students analyze the results and make inferences from the data.

? Why are we using a bar graph to display our owl pellet data? (A bar graph compares totals. Each bar represents the total number of each type of animal. We can easily compare the totals of each type by looking at the bars.)

? What animal was found most frequently in the owl pellets?

? Why do you think the owls ate more of these animals than any other?

Students may now add "learnings" to the "L" column of the O-W-L chart.

explain

Food Webs

Write an example of a simple food chain on the board:

SEED ⟶ MOUSE ⟶ OWL

Explain to students that when one animal eats another animal or plant, they both become part of a *food chain*. A food chain is the path that energy takes as one living thing eats another. The arrows represent the direction of the energy flow; in this case, the energy flows from the seed to the mouse to the owl. The Sun is the source of all the energy in a food chain. Plants use the Sun's energy to make food. Animals eat plants to get some of that energy. Some animals eat those animals to get some of that energy, and so on.

There are some simple food chains in nature, but usually two or more food chains link to form a *food web*. A food web is made of many food chains put together. Write another simple food chain below the first. Ask students how you could link the two chains to make a food web. For example:

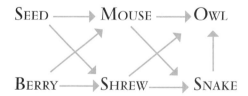

Then ask students

? What is missing from the food web on the board? (the Sun)

Draw a picture of the Sun on the food web with arrows pointing to the seed and the berry.

Food Web Poster

Using the evidence from their owl pellets and their knowledge of food chains and webs, have students work in pairs to create a labeled, pictorial "Owl Food Web Poster" including the owl, its prey, the food of the prey, the Sun, and energy flow arrows. Explain that the arrows on their food chains show the direction of the energy flow. In other words, the arrows (energy) go from a plant or animal to the animals that consume it. Have students explain their posters to other teams. Use the following guiding questions as you encourage students to explain the food web posters in their own words:

? What did your owl eat? What is your evidence? (Answers will vary.)

? Why did your owl eat? (to get energy)

? Where did the animals the owl ate get their energy? (from eating plants or other animals)

? Why is the Sun an important part of your food web? (The Sun is the source of all the energy in a food web. Plants use the Sun's energy to make food.)

elaborate

Butternut Hollow Pond

 Inferring

Hold open the front and back covers of *Butternut Hollow Pond,* which together give a panoramic view of a pond scene. Model the inferring strategy by making observations about the picture on the cover showing the hawk and the woodchuck and then inferring from your observations and your prior knowledge what the book might be about. For example, "I see a hawk flying close to the ground with its talons open. I also see a fat woodchuck running from the hawk. I think that the hawk is hunting the woodchuck. I wonder if this book might be about food chains and webs."

 Visualizing

Then model the visualizing strategy by closing your eyes and sharing what you might see, feel, smell, and hear if you were at the pond. For example, "I feel a light breeze blowing through my hair and the warm sun on my face. I hear the buzz of insects as they flit around the edge of the pond. I smell the wildflowers growing on the grassy bank. I see the shadow of a large bird as it passes overhead. I hear a rustling sound in the bushes as a woodchuck takes cover." Then ask students to close their eyes and visualize the scene.

This book is especially useful for having students practice the strategies of inferring and visualizing. After you have modeled these strategies, you may want to stop reading periodically to have students visualize, make predictions and inferences—or Sketch to Stretch by drawing a picture.

 Determining Importance

Next, ask students to listen for the different organisms in the pond food web as you read aloud *Butternut Hollow Pond*.

? What are some of the plants in the food web?

? What are some of the animals in the food web?

 Word Sort

Word sorts help learners understand the relationships among key concepts and help teach classification. Classifying and then reclassifying helps students extend and refine their understanding of the concepts studied. Students can apply the scientific concepts they have learned about food webs from the owl pellet inquiry to a new situation through the following word sort activity.

Open Sort: Give pairs of students the *Butternut Hollow Pond* Word Sort Cards. Ask students to sort the words into different categories. At this point, it should be an open sort,

in which students group words into categories of their choice and then create their own labels for each category (don't tell them the significance of the gray cards yet). As you move from pair to pair, ask students to explain how they categorized the words. This can help you become aware of students' prior knowledge and misconceptions about the relationships of organisms in a food web.

Closed Sort: In a closed sort, the teacher provides the categories into which students assign words. The closed sort categories can be found on the gray cards: *producer, consumer, omnivore, herbivore,* and *carnivore.* Write each of these terms and their definitions on the board.

Producer—a living thing that makes its own food (plant)

Consumer—a living thing that eats other living things

Carnivore—an animal that eats only other animals

Herbivore—an animal that eats only plants

Omnivore—an animal that eats both plants and animals

As you discuss each term on the gray cards, ask pairs to locate one example of that term from their word sort cards and hold it up. Have students explain why they chose that example, and redirect them if they have made incorrect choices. Students may need to refer back to *Butternut Hollow Pond* to find the role of some of the organisms in the pond food web.

Although students may classify raccoons and opossums as carnivores because, in the book, they are eating other animals, both are omnivores. The raccoon in the book eats crayfish, but tell students that raccoons also eat grubs, insects, fruits, and vegetables. The opossum in the book eats a tiger beetle, but tell students that opossums also eat insects, snails, earthworms, fruit, nuts, seeds, and grasses. Try to have several copies of *Butternut Hollow Pond* available for students to refer to. You may also want to give them additional resources to research the diet of some of the animals mentioned on the cards.

Next, provide some time for students to sort the rest of their words into the five categories found on the gray cards. Informally assess their understanding of the terms as you move from pair to pair, and have them explain their reasoning. Ask clarifying questions such as

? What does that animal eat?

? Why did you place that organism in that category?

? Can that organism be placed in more than one category?

The relationship of the main categories on the gray cards to the rest of the cards is shown on the chart below:

Explain that *decomposers* are organisms that feed on the tissues of dead organisms, and on the waste products of living organisms. They live in or on their food source. Decomposers cause things to rot or decay, and eventually become part of the soil. Ask

? What would it be like if leaves never decayed after they fell from trees?

? What would it be like if dead animals never decomposed?

? What would it be like if apple cores, banana peels, and other garbage never rotted?

Tell students that decomposers play a major role in food webs because they recycle nutrients back into the soil. Some examples of decomposers are Fungi, such as molds and mushrooms, and microscopic organisms, such as protozoans and bacteria.

Closed Sort Key

Producer	Consumer		
green algae	**Herbivore**	**Carnivore**	**Omnivore**
wildflower	woodchuck	dragonfly	fisherman
water shamrock	mallard duck	largemouth bass	raccoon
grass	deer	pickerel frog	opossum
		snapping turtle	
		heron	
		brown bat	
		marsh hawk	

After the word sort, tell students that every food web has some very important organisms that you haven't discussed yet. Ask

? Does anyone know what's missing from the food webs we've discussed? (decomposers)

Butternut Hollow Pond Food Web

Have students complete the *Butternut Hollow Pond* Food Web student pages. Answers follow.

1 (b) The grasses

2 (c) The grasses are eaten by the woodchuck and the woodchuck is eaten by the hawk.

3 (b) consumer

4 (a) from the dragonfly, the moth, and the mosquito

5 The animals that eat insects would starve or leave the pond to find food elsewhere. Eventually, the animals that eat the insect eaters would starve or leave the pond to find food elsewhere. The entire food web would be affected by the elimination of the insects.

evaluate

Food Web Posters

Students can now place any of the appropriate key words—*producer, consumer, herbivore, omnivore,* or *carnivore*—on their owl food web posters, thereby attaching scientific terminology to concepts learned through exploration. Food web posters should demonstrate understanding of the relationships among producers, consumers, and the Sun and should include accurate use of terminology and proper placement of energy flow arrows.

evaluate

Food Web Quiz

As a final evaluation, give the Food Web Quiz. Answers follow.

1 (a) corn

2 (b) consumer

3 (a) Energy flows from the Sun to the corn to the mouse to the owl.

4 grasses and seeds

5 The Sun

6 Answers will vary.

7 The numbers of grasshoppers, sparrows, and mice will increase, because their consumers have been eliminated. The numbers of grasses and seeds will then decrease because they will be eaten by more grasshoppers, sparrows, and mice. (Students may also respond that the numbers of grasshoppers, sparrows, and mice will eventually decline because they will become overpopulated and have to compete for increasingly scarce grasses and seeds.)

Inquiry Place

Place several different types of bird feeders on the school grounds. Make daily observations of the numbers and types of birds that visit the feeders. Have students keep careful records of observations in an organized form. Have students brainstorm "investigatable" questions such as

? Which type of feeder do most birds prefer?

? Do birds feed more in the morning or afternoon?

? What is the effect on the numbers of birds if an artificial owl is placed near the feeders?

? How are other local organisms linked to the birds' food chain?

Then have students select a question to investigate as a class, or have groups of students vote on the question they want to investigate as teams. After they make their predictions, have them collect data to test their predictions. Students can present their findings at a poster session.

Classroom FeederWatch is a school program sponsored by the Cornell Lab of Ornithology. Students can count the kinds and numbers of bird species that visit feeders placed in their school yard. Using Web-based submittal and retrieval forms, they share their bird data with the lab and with other students doing the project. Their analyses help scientists and other student participants answer questions about changes in populations of bird species from month to month, year to year, and place to place. Go to *http://www. birds.cornell.edu/cfw/* for information about signing up. Check out the "Classroom Birdscope Webzine" for some outstanding examples of student inquiry projects.

Web Sites

Owl Resource Guide (including bone charts)
www.carolina.com/owls/guide/owl_guide_intro.asp

More Books to Read

Johnston, Tony. 2000. *The barn owls*. Watertown, MA: Charlesbridge Publishing.
Summary: The poetic text describe the lives of barn owls, who have slept, hunted, called, raised their young, and glided silently above the wheat fields around an old barn for many generations.

Kalman, Bobbie. 1998. *What are food chains and webs?* New York: Crabtree Publishing.
Summary: Clear photographs, illustrations, charts, and short chapters introduce children to food chains and webs.

Lauber, Patricia. 1995. *Who eats what? Food chains and food webs*. New York: HarperCollins.
Summary: Explains the concept of a food chain and how plants, animals, and humans are ecologically linked.

Yolen, J. 1987. *Owl moon*. New York, NY: Philomel Books.
Summary: The simple, melodious text and soft watercolors describe how a father and daughter hike the woods under a full moon to see the Great Horned Owl.

Reference

Kaufman, D. G., and C. M. Franz. 2000. *Biosphere 2000: Protecting our global environment, 3rd edition*. Dubuque, IA: Kendall Hunt Publishing.

Name: _____

O-W-L Chart

O	W	L
What do you **OBSERVE** about the object? (Don't forget to measure.)	What do you **WONDER** about the object?	What did you **LEARN** about the object?

Owl Pellet

Bar Graph

Number of Skulls

Types of Prey Found

Butternut Hollow Pond
Word Sort Cards

dragonfly	**herbivore**
largemouth bass	**mallard duck**
omnivore	**heron**
woodchuck	**water shamrock**
pickerel frog	**green algae**

NATIONAL SCIENCE TEACHERS ASSOCIATION

Butternut Hollow Pond

Word Sort Cards cont.

deer	producer
wildflower	snapping turtle
brown bat	fisherman
consumer	grass
marsh hawk	raccoon
opossum	carnivore

Name: _____

Butternut Hollow Pond
Food Web

When one animal eats another living thing, they both become part of a food chain. A **food chain** is the path that energy takes as one organism eats another. There are some simple food chains in nature. But usually two or more food chains overlap and link, forming a food web. A **food web** is made of many food chains put together. All food webs include plants. Plants are **producers** and can make their own food. They get their energy from the Sun. Animals are **consumers**. They cannot make their own food so they must consume plants or other animals. **Decomposers** are consumers that break down the tissues of dead organisms. They feed on everything that dies in a food web. Some examples of decomposers are bacteria and fungi (not shown on food web below).

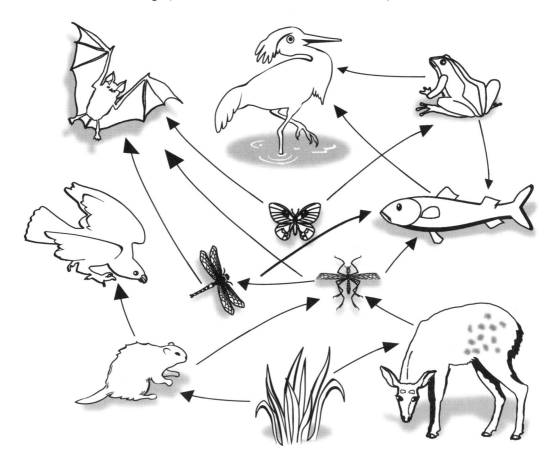

Butternut Hollow Pond

Food Web cont.

Look through *Butternut Hollow Pond* to identify each organism in the food web. Then use the food web to answer the questions below.

1 What are the producers in the food web?
   a. The heron and the hawk
   b. The grasses
   c. The moth and the mosquito

2 Which food chain in the web is in the correct order?
   a. The moth is eaten by the deer and the deer is eaten by the grass.
   b. The heron is eaten by the fish and the fish is eaten by the mosquito.
   c. The grasses are eaten by the woodchuck and the woodchuck is eaten by the hawk.

3 In this food web, the fish is a
   a. producer
   b. consumer
   c. decomposer

4 Where does the bat in this food web get its energy?
   a. from the dragonfly, the moth, and the mosquito
   b. from the cattails and the grass
   c. from the hawk and the heron

5 How would the food web be affected if someone sprayed pesticide around the pond and all of the insects died? Explain your answer.

_____

_____

_____

_____

Name: _____

Food Web Quiz

Use the food chain diagram below to answer questions 1 to 3.

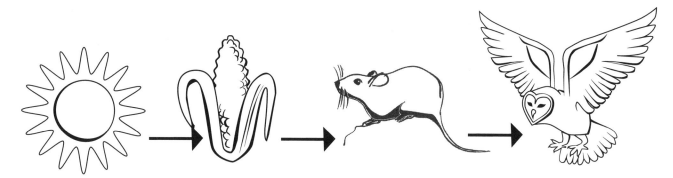

1 Which organism is the producer in this food chain?

a corn

b mouse

c owl

2 In this food chain, the owl is a

a producer

b consumer

c decomposer

3 Which statement describes the movement of energy in the diagram above?

a Energy flows from the Sun to the corn to the mouse to the owl.

b The owl gets its energy directly from the Sun.

c Energy flows from the owl to the mouse to the corn.

Name: _____

Food Web
Quiz cont.

Use the food web diagram at the bottom of the page to answer questions 4 through 7.

4 What are the producers in the food web below? _____

5 What is the source of all the energy in the food web? _____

6 Write down any food chain with three links in the food web:

_____

7 What will happen to the other organisms in the food web if all of the snakes and owls are killed by someone? Explain your answer.

_____

_____

_____

_____

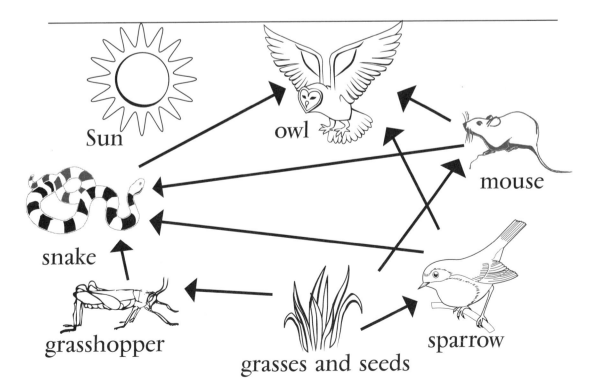

Sun

owl

mouse

snake

grasshopper

grasses and seeds

sparrow

Close Encounters
of the Symbiotic Kind

Description
Learners explore how some organisms interact with other organisms through symbiotic relationships by observing "mystery objects" (plant galls) collected from the local ecosystem.

Suggested Grade Levels: 4–6

Lesson Objectives Connecting to the Standards

**Content Standard A:
Science as Inquiry**

K–4: Ask a question about objects, organisms, and events in the environment.

5–8: Develop descriptions, explanations, predictions, and models using evidence.

5–8: Think critically and logically to make the relationships between evidence and explanations.

Content Standard C: Life Science

K–4: Understand that all organisms cause changes in the environment where they live. Some of these changes are detrimental to the organism or other organisms, whereas others are beneficial.

5–8: Understand that biological adaptations include changes in structures, behaviors, or physiology that enhance survival and reproductive success in a particular environment.

Featured Picture Book

Title	***Weird Friends: Unlikely Allies in the Animal Kingdom***
Author	**Jose Aruego and Ariane Dewey**
Illustrator	**Jose Aruego and Ariane Dewey**
Publisher	**Harcourt**
Year	**2002**
Genre	**Narrative Information**
Summary	**Details some of the amazing symbiotic relationships found in the animal kingdom**

Time Needed

This lesson will take several class periods. Suggested scheduling is as follows:

Day 1: **Engage** and **Explore** with mystery objects, and **Explain** with Close Encounters Dichotomous Key

Day 2: **Explore** and **Explain** with Close Encounters of the Symbiotic Kind article

Day 3: **Elaborate** with *Weird Friends,* and **Evaluate** with Symbiosis Quiz

Materials

This lesson uses "mystery objects" to engage the students and lead them into an inquiry on symbiotic relationships in nature. The mystery objects are plant galls. If goldenrod grows in your area, you can probably find galls on it. The spherical goldenrod gall is caused by a tiny fly. The spindle gall is caused by a kind of moth. The galls are often located about two-thirds of the way up the stem and can be seen easily, especially in the winter when the foliage has died. Another easy way to collect galls is to find them on oak trees, which play host to hundreds of different gall-forming organisms. Keep the galls attached to the leaves or twigs if possible, to help with identification. See *www.cals.ncsu.edu/course/ent525/close/gallpix/index.htm* for color photographs of some common galls. (Safety note: Goldenrod is usually not responsible for allergies. The pollen is heavy and sticky, designed for insect pollination, not wind. Wind-blown ragweed pollen is the most common culprit for allergies.)

You will need to collect several specimens of at least two kinds of galls from the local ecosystem, such as the common galls pictured at right.

GOLDENROD
BALL GALL

GOLDENROD
SPINDLE GALL

Other Materials

- Centimeter rulers and/or tape measures (1 per pair)
- Hand lenses (1 per student)
- Small knife or dissecting scalpel (for adult use only)
- Cutting board to use when cutting galls open (for adult use only)
- Symbiosis Quiz Key (for teacher use)

Student Pages

- O-W-L Chart
- Close Encounters Dichotomous Key
- Close Encounters Sorting Cards
- Close Encounters Article
- *Weird Friends*
- Symbiosis Quiz

OAK LEAF GALL

OAK APPLE GALL

engage

Mystery Objects

Pass out a mystery object (goldenrod ball gall, oak apple gall, or other plant gall) to each student or pair of students. Do not tell them what the mystery objects are. Pass out an O-W-L chart to each student. Give students several minutes to carefully take measurements and write observations in the first column and then write their "wonderings" about the objects in the second column.

Ask several students to share their observations. Then ask whether the observations were truly *observations* based upon measurements and the senses, or whether some of them were actually *inferences*. Explain that, when you make an inference, you use past experiences to draw a conclusion based on your observations. So if any of the observations were guesses about the identity of the mystery ob-

jects, then those statements were actually inferences. Students who wrote inferences in the "Observations" column of the O-W-L chart can rewrite them into questions in the "Wonderings" column instead. For example, "I wonder if this is an insect living inside a plant?"

explore

Demonstrate how to safely cut open a gall. You will most likely want to open the galls for each student, especially the hardened goldenrod gall, because of safety concerns. Ask a parent volunteer to help. Use a sturdy cutting board and a small sharp knife or dissecting scalpel. Carefully insert the knife blade part way into a gall along its circumference. Twist the knife until the gall pops open. Galls can usually be opened this way without damaging the larvae inside.

Have students make observations of the opened objects and compare them with the observations of other students. Then have them add to the "Observations" and "Wonderings" columns of the O-W-L chart.

explain

Close Encounters Dichotomous Key

Ask students if they are ready to develop some explanations about their mystery objects.

? Was anything inside your mystery object? Is it still there?

? How do you think it got inside? What do you think it was doing in there?

? What do you think it is?

Tell students they are going to do some research to clear up the mystery surrounding their objects. Pass out copies of the Close Encounters Dichotomous Key. Explain that the word *dichotomous* means dividing into two parts. A dichotomous key has two choices at every step. Discuss the different characteristics used in the key such as spherical, elliptical, encircling twig, and horns. Then tell students to start with number one, make a choice based on their observations, and follow the steps of the key until they have identified the object. They can find out more about their objects by reading the rest of the student page.

Oak galls can be difficult to identify because there are hundreds of varieties. It is sufficient for the students to identify them as "oak galls" if they cannot tell which type they have.

Students can now fill out the "Learnings" column of the O-W-L chart. Have students communicate their findings about their mystery objects by presenting their completed O-W-L charts in small groups to other students.

Discuss the following questions with the whole class.

❓ What is your mystery object?

❓ How did the insect get inside the plant?

❓ Is the insect helped or hurt by the plant? How?

❓ Is the plant helped or hurt by the insect? How?

Tell students that the name for this type of "close encounter" between different organisms is called *symbiosis*. Explain that symbiotic relationships occur when one organism lives near, on, or, in some cases, inside another organism and when at least one organism benefits from the relationship.

❓ How does your mystery object show symbiosis? (An insect is living on or in a plant and getting food, shelter, and protection from the plant.)

Some students may have concerns about the survival of the organisms they are studying in this inquiry. You may want to take the class outside to a natural area or bird feeder where students can gently return their organisms to the food chain, but make sure you are not introducing an organism into a habitat where it doesn't belong.

Initiate a discussion on biological adaptations: changes in structures, behaviors, or physiology that enhance survival and reproductive success in a particular environment.

Discuss biological adaptations: changes in structures, behaviors, or physiology that help organisms survive in their environment. For example, camouflage is an adaptation in body structure (shape, color, or pattern) that helps many animals survive. Camouflage can help a predator stay hidden from its prey as it hunts. A polar bear's white fur blends in with the snow and ice so that it can sneak up on seals. Camouflage can help a prey animal stay hidden from its predators. A fawn's spots match the sun and shade that dapple the ground where it hides. Camouflage can also be an adaptation in behavior. Recently, scientists have discovered that some species of octopus camouflage themselves by walking on two arms instead of using all eight. One kind of octopus walks backward on two arms while holding the others above its head—camouflage that makes the creature look like a floating clump of algae. Another species holds six arms under its rounded body while walking on two, giving the animal the appearance of a coconut—and coconuts are everywhere on the sea floor where it lives. Have students describe more examples of camouflage, both structural and behavioral.

Discuss other types of structural adaptations, such as the way specialized beaks and feet help birds survive. Discuss other behavioral adaptations, such as the tendency of some animals such as elephants to live in herds for protection whereas others such as wolves and lions roam in packs for efficient hunting. Then discuss how adaptations help organisms live in symbiotic relationships, such as how sucking mouthparts are structural adaptations on some parasites and how laying eggs on the right species of plant is a behavioral adaptation of gall-making insects. Ask

? What are some adaptations that help gall-making insects live symbiotically with their host plant species? (the ability to produce special chemicals which cause their host plant to form a gall, structures which allow them to breathe and eat within galls, behaviors such as crawling or flying to the appropriate host plant)

? What might happen to an insect if its host species—for example, goldenrod—died out suddenly? Do you think it would be able to adapt to a new species of host plant? (No, because gall-making insects are suited to a particular species of host plant. Their special structures and behaviors would most likely not function as well on a different host species, and the insect would die.)

For more information on adaptations, see *Life on Earth: The Story of Evolution, How do Animals Adapt?* and *Adaptation*, in "More Books to Read" at the end of this lesson.

explore

Symbiosis Word Sort and Article

 ### Word Sort

Tell students they are going to do an activity to explore symbiosis. Divide students into pairs. Pass out the Close Encounters Sorting Cards to each pair.

Open Sort: First, have students do an open sort of the cards. In an open sort, students group words into categories and create their own labels for each category. Have students explain their reasoning as they are sorting. An open sort helps students to become familiar with the words, to begin thinking about relationships among the words, and to listen for the words in the reading. As you circulate, ask students to explain why they grouped the words the way they did. This can help you determine their prior knowledge about the meanings of the words on the cards.

Pairs Read

Pass out the Close Encounters of the Symbiotic Kind article. This article will give them the necessary information to do a

Relationship of Words in the Closed Sort

SYMBIOSIS		
Parasitism	**Commensalism**	**Mutualism**
Dog—Tick	Orchid—Kapok Tree	Clown Fish—Sea Anemone
Cat—Flea	Remora—Shark	
Human—Mosquito		
Bark Beetle—Elm Tree		

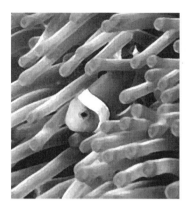

closed sort with their cards. Have students take turns reading aloud from the article. While one student reads a paragraph, the other listens and then summarizes. Then they switch roles.

Closed Sort: Next, have students perform a closed sort of the cards. In a closed sort, the teacher provides categories into which students assign the words. In this case, the article outlines three categories of symbiosis into which the organisms on the cards can be sorted: parasitism, commensalism, and mutualism.

explain

Ask students to justify how they sorted their cards to you as you move around to each team. Students should recognize that there are three types of symbiosis, and identify which organisms belong in each category. Discuss the following questions:

? Why do you think it is beneficial to the parasite not to kill its host?

? Could these organisms survive without each other? Why or why not?

? How do you think these organisms became adapted for living so closely together?

? How is a human's relationship to a pet an example of symbiosis? What type of symbiosis? Why?

elaborate

Weird Friends
Tell students that they are going to learn more about the fascinating world of *mutualism,* a relationship that is beneficial to both partners. Mutualism can seem very strange because the most unlikely creatures do amazing things to help each other survive. Some act as bodyguards or booby traps, others as hairdressers or housekeepers. Ask students if they can think of other examples of mutualism in addition to the clown fish and the sea anemone featured in the symbiosis article.

Inferring/Making Connections
Show students the cover of *Weird Friends: Unlikely Allies in the Animal Kingdom.* Ask students to infer from the title what the book is about. Then ask them what they think it might have to do with the previous activity on plant galls.

Determining Importance
Pass out the *Weird Friends* student page. Ask pairs of students to read through the examples listed and briefly discuss some predictions of how each partner might benefit from the relationship. Then tell students to listen for the relationships mentioned on the worksheet as you read the book aloud. Read aloud *Weird Friends,* and pause after each relationship is described to give students time to record their responses on the student page, listing the benefit for each partner

evaluate
Symbiosis Quiz
Review the differences among the types of symbiosis, and then administer the Symbiosis Quiz. Use the Symbiosis Quiz Key to grade the quiz.

Inquiry Place

Students can investigate goldenrod galls further by doing some field studies in a natural area containing many goldenrod plants. Have students brainstorm "investigatable" questions such as

?   Can the gall fly larvae survive being frozen over the winter?

?   Do gall fly larvae distinguish up from down? Do they make more exit tunnels in the upper or lower part of the gall, or are the tunnels randomly placed on the galls?

?   At what height on the plant do most galls occur?

?   What is the average circumference of the goldenrod galls?

?   Are goldenrods without galls on average taller than goldenrods with galls?

Students can select a question to investigate as a class, or groups of students may choose a question they want to investigate as teams. After they make their predictions, they will design an investigation and collect data to test their predictions. Students can present their findings at a poster session.

More Books to Read

Darling, K. 2000. *There's a zoo on you.* Brookfield, CT: Millbrook Press.
Summary: A fascinating introduction to the microorganisms that have symbiotic relationships with the human body. Explains that most of these microbes are harmless and may actually be helpful.

Hines, JG. 2004. *Friendships in nature.* Chanhassen, MN: NorthWord Press.
Summary: Richly detailed paintings bring life to fascinating symbiotic relationships in nature.

Jenkins, S. 2002. *Life on Earth: The story of evolution.* New York, NY: Houghton Mifflin.
Summary: Jenkins' trademark collages illustrate this oversized book describing the origins of life on earth and the basics of evolution. Concepts such as variation, mutation, and Darwin's theory of natural selection are explained in simple language.

Kalman, B. 2000. *How do animals adapt?* New York, NY: Crabtree Publishing.
Summary: This fact-filled book describes how animals adapt to survive. It details camouflage, mimicry, poisons, and adaptations to climate, feeding, and mating. Includes full-color photographs, informational insets, and words to know.

Parker, S. 2001. *Adaptation: Life processes series.* Chicago, IL: Heinemann Library.
Summary: This informational book describes how living things develop habits and physical features that help them live where they do. It reveals how animals' bodies have adapted to help them live in their environment, and explains what would happen to the animals if they continued to adapt.

Parasites and Partners Series
Summary: Introduces unique symbiotic relationships to readers in grades 5–7. Each book takes one broad relationship type and discusses it in an easy to understand way within a framework packed with full-color photographs and fascinating examples.

Giles, B. 2003. *Parasites and partners: Lodgers and cleaners.* Chicago, IL: Raintree.

Harman, A. 2003. *Parasites and partners: Farmers and slavers.* Chicago, IL: Raintree.

Hoare, B. 2003. *Parasites and partners: Breeders.* Chicago, IL: Raintree.

Houston, R. 2003. *Parasites and partners: Feeders.* Chicago, IL:

Raintree. Martin, J. W. R. 2003. *Parasites and partners: Killers.* Chicago, IL: Raintree.

Pitts, K. 2003. *Parasites and partners: Hitchers and thieves.* Chicago, IL: Raintree.

Name: _____

O-W-L Chart

O	W	L
What do you **OBSERVE** about the object? (Don't forget to measure.)	What do you **WONDER** about the object?	What did you **LEARN** about the object?

NATIONAL SCIENCE TEACHERS ASSOCIATION

Close Encounters
Dichotomous Key

Directions: Use the dichotomous key below to identify your mystery object. Then read more about it!

1 Found in middle of goldenrod stem .... go to 2

Found on oak leaf or twig .... go to 3

2 Spherical (ball-shaped) growth .... GOLDENROD BALL GALL

Elliptical (oval-shaped) growth .... GOLDENROD SPINDLE GALL

3 Found on oak twig, leaf stem, or central vein .... go to 4

Found growing directly on oak leaf .... (a type of) Oak Leaf Gall

4 Growth encircling twig .... go to 5

Growth hanging from twig or leaf stem .... go to 6

5 Hard, woody swelling with small "horns" .... HORNED OAK GALL

Hard, woody swelling with no "horns" .... GOUTY OAK GALL

6 Round, bumpy, and hard .... OAK BULLET GALL

Round with thin, papery shell and spongy center ..... OAK APPLE GALL

Name: _____

Close Encounters
Dichotomous Key cont.

What Are Galls?

Imagine living inside a windowless, globelike room made out of your favorite food. The room gives you shelter, protection, and all the nutrition you need to grow into an adult. When the time is right to leave, you just eat your way out! That's what it would be like to trade places with a gall-making insect.

Galls are abnormal growths on a plant usually caused by insects, mites, bacteria, or fungi. Sometimes the plant is harmed by the galls, but in many cases the plant is not affected. Gall-making insects lay eggs on or in their host plant. The eggs hatch into larvae, and chemicals in the insects cause the plant to form protective growths around them. After metamorphosis, the adult insects crawl out, leave their host plant, and start the cycle all over again.

Types of Galls

Galls come in a wide variety of shapes and colors. By looking at the gall's shape, color, and location on the plant, you can determine what organism caused it. For example, if you observe an oval-shaped gall growing in the stem of a goldenrod plant, then it was made by a kind of moth. If the gall is ball-shaped, it was made by a tiny goldenrod gall fly. Inside either kind of goldenrod gall you may find a tiny white insect larva.

Oak galls are usually caused by different species of gall wasps. The wasp lays an egg on the oak leaf, on the leaf stem or vein, or on a twig. When the larva hatches, it causes the leaf or twig to grow a swelling around it. The larva gets shelter and food inside the gall until it hatches into an adult wasp. Don't worry—these tiny wasps will not sting humans!

There are hundreds of different kinds of oak galls, so identification can be a real challenge! Your gall could be a hairy oak leaf gall, spiny vase oak gall, wooly fold oak gall, oak saucer gall, or oak spangle gall, to name a few.

My mystery object is most likely a_____

made by a _____

Close Encounters
Sorting Cards

Directions: Cut out the cards below and sort them into different categories (choose any categories you want). Then read the article "Close Encounters of the Symbiotic Kind" and sort them a different way!

parasitism	commensalism
mutualism	symbiosis
tick	elm tree
sea anemone	dog

Close Encounters

Sorting Cards cont.

shark	bark beetle
remora	cat
clown fish	flea
orchid	human
mosquito	kapok tree

Name: _____

Close Encounters
of the Symbiotic Kind

A bright little clown fish darts in and out of a deadly sea anemone's tentacles. A bark beetle bores into an elm tree to lay its eggs, which will hatch into hungry, wood-eating larvae. A beautiful flower called an orchid survives in the shadowy rain forest by growing high on the trunk of a giant kapok tree. What do these things have in common? They are all examples of **symbiosis**, a close relationship between two organisms in which one organism lives near, on, or even inside the other. In symbiosis, at least one organism benefits from the relationship. This article describes three types of symbiosis.

Has your dog had ticks? Has your cat had fleas? Have you ever been bitten by a mosquito? If so, you and your pets have been victims of parasites. **Parasitism** is a type of symbiosis in which one organism (the **parasite**) lives on or in a much larger organism (the **host**) and feeds on it while the host is still alive. Parasites don't usually kill their host.

Commensalism is a type of symbiosis in which one of the organisms is helped while the other is not affected. For example, an orchid gets support and sunlight by living on the trunk or branches of a tall rain forest tree. The tree is neither helped nor harmed by the orchid. A remora is a hitchhiking fish that often attaches itself to the body of a shark. The remora gets a free ride, protection from predators, and food scraps left by the shark. The shark is not affected by the remora.

In **mutualism**, both organisms benefit from their close encounter. The clown fish has a slimy coating that protects it from the stinging tentacles of the sea anemone. This colorful fish hides among the tentacles to gain protection from predators. The anemone benefits by eating leftovers from the fish's meals, and the fish helps keep it clean. The sea anemone gets one other benefit. Its enemy, the butterfly fish, is afraid of the little clown fish's nasty bite!

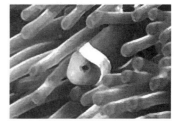

Name: _____

Weird Friends
Unlikely Allies in the Animal Kingdom

As your teacher reads the book *Weird Friends*, listen for how each partner benefits from the relationship. Beneath the name of each partner, list the benefit. The first one is done for you.

1	Clown Fish Protection	Sea Anemone Protection
2	Rhino	Cattle Egret
3	Blind Shrimp	Goby
4	Ostrich	Zebra
5	Red Phalaropes	Sperm Whale
6	Red Ants	Large Blue Butterfly
7	Hermit Crab	Sea Anemones
8	Impalas	Baboons
9	Horse Mackerel	Portuguese Man-of-War
10	Forest Mouse	Beetles
11	Hippo	Oxpeckers Black Labeo Fish
12	Wrasse	Google-Eye Fish
13	Tuatara	Snooty Shearwater

Symbiosis Quiz

Three types of symbiosis are parasitism, mutualism, and commensalism.
After reading each example, circle the type of symbiosis described and
explain how each organism is hurt or helped by the relationship.

1 African tickbirds can often be found sitting on the backs of large
grazing animals such as Cape buffalo. The tickbirds eat bloodsucking
ticks found on the skin of the large animals. What type of symbiosis
is shown by the tickbirds and the Cape buffalo?

   a parasitism

   b mutualism

   c commensalism

   Explain _____

   _____

2 A male golden weaver bird builds a hanging nest made of grass and
straw high on the branches of a thorny acacia tree. The tree is not
affected by the nest. What type of symbiosis is shown by the weaver
bird and the acacia tree?

   a parasitism

   b mutualism

   c commensalism

   Explain _____

   _____

Name: _____

Symbiosis Quiz cont.

3 Aphids are tiny bugs that live on plants. They excrete a sugary liquid called honeydew from their abdomens. Ants find the honeydew both nutritious and delicious. Some kinds of ants protect herds of aphids from predators such as ladybugs. When danger threatens, the ants carry the aphids to safety on their backs or in their mouths! When the ants want to feed, they tickle the aphids into producing honeydew. What type of symbiosis is shown by the ants and the aphids?

a parasitism

b mutualism

c commensalism

Explain _____

_____

4 Tapeworms are long flatworms that live in the guts of animals, including humans. Tapeworms absorb nutrients through their skin. They stretch out their narrow bodies in order to reach the right kind of food, food that has been broken down by the host's digestive system. They dig their heads into the gut wall to avoid being swept away. Humans can lose many nutrients when infected by tapeworms, leading to disorders of the blood, brain, and nerves. What type of symbiosis is shown by the tapeworms and the humans?

a parasitism

b mutualism

c commensalism

Explain _____

_____

Symbiosis Quiz cont.

5 Flower mites are tiny animals that feed on the nectar and pollen of certain plants. When the plant stops flowering, the mites must move on. They rely on hummingbirds to carry them from plant to plant. When a hummingbird stops to feed at a flower, the tiny mites run up the bird's beak and climb into its nostrils. The hummingbird doesn't even know the mites are there. When the hummingbird stops at the right kind of flower, the mites sense the flower's perfume and run back down the beak and into the flower. What type of symbiosis is shown by the mites and the hummingbird?

a parasitism

b mutualism

c commensalism

Explain _____

_____

6 Some wasps lay their eggs on or inside living caterpillars. When the eggs hatch, the wasp larvae feed on the bodies of the caterpillars. What type of symbiosis is shown by the wasps and the caterpillars?

a parasitism

b mutualism

c commensalism

Explain _____

_____

Symbiosis Quiz

Answer Key

Three main types of symbiosis are parasitism, mutualism, and commensalism. After reading each example, circle the type of symbiosis described and explain how each organism is hurt or helped by the relationship.

1 African tickbirds can often be found sitting on the backs of large grazing animals such as Cape buffalo. The tickbirds eat bloodsucking ticks found on the skin of the large animals. What type of symbiosis is shown by the tickbirds and the Cape buffalo?

a parasitism

b mutualism

c commensalism

Explain: **The tickbirds are helped because they get food by eating the ticks, and the Cape buffalo are helped because the tickbirds remove the bloodsucking parasites.**

2 A male golden weaver bird builds a hanging nest made of grass and straw high on the branches of a thorny acacia tree. The tree is not affected by the nest. What type of symbiosis is shown by the weaver bird and the acacia tree?

a parasitism

b mutualism

c commensalism

Explain: **The weaver bird is helped because it has a safe place to build its nest, but the tree is neither hurt nor helped.**

Symbiosis Quiz
Answer Key cont.

3 Aphids are tiny bugs that live on plants. They excrete a sugary liquid called honeydew from their abdomens. Ants find the honeydew both nutritious and delicious. Some kinds of ants protect herds of aphids from predators such as ladybugs. When danger threatens, the ants carry the aphids to safety on their backs or in their mouths! When the ants want to feed, they tickle the aphids into producing honeydew. What type of symbiosis is shown by the ants and the aphids?

a parasitism

b mutualism

c commensalism

Explain: **The ants are helped because they get food from the aphids, but the aphids are not harmed. Instead, they are helped because the ants protect them.**

---

4 Tapeworms are long flatworms that live in the guts of animals, including humans. Tapeworms absorb nutrients through their skin. They stretch out their narrow bodies in order to reach the right kind of food, food that has been broken down by the host's digestive system. They dig their heads into the gut wall to avoid being swept away. Humans can lose many nutrients when infected by tapeworms, leading to disorders of the blood, brain, and nerves. What type of symbiosis is shown by the tapeworms and the humans?

a parasitism

b mutualism

c commensalism

Explain: **The tapeworms are helped because they get food and a place to live. The humans are hurt because the tapeworms feed on them and can cause disorders.**

Name: _____

Symbiosis Quiz
Answer Key cont.

5 Flower mites are tiny animals that feed on the nectar and pollen of certain plants. When the plant stops flowering, the mites must move on. They rely on hummingbirds to carry them from plant to plant. When a hummingbird stops to feed at a flower, the tiny mites run up the bird's beak and climb into its nostrils. The hummingbird doesn't even know the mites are there. When the hummingbird stops at the right kind of flower, the mites sense the flower's perfume and run back down the beak and into the flower. What type of symbiosis is shown by the mites and the hummingbird?

a parasitism

b mutualism

c commensalism

Explain: The mites are helped because they get transportation from the hummingbirds. The hummingbirds are neither helped nor hurt.

6 Some wasps lay their eggs on or inside living caterpillars. When the eggs hatch, the wasp larvae feed on the bodies of the caterpillars. What type of symbiosis is shown by the wasps and the caterpillars?

a parasitism

b mutualism

c commensalism

Explain: The wasp larvae are helped because they get food from the caterpillars' bodies. The caterpillars are hurt because the wasp larvae eat them and they probably die.

Turtle Hurdles

Description

By taking part in a simulation, learners explore the many threats to sea turtles and the ways humans can help them survive. Learners identify which dangers result from human actions and which dangers are natural. Learners also explore the life cycles of sea turtles through literature.

Suggested Grade Levels: 3–4

Lesson Objectives Connecting to the Standards

Content Standard C: Life Science

K–4: Understand that humans change environments in ways that can be either beneficial or detrimental for themselves or other organisms.

K–4: Understand that animals have life cycles that include being born, developing into adults, reproducing, and eventually dying.

Content Standard F: Science in Personal and Social Perspectives

K–4: Understand that changes in environments can be natural or influenced by humans. Some changes are good, some are bad, and some are neither good nor bad.

Featured Picture Books

Title	**Turtle Bay**
Author	**Saviour Pirotta**
Illustrator	**Nilesh Mistry**
Publisher	**Farrar, Straus, and Giroux**
Year	**1997**
Genre	**Story**
Summary	**Taro is fascinated by old Jiro-San, who sweeps the beach while waiting for the arrival of sea turtles ready to lay their eggs.**

Title	**Turtle, Turtle, Watch Out!**
Author	**April Pulley Sayre**
Illustrator	**Lee Christiansen**
Publisher	**Orchard Books**
Year	**2000**
Genre	**Narrative Information**
Summary	**From before she hatches until she returns to the same beach to lay eggs of her own, a sea turtle escapes from danger with help from human hands.**

Time Needed

This lesson will take several class periods. Suggested scheduling is as follows:

Day 1: **Engage** with read aloud of *Turtle Bay* and K-W-L chart

Day 2: **Explore** with *Turtle, Turtle, Watch Out!*

Day 3: **Explain** with Turtle T-Chart

Day 4: **Elaborate** and **Evaluate** with Write a Letter

Materials

- Think pads (pads of sticky notes—1 per student)
- Turtle-shaped K-W-L chart
- Turtle Line Graph (copied onto an overhead transparency)
- Overhead projector
- Overhead markers of at least three different colors
- Dice chart
- One die
- Optional: CD of ocean sounds

Student Pages

- Optional: Sea Turtle Headband
- How to Make a Fortune-Teller
- Fortune-Teller Templates 1 and 2
- How to play "Turtle, Turtle, Watch Out!"
- Turtle Line Graph
- Turtle T-Chart
- Write a Letter!

Background

The turtles in the featured books *Turtle Bay* and *Turtle, Turtle, Watch Out!* are loggerhead turtles, one of seven different kinds of turtles that live in the sea. Sea turtles are becoming rare and are in danger of extinction. Scientists estimate that only one in 2,500 sea turtles survives to breeding age. For more background information about sea turtles, read the last page of each of the two books featured in this lesson.

Engage

Read Aloud and K-W-L Chart

Use paper to hide the cover of the book *Turtle Bay* in advance, and don't tell students the title of the book.

Tell students you have a very interesting book to share and you want them to make some predictions about the story without seeing the cover yet. Then begin reading aloud *Turtle Bay* using the suggested reading strategies. Make sure each student has a sticky note "think pad" to write on.

SEA TURTLE K-W-L

Questioning

After reading page 5 (Jiro-San says his old friends are coming) and showing the pictures, model your students' thinking by asking aloud:

❓ I wonder who Jiro-San's friends are?

Inferring

As you read pages 6 through 16 (Jiro-San and Taro are cleaning the beach and different animals are coming to the beach), periodically stop reading and have students get out their think pads to "stop and jot" their inferences about who Jiro-San's friends might be. Remind them to use clues from the text and the pictures.

Visualizing

Hide the illustrations as you read pages 23 through 25 (the sea turtles are hatching). Have students sketch to stretch: visualize what the teacher is reading and draw a sketch of what they think it might look like.

K-W-L Chart

Make a large K-W-L chart on sea turtles, a turtle-shaped chart as pictured if you like. Ask students what they know and what they are wondering about sea turtles to fill out the first two columns of the chart.

Explore

Turtle, Turtle, Watch Out!

Determining Importance

Introduce the author and illustrator of *Turtle, Turtle, Watch Out!* Tell students that as you read the book they should call out "Turtle, turtle, watch out!" when that phrase appears in the book. Also, tell students to signal by touching their noses when they hear an example of a human's changing the turtle's habitat. Read the book aloud.

Tell students they are getting ready to play a game in which they will pretend to be sea turtles. (Optional for younger students: Have them make a turtle headband to wear during the game using the Sea Turtle Headband student page.) Distribute the fortune-teller templates, randomly giving students either

Making a fortune-teller. Read all eight steps on p. 161.

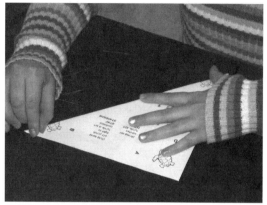

Step 2

Step 5

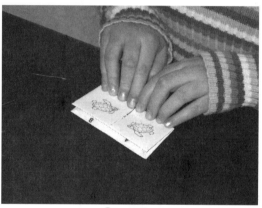

Step 6

Step 8

Template 1 or Template 2. To save time you can precut the fortune-teller templates on a paper cutter. Using the How to Make a Fortune-Teller sheet, have students cut and fold their fortune-tellers. You may want to read the directions together and model the steps.

Next, place the Turtle Line Graph on the overhead projector and turn off the classroom lights to simulate nightfall on the beach. Play a CD of ocean sounds if you wish. Then set the stage for the students:

"Please stand to play a game called 'Turtle, Turtle, Watch Out!' You are now baby sea turtles. Your goal is to hatch safely, crawl across the beach to the ocean, and swim to deep wa-ter, all under the cover of darkness. You will face many hurdles. If your fortune-teller opens up to reveal that your turtle has been helped by a human or natural factor, stay standing for that turn. But if your fortune-teller opens up to reveal bad news for your turtle, sit down until the game is over. You may continue to follow along with your fortune-teller, but you must stay seated to represent the loss of that baby turtle. If you are still standing after five turns, you have made it to deep water. I will graph on the overhead how many turtles are left standing after each turn. Before we start, I want you to predict how many turtles will make it to the deep ocean after five turns."

Discuss student predictions. Be ready to reassure any student who becomes unusually discouraged if he or she is a turtle who gets bad news.

Directions for "Turtle, Turtle, Watch Out!" Game:

1 Have students stand up and spread out, holding their assembled fortune-tellers.

2 Before each turn, call out "Turtle, turtle, watch out!" in unison.

3 Hold a die about one inch above the star on the dice chart and drop it.

4 Call out the number on the die. Have students open and close their fortune-tellers that many times.

5 Call out the letter that the die landed on. Have students open the panel under the corresponding letter on their fortune-tellers and read their turtle's fate. If their turtle survives, they remain standing. If their turtle dies, they sit down. (Seated students can still follow along with their turtle fortune-tellers.)

6 Count the number of students standing after each turn and graph that number on the Turtle Line Graph.

7 The game ends after five turns or when no one is left standing.

8 Repeat game several times, using a different colored marker to graph results each time.

explain

Turtle T-Chart

You can use the information on the last page of both *Turtle Bay* and *Turtle, Turtle, Watch Out!* in your discussion of the game. Modify the explanations for students as needed.

Discuss the results of the game using the Turtle Line Graph.

? Why did we use a line graph to display our turtle data? (A line graph shows changes over time. Each turn represented a point in time, and we used the line graph to show the change in the number of turtles as time passed.)

? How many turtles survived each time? How did those numbers compare to your predictions?

? What kinds of dangers did the turtles encounter?

? Why do you think sea turtles lay so many eggs?

? How were some of the turtles helped?

? Why did the results change when we played the game again? How do you think this compares to real life?

? What things can people do to help sea turtles?

Next, have students open up their fortune-tellers to read all of the factors that could have affected them during the game. Give each student a Turtle T-Chart, and have them list all the natural factors that helped or harmed their turtles on one side and all the human factors that helped or harmed their turtles on the other.

After discussing the results of the game, have students answer the questions at the bottom of the Turtle T-Chart.

? Do human actions help or harm sea turtles? Explain. (Discuss the results of human actions on sea turtles. Students should realize that some human actions help sea turtles and others harm sea turtles. Students can debate whether human actions are mostly positive or mostly negative.)

? Do you think humans should interfere with nature by helping sea turtles? Why or why not? (Answers will vary. Some students may justify human interference by saying that it can help "un-do" some of the harm we have caused to the sea turtles and their habitat.)

 K-W-L Chart

Next, ask students what they have learned about sea turtles from the book and the game and add to the "L" column of the K-W-L chart. They may also want to add more wonderings to the chart to explore through further research.

Elaborate & Evaluate

Write a Letter

Many students will be very concerned about the plight of sea turtles, and will want to know what they can do to help them. Give students the Write a Letter! student page. Have each student write a letter to one of the organizations listed asking for information about helping endangered sea turtles. They should include the following in their letters:

- 3 facts about sea turtles
- 3 ways sea turtles are harmed by human actions
- 1 reason endangered sea turtles should be helped
- 1 question asking how kids can help sea turtles
- teacher's name and school address

When sending the letters to the various marine conservation organizations, be sure to use the teacher's name and school address for the return address so that responses come back to the school. Many marine conservation groups have limited budgets and may not be able to send each child a response. You can help them by sending all letters to an organization together with just one request for a reply. Include a self-addressed stamped envelope.

Scoring Rubric for Letter

4 Point Response	The student's letter includes three important facts about sea turtles, clearly demonstrates understanding of three ways sea turtles are harmed by human actions, effectively communicates one reason sea turtles should be helped, and requests information about how kids can help sea turtles.
3 Point Response	The student's letter demonstrates a flaw in the understanding of the concepts, OR is missing one or two elements.
2 Point Response	The student's letter demonstrates a flaw in the understanding of the concepts and is missing one or two elements, OR is missing three or four elements.
1 Point Response	The student's letter demonstrates a flaw in the understanding of the concepts and is missing three or four elements OR is missing five elements.
0 Point Response	The student shows no understanding of the concepts OR does not write a letter.

The information the students receive in response to their letters can be added to the K-W-L chart and posted on a marine conservation bulletin board. Optional: Begin a class or schoolwide fundraiser for marine conservation efforts. Go to *www.cccturtle.org* for information on the Caribbean Conservation Corporation's Adopt-a-Turtle! program.

Inquiry Place

Some questions related to science cannot be answered by experimentation in the classroom. Students will have many questions about sea turtles, but it is not possible for them to observe or experiment with sea turtles in the classroom. The questions below are examples of research-type questions students can answer by doing Internet or library research. Have students brainstorm researchable questions such as

? How do scientists track sea turtles? What are the advantages and disadvantages of their methods?

? Which sea turtle species travels the farthest in its migration?

? What are some theories on how sea turtles navigate? Which theory do you think is most probable? Why?

Students can select a question to research individually or as teams. They should collect and analyze information from a variety of sources. Students can present their findings at a poster session.

Web Sites

Caribbean Conservation Corporation
www.cccturtle.org

HEART (Helping Endangered Animals—Ridley Turtles) *www.ridleyturtles.org*

The Ocean Conservancy
www.oceanconservancy.org

Sea Turtle Rescue and Rehabilitation Center
www.seaturtlehospital.org

Sea Turtle Restoration Project
www.seaturtles.org

World Wildlife Fund
www.worldwildlife.org

More Books to Read

Davies, N. 2001. *One tiny turtle.* New York, NY: Candlewick Press.
Summary: This introduction to the life cycle of the loggerhead turtle is written in poetic, informative text.

Gibbons, G. 1998. *Sea turtles.* New York, NY: Holiday House.
Summary: This informative book describes the types, features, nesting, and protection of sea turtles.

Guiberson, B. Z. 1996. *Into the sea.* New York, NY: Henry Holt.
Summary: Takes the reader through the life cycle of a turtle, from hatching to migration to returning to the beach to lay her eggs.

Lasky, K. 2001. *Interrupted journey: Saving endangered sea turtles.* New York, NY: Candlewick Press.
Summary: This photo essay depicts the efforts to save an endangered Kemp's ridley turtle rescued on a Cape Cod beach. Distinctive, full-color photographs carefully document each step of the extensive rescue procedure.

Sea Turtle
Headband

Directions for Making a Sea Turtle Headband:

1 Color the sea turtle and cut it out.

2 Cut a strip of paper 5 cm wide and long enough to fit around your head.

3 Tape the turtle to the strip of paper and you have a turtle headband!

4 Wrap the headband around your head and tape it in the back.

How to Make a
Fortune-Teller

1 Cut the fortune-teller template at the dotted line to make a square.

2 Lay the paper square with the turtle side down. Fold the square in half to make a triangle, crease it, and then open it back up.

3 Lay the paper square with the turtle side down again. Fold the other corners into a triangle and crease again. Unfold so you are back to the square (turtle side down).

4 Next, fold each corner point into the center of the creases.

5 Flip it over (turtle side down). Fold all four corner points into the center again.

6 Fold the square in half to make a rectangle and crease.

7 Open it back up to the square. Fold the other way to make a rectangle and crease.

8 Stick your two thumbs and two forefingers into each of the four turtle flap pockets. Fingers should press center creases so that all four flaps meet at a point in the center.

Now you are ready to play "Turtle, Turtle, Watch Out!"

Fortune-Teller
Template 1

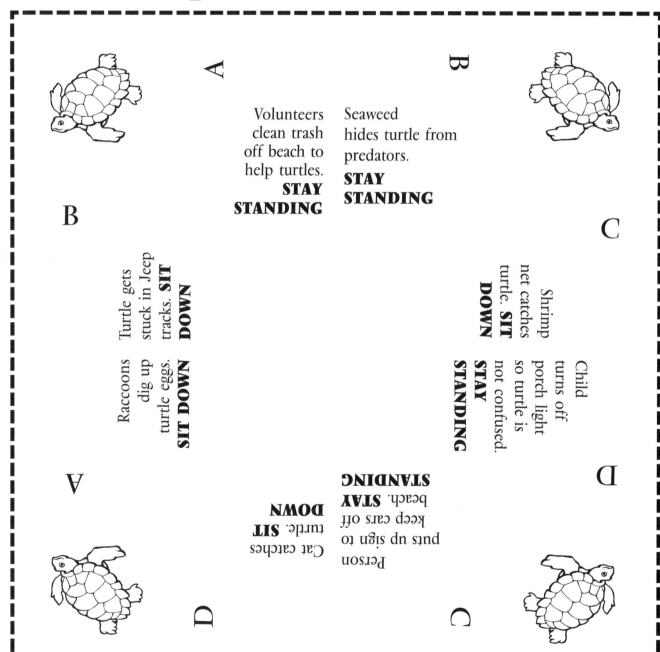

A

Volunteers clean trash off beach to help turtles. **STAY STANDING**

B

Seaweed hides turtle from predators. **STAY STANDING**

B

Turtle gets stuck in Jeep tracks. **SIT DOWN**

Raccoons dig up turtle eggs. **SIT DOWN**

C

Shrimp net catches turtle. **SIT DOWN**

Child turns off porch light so turtle is not confused. **STAY STANDING**

A

Cat catches turtle. **SIT DOWN**

Person puts up sign to keep cars off beach. **STAY STANDING**

D

C

Cut off at the dotted line to make a square.

NATIONAL SCIENCE TEACHERS ASSOCIATION

Fortune-Teller
Template 2

A

B

Moonlight attracts turtle to the ocean. **STAY STANDING**

Raccoons dig up turtle eggs. **SIT DOWN**

B

C

Ocean waves carry turtle away from beach predators. **STAY STANDING**

Turtle eats plastic bag floating in ocean. **SIT DOWN**

Child protects nest with wire mesh. **STAY STANDING**

Jeep runs over eggs. **SIT DOWN**

A

D

Shark catches turtle. **SIT DOWN**

Person picks up trash in ocean. **STAY STANDING**

D

C

Cut off at the dotted line to make a square.

How to play "Turtle, Turtle, Watch Out!"

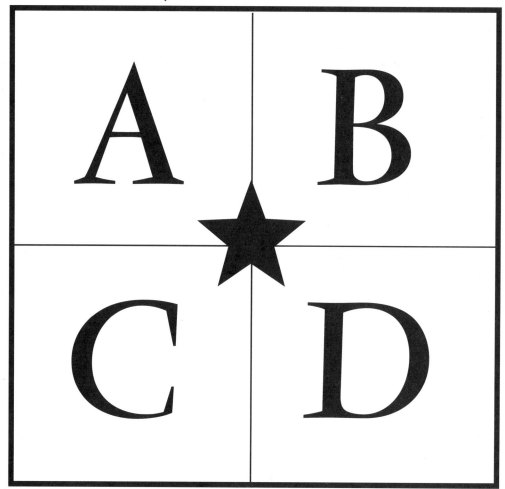

1 Have students stand up and spread out holding their assembled turtle fortune-tellers.

2 Before each turn, call out "Turtle, turtle, watch out!" in unison.

3 Hold a die about one inch above the star and drop it.

4 Call out the number on the die. Have students open and close their fortune-tellers that number of times.

5 Call out the letter that the die landed on. Have students open the panel under the letter and read their turtle's fate. If their turtle survives, they remain standing. If their turtle dies, they sit down. (Seated students can still follow along with their turtle fortune-tellers.)

6 Count the number of students standing after each turn and graph that number on the Turtle Line Graph.

7 The game ends after five turns or when no one is left standing.

8 Repeat game several times, using a different color to graph results each time.

9 Discuss results.

Turtle Line Graph

Number of Turtles Standing

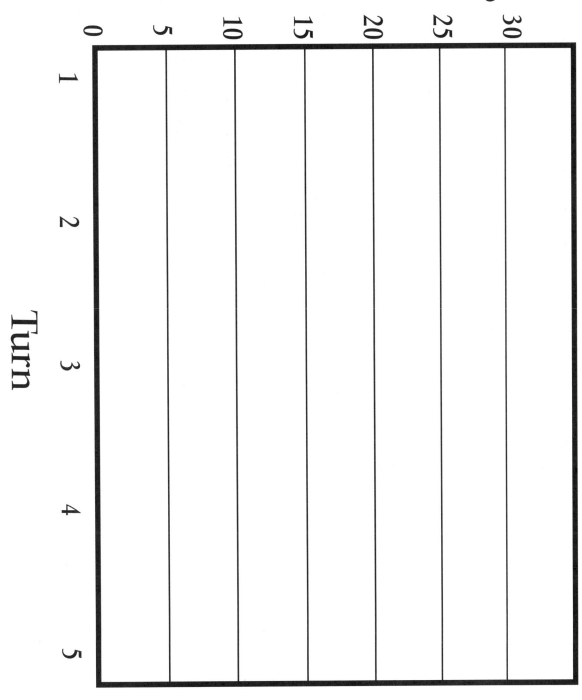

Name: _____

Turtle T-Chart

After playing "Turtle, Turtle, Watch Out!," open your fortune-teller and read all the factors that could have affected your turtle during the game. Fill out the T-Chart, and answer the questions below.

Natural Factors	Human Factors
Helped the turtle:	Helped the turtle:
Harmed the turtle:	Harmed the turtle:

1 Do human actions help or harm sea turtles? Explain. _____

_____

_____

2 Do you think humans should interfere with nature by helping sea turtles? Why or why not? _____

_____

Name: _____

Write a Letter!

Write a letter to one of the organizations listed below asking for information about helping endangered sea turtles. Include the following in your letter:

- 3 facts you learned about sea turtles
- 3 ways sea turtles are harmed by human actions
- 1 reason endangered sea turtles should be helped
- 1 question asking how kids can help sea turtles
- Your teacher's name and school address (Ask them to send the information to your teacher at your school address.)

Marine Conservation Organizations

Sea Turtle Restoration Project
PO Box 400
Forest Knolls, CA 94933

HEART (Helping Endangered
Animals—Ridley Turtles)
PO Box 681231
Houston, TX 77268-1231

The Ocean Conservancy
1725 DeSales Street, Suite 600
Washington, DC 20036

Sea Turtle Rescue and
Rehabilitation Center
PO Box 3012
Topsail Beach, NC 28445

World Wildlife Fund
1250 Twenty-Fourth Street, NW
PO Box 97180
Washington, DC 20037

Oil Spill!

Description

Learners explore the effects of oil spills on plants, animals, and the environment and investigate cleanup methods through a simulated oil spill. Learners also use creative writing and letter writing to demonstrate their understandings about the effects of oil spills.

Suggested Grade Levels: 3–6

Lesson Objectives Connecting to the Standards

Content Standard A: Scientific Inquiry

K–4: Plan and conduct a simple investigation.

5–8: Design and conduct a scientific investigation.

Content Standard F: Science in Personal and Social Perspectives

K–4: Understand that pollution is a change in the environment that can influence the health, survival, or activities of organisms, including humans.

5–8: Understand the risks associated with chemical hazards such as pollutants in water.

Featured Picture Books

Title	**Prince William**		Title	**Oil Spill!**
Author	**Gloria Rand**		Author	**Melvin Berger**
Illustrator	**Ted Rand**		Illustrator	**Paul Mirocha**
Publisher	**Henry Holt & Company**		Publisher	**HarperCollins**
Year	**1994**		Year	**1994**
Genre	**Story**		Genre	**Narrative Information**
Summary	**On Prince William Sound in Alaska, Denny rescues a baby seal hurt by an oil spill and watches it recover in a nearby hospital.**		Summary	**Explains why oil spills occur and how they are cleaned up and suggests strategies for preventing oil spills in the future**

Time Needed

This lesson will take several class periods. Suggested scheduling is as follows:

Day 1: **Engage** with read aloud of *Prince William*

Day 2: **Explore** and **Explain** with read aloud of *Oil Spill!* and Oil Spill Cleanup Checkpoint Lab

Day 3: **Elaborate** with Animal Rescue

Day 4: **Evaluate** with Thank a Rescuer

Materials

For Oil Spill Cleanup Checkpoint Lab

- In advance, make black oil by adding 8 teaspoons of powdered black tempera paint to a gallon jug half full of vegetable oil. With the lid tightly in place, shake the jug to mix the powder with the vegetable oil. This will make enough oil for 8 teams.

- Newspaper

- Disposable aluminum pie pans (3 per team)

- Rocks each no bigger than a deck of cards (3 per team)

- Leafy carrot or celery tops or plastic aquarium plants (3 per team)

- Pipe cleaners

- Water

- 3 cups for collecting removed oil for measuring

- Metric measuring cups

- Red cup and green cup with the openings taped together (1 per team)

- Zipper baggies filled with these supplies (1 per team):
  - Spoon
  - Fork
  - Yarn (about 50 cm)
  - 10 cm strip of nylon stocking
  - Cotton ball
  - Disposable pipettes
  - Coffee filter
  - 5-cm-wide strip of paper towel

Student Pages

- Oil Spill Cleanup Checkpoint Lab

- Animal Rescue

- Thank a Rescuer

Engage

Read Aloud

 Inferring

Show students the cover of the book *Prince William*. Then ask

? What do you think this book might be about?

? Who do you think Prince William is?

 Questioning

Say, "As I'm reading, I'm going to be telling you what I'm wondering because good readers ask questions as they read."

Begin reading to the class. Stop periodically to model some questions that come to your mind as you read. For example:

? What would an oil-covered beach look and smell like?

? Why does Denny hear a baby crying on the beach?

? What would it be like to pick up a slippery baby seal?

? Will Prince William survive?

Be sure to read the author's note at the end of the book, which explains that *Prince William* is based on true events and that schoolchildren really did help with the seal recovery efforts.

 Text-to-Self:

Think-Pair-Share

After reading the story, model some text-to-self connections. For example, tell what you remember about the *Exxon Valdez* oil spill or tell about a time you helped an injured animal. Ask students if they have ever helped an animal like Denny helped Prince William. Give them a minute to think about it, and then share their experiences with a partner.

Explore & Explain

Read Aloud and Oil Spill Cleanup Checkpoint Lab

Determining Importance

Introduce the author and illustrator of *Oil Spill!* Have students jot down the methods and materials used by oil spill cleanup crews as you read *Oil Spill!* to the class.

? What methods and materials were described in the book? (using booms, skimmers, and pads; setting the oil on fire; spreading chemicals; spraying the shore; adding bacteria; or taking no action)

? Which method do you think works the best? Why? (answers will vary)

? Are there any disadvantages to any of these methods? (Pads are difficult to dispose of; fire sends smoke and gas into the air and leaves ash in the water; chemicals add poison to the water; hot spray pushes water far-

CLEANING UP A SIMULATED OIL SPILL

ther into the rocks and sand; and using bacteria requires huge amounts of it.)

After discussing *Oil Spill!*, tell students they are going to be members of an oil spill response team. An oil spill has just occurred in their region, and they must spring into action to find out which methods will work best to clean up the oil.

In advance, prepare the materials for the Oil Spill Cleanup Checkpoint Lab. See "Teaching Science Through Inquiry," Chapter 3, for a list of tips for managing a checkpoint lab.

Oil Spill Cleanup Checkpoint Lab

Divide students into four-person teams. Give each member of the team a copy of the Oil Spill Cleanup Checkpoint Lab. Explain that they will be following the directions on the student page. As they are working, they should keep their cups green side on top. If they need help or if they are at a checkpoint, they should put their cups red side on top. Each member of the group is responsible for recording data and writing responses. Before you give a team a check mark or stamp so that they can move ahead in the lab, informally evaluate the students by asking probing questions to different members of the team. Redirect their investigations when necessary.

When all groups are finished with the checkpoint lab, discuss the following questions:

? What did you learn about designing an experiment?

? Would you make any changes in your experimental design?

? Can you propose any new methods for cleaning up oil spills?

? What do you think it would be like to clean up a real oil spill like the *Exxon Valdez* spill we have been reading about?

elaborate

Animal Rescue

Rereading

Reread pages 10 through 13 of *Oil Spill!* Then ask

? What types of animals were harmed by the oil spill in the book? (seabirds such as ducks and geese, fish, shrimp, crabs, sea otters, sea lions, harbor seals, and killer whales)

? How do oil spills harm birds? (The oil sticks to their feathers so they can't swim or fly.)

? How do oil spills harm fish, shrimp, and crabs? (Oil gets into their bodies and poisons them.)

? How do oil spills harm sea mammals? (They swallow oil and breathe poisonous fumes. The oil also coats their bodies.)

Reread the following pages in *Prince William*: pages 10 (about the doctor and volunteer), 19 (about the other animals being washed), and 20 (about Denny finding the empty incubator). Then ask

? Imagine that you are cleaning a real, live animal that has been oiled. What things would you need to consider to keep you and the animal safe?

? What would your day be like if you were an animal rescuer?

? What would you enjoy about being a rescuer?

? What parts of the job would be difficult?

Pass out the Animal Rescue student page. Tell students to imagine they are animal rescuers. Have them write a short story describing their rescue experiences. They should draw a picture to illustrate their story and write a caption for the drawing.

evaluate

Thank a Rescuer

Pass out the Thank a Rescuer student page. Students will write letters to oil spill animal rescue organizations thanking the oil response team employees and volunteers. Use the rubric below to evaluate the letters.

Scoring Rubric for Letter

4 Point Response	The student's letter includes a statement thanking the rescuer, clearly demonstrates understanding of the oil spill activity, lists two ways oil spills can affect the health and survival of organisms, effectively communicates his or her concern about oil spills, and requests information about how kids can support cleanup efforts or prevent oil spills.
3 Point Response	The student's letter demonstrates a flaw in the understanding of the concepts OR is missing one or two elements.
2 Point Response	The student's letter demonstrates a flaw in the understanding of the concepts and is missing one or two elements OR is missing three or four elements.
1 Point Response	The student's letter demonstrates a flaw in the understanding of the concepts and is missing three or four elements OR is missing five elements.
0 Point Response	The student shows no understanding of the concepts OR does not write a letter.

Inquiry Place

Have students brainstorm "investigatable" questions such as:

? Which brand of detergent is best for cleaning oiled material?

? Which is best for insulating a marine animal: fur, feathers, or blubber?

? Do all types of oil float on water? Of the following types of oil, olive oil, corn oil, and baby oil, which is the most dense? the least dense?

Students can select a question to investigate as a class, or have groups of students vote on the question they want to investigate as teams. After they make their predictions, students can design an experiment to test their predictions. Students can present their findings at a poster session.

Web Sites

Photos from the *Exxon Valdez* oil spill
www.oilspill.state.ak.us/facts/photos.html

Map of the *Exxon Valdez* Oil Spill Area
www.conservationgiscenter.org/maps/html/
exxon_spill.html

How Oil Affects Birds
www.ibrrc.org/oil_affects.html

Clean the Oiled Sea Otter Activity
www.marinemammalcenter.org/learning/
education/teacher_resources/cleanseaotter.asp

Effects of Oil on Wildlife
www.tristatebird.org/oilspill/effects_of_oil.htm

More Books to Read

D'Lacey, C. 2002. *A break in the chain.* New York, NY: Crabtree Publishing Company.
Summary: This illustrated chapter book reveals how a terrible oil spill in the Arctic, a lesson about food chains, and a computer game featuring a polar bear turn into a magical adventure for Billy, whose class uses e-mail and a fundraiser to help rescue the Arctic animals. A compelling story about environmental protection and how children can make their voices heard.

Hodgkins, F. 2000. *The orphan seal.* Camden, ME: Down East Books.
Summary: This beautifully illustrated picture book tells the true story of Howler, an abandoned harbor seal pup who was separated from his mother in a storm. Howler is rescued and rehabilitated by the New England Aquarium and eventually released back into the wild.

Meeker, CH. 1999. *Lootas: Little wave eater.* Seattle, WA: Sasquatch Books.
Summary: This fascinating photo essay describes how a young sea otter pup is rescued after its mother is accidentally killed by a motorboat. The pup, Lootas, is taken to a U.S. Fish and Wildlife Service office after her rescue and eventually finds a home in the Seattle Aquarium. Includes insets with facts about sea otters.

Smith, R. 2003. *Sea otter rescue: The aftermath of an oil spill.* New York, NY: Puffin.
Summary: When the *Exxon Valdez* struck the rocks in Prince William Sound, Alaska, nearly 11 million gallons of crude oil spilled into the water. The result was an oil slick that threatened all of the area wildlife, especially the sea otters. This is the story of the animal rescue experts who went to Alaska to help out. Illustrated with the author's own photographs, this book is a fascinating firsthand account of the heroic measures taken to save the lives of hundreds of sea otters.

Name: _____

Oil Spill Cleanup Checkpoint Lab

You are a member of an oil spill response team. An oil spill has just occurred in your region and you must spring into action to find out which methods will work best to clean up the oil! If your team is working, put the green cup on top. If you have a question, put the red cup on top. If you are finished with a part and you are ready for a check from your teacher, put the red cup on top.

Part A Setting Up an Oil Spill Simulation

☑ *Check the boxes as your team completes each step.*

☐ Cover your work area with newspaper.

☐ Get three aluminum pie pans from your teacher.

☐ Place one rock in each of the pans to represent the shore.

☐ Place a plant in each to represent shoreline plants.

☐ Make three models of animals out of pipe cleaners, and place the pipe cleaner animals on the edge of the rocks.

☐ Fill the pan with 250 ml of water.

☐ Get some simulated black oil from your teacher, and add 75 ml of the black oil mixture to each pan. Have one person from your group gently blow across the top of the pan to simulate wind and waves.

Note: The reason you are not using real petroleum oil is that it is toxic and should never be handled by children.

Describe what happens when someone blows across the water.

_____

_____

Checkpoint A ☐

Name: _____

Oil Spill Cleanup
Checkpoint Lab cont.

Part B Design an Experiment to Test Cleanup Materials

1 Your job is to find out which material will remove the most oil from the pan. Choose three materials to test from the list below.

Circle your choices:

Spoon	Cotton balls
Fork	Disposable pipettes
Nylon stockings cut into strips	Coffee filters
Paper towels cut into strips	Yarn

2 Make a prediction about which of the three materials will remove the most oil from the pan. Explain why you chose that material.

_____

_____

3 How will you decide which material removed the most oil? You can use the 3 plastic cups for measuring removed oil.

_____

_____

4 Write a step-by-step procedure for your experiment:

_____

_____

_____

_____

Checkpoint B ☐

Name: _____

Oil Spill Cleanup
Checkpoint Lab cont.

Part C Data and Conclusions

1 You are now ready to test three cleanup materials. Collect your data and organize it in a table below.

2 What effects did the oil spill have on the simulated environment?

_____

_____

3 Conclusion: Which material was best for cleaning up the oil spill? What is your evidence?

_____

_____

4 If you were going to repeat this experiment, what would you do differently? Why?

_____

_____

_____

Checkpoint C ☐

Author:_____

Animal Rescue

Imagine that you are an animal rescuer. Write a short story describing your rescue experiences. Draw a picture to illustrate your story, and write a caption for the picture.

Caption _____

_____

_____

Author:_____

Animal Rescue
cont.

Story _____

_____

_____

_____

_____

_____

_____

_____

_____

_____

_____

_____

_____

_____

_____

_____

_____

_____

_____

_____

_____

_____

_____

Thank a Rescuer

Write a letter thanking an oil spill animal rescue worker or volunteer involved in one of the organizations listed below. Include the following in your letter:

- a statement thanking the oil spill rescue worker
- a description of the activity you did to clean up an oil spill and what you learned
- 2 ways oil spills affect the health and survival of organisms
- what concerns you most about oil spills
- a request for information on how kids can help support cleanup efforts or prevent oil spills (Ask them to send the information to your teacher at your school address.)

Oil Spill Animal Rescue Organizations

International Bird Rescue
Research Center
4369 Cordelia Road
Fairfield, CA 94534

Marine Mammal Center
1065 Fort Cronkhite
Sausalito, CA 94965

Oiled Wildlife Care Network
Wildlife Health Center
University of California
Davis, CA 95616

SeaWorld & Busch Gardens
Conservation Fund
c/o Hubbs-SeaWorld Research
Institute
2595 Ingraham Street
San Diego, CA 92109

Tri-State Bird Rescue & Research
110 Possum Hollow Road
Newark, DE 19711

Sheep in a Jeep

Description

Learners investigate forces and motion using ramps, toy jeeps, and small plastic farm animals, and share their findings in a poster session. Learners also design and evaluate a device to slow the motion of a falling object.

Suggested Grade Levels: 3–4

Lesson Objectives Connecting to the Standards

Content Standard A:
Scientific Inquiry

K–4: Plan and conduct a simple investigation.

K–4: Employ simple equipment and tools to gather data and extend the senses.

K–4: Use data to construct a reasonable explanation.

K–4: Communicate investigations and explanations.

Content Standard B:
Physical Science

K–4: Understand that an object's motion can be described by tracing and measuring its position over time.

K–4: Understand that the position and motion of objects can be changed by pushing or pulling.

Content Standard E:
Science and Technology

K–4: Propose a solution.

K–4: Implement a proposed solution.

K–4: Evaluate a product or design.

Featured Picture Book

Title	***Sheep in a Jeep***
Author	**Nancy Shaw**
Illustrator	**Margot Apple**
Publisher	**Houghton Mifflin Company**
Year	**1997**
Genre	**Story**
Summary	**Records the misadventures of a group of sheep who go riding in a jeep**

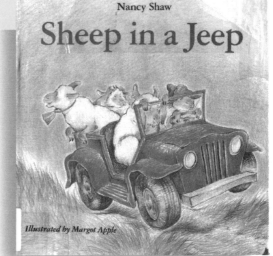

Nancy Shaw

Sheep in a Jeep

Illustrated by Margot Apple

Time Needed

This lesson will take several class periods. Suggested scheduling is as follows:

Day 1: **Engage** with read aloud of *Sheep in a Jeep,* and **Explore** with Checkpoint Lab, Part A and Part B

Day 2: **Explore** with Checkpoint Lab Part C and Part D, and **Explain** with Poster Session (from Checkpoint Lab, Part E)

Day 3: **Explore** and **Explain** with Motion and Forces Sentence Cards

Day 4: **Elaborate** with Sheep Leap, and **Explain** with Sheep Leap Diagram

Day 5: **Evaluate** with Review and Motion Quiz

Materials

For the Sheep in a Jeep Checkpoint Lab:

- Toy jeeps or toy diecast cars (1 per team)
- Small plastic animals (1 per team)
- Wooden ramps (1 per team)
- Books to build ramps and chutes (about 5 per team)
- Rough sandpaper (2 sheets per team)
- Tape (1 roll per team)
- Team task cards precut
- Red cup and green cup with the openings taped together (1 per team)
- Calculators (1 per team)
- Poster-size paper (1 piece per team)

For the Sheep Leap elaboration activity (per pair):

- String
- Plastic bag
- Scissors
- Piece of paper
- Tape
- Paper bag

Sheep Leap Diagram (copied onto an overhead transparency)

Student Pages

- Sheep in a Jeep Team Task Cards
- Sheep in a Jeep Checkpoint Lab
- Motion and Forces Sentence Cards
- Motion and Forces Article
- Sheep Leap
- Motion Quiz

The Sheep in a Jeep Checkpoint Lab is ideally done on tile floors. If your classroom floors are carpeted, try to find other areas in your school that have smooth surfaced floors, such as in the hallways, gymnasium, and cafeteria.

engage

Read Aloud

 Determining Importance

Tell students that you will be reading a funny book called *Sheep in a Jeep* because it can help them learn about force and motion. Ask them to give a "thumbs up" when they think they hear an example of a *force* or a *motion* in the book. The purpose of this is to determine students' prior knowledge about the meanings of the words *force* and *motion*. Then read *Sheep in a Jeep* aloud to the class.

Make a T-chart on the board. Label it "Force" on the left side and "Motion" on the right. Discuss their ideas about force and motion using the guiding questions below:

❓ What is a force? (A force is a push or a pull on an object.)

❓ What things can forces do? (They can make things move. They can make things speed up. They can make things slow down. They can make things change direction. They can make things move back and forth or around and around.)

❓ Is gravity a force? (Yes.)

❓ How do you know? (Gravity pulls all objects toward Earth.)

❓ What is motion? (Motion is a change in the position of an object. When you say that something has moved, you are describing its motion.)

Next, ask students to name examples of force or motion from the book. List the examples on the T-chart. If students name a force, ask them to identify the resulting motion. If the students name a motion, ask them to identify what force caused the motion.

explore

Sheep in a Jeep Checkpoint Lab

In advance, prepare the supplies for the Sheep in a Jeep Checkpoint Lab. See "Teaching Science Through Inquiry," Chapter 3, for a list of tips for managing a checkpoint lab.

Tell students they will be exploring some things that affect motion. Divide students into four-person teams. Give each member of the teams a copy of the Sheep in a Jeep Checkpoint Lab. Explain that they will be following the directions on the worksheet. Give each team member a Team Task Card. Assign tasks to each person on the team:

Reader—reads the directions as the group is working and is in charge of the green and red cups

Sample Force and Motion T-Chart

Force	Motion
Sheep push on jeep	Jeep moves down hill
Gravity pulls on sheep	Sheep move down hill
Sheep tug on jeep	Jeep won't move
Pigs push on jeep	Jeep moves
Wheels push jeep forward	Jeep moves
Jeep runs into tree	Jeep stops moving

Releaser/Calculator—releases the jeep from the top of the ramp without pushing it and calculates average distances in Parts B and C using a calculator

Part B Measurer—measures the distance in centimeters the jeep travels from the end of the ramp in Part B

Part C Measurer—measures the distance in centimeters the jeep travels from the end of the ramp in Part C

Distribute the materials for the lab. Demonstrate how to release a jeep from the top of a ramp without pushing it. Before students begin working, discuss the following questions:

? How should you measure the distance the jeep rolls from the bottom of the ramp—from the front of the jeep or the back of the jeep? (It doesn't matter, as long as you measure in centimeters from the same point each time.)

? What will you do if the jeep falls off the ramp before it reaches the bottom, or it gets stuck, or it hits something? (We won't record that trial, and we will do it over.)

Discuss the concept of *variability*. Say, "Scientists do the same experiment over and over to make sure of their results. Your results probably won't be exactly the same for every trial—scientists call that variability. Your results will vary a little each time. That's why you are doing several trials and taking an *average* to find out about how far the jeep will usually roll. We're going to take the average of three trials for each setup. Scientists always repeat their experiments many, many times. We will repeat them only three times because of our time constraints."

? How do you calculate an average? (Add up the distances of all trials, and then divide by the number of trials.)

Have students begin the checkpoint lab. Observe and listen to the students as they interact. While they are working, they should keep the green side of their cups on top. If they need help, or if they are at a checkpoint, they should put the red side on top. Each member of the group is responsible for recording data and writing responses. Before you give a team a check mark or stamp so they can move ahead in the lab, informally evaluate the students by asking probing questions of each member of the team.

RELEASING THE JEEP DOWN THE RAMP

explain

Poster Session

After each team has completed parts A through D of the checkpoint lab, it should begin its Poster Session assignments (Part E). At this point students do not need to apply scientific terminology. Encourage students to use their own words, their recorded observations from the checkpoint lab, and their prior knowledge of motion as a basis for explaining concepts. Have students present their posters. Encourage the audience to listen carefully, ask thoughtful questions, examine the evidence, identify faulty reasoning, and suggest alternative explanations to presenters in a polite, respectful manner.

After the poster session, ask students if they have ever heard of a man named Isaac Newton. Explain that Newton was born in England about 360 years ago. When he was 23, as the story goes, he saw an apple fall to the ground, which led him to write a scientific law about gravity. Later he wrote the three famous laws describing motion that we call Newton's laws of motion. Tell students that they are going to do an activity to help them learn more about motion and forces.

explore & explain

Motion and Forces Sentence Cards

 ### Word Sorts

Word sorts help learners understand the relationships among key concepts and help teach classification. Classifying and then reclassifying help students extend and refine their understanding of the concepts studied. Distribute a set of Motion and Forces Sentence Cards to each pair of students for an "open sort." Instruct students to cut out the cards and see if they can make some sentences with them. As you move from pair to pair, ask students to explain the meaning of their sentences.

 ### Pairs Read

Then pass out the Motion and Forces Article. Have students take turns reading aloud from the article. While one person reads a paragraph, the other listens and then summarizes.

For this "closed sort," you provide the categories into which students are to assign words. In this case, the categories come from the meanings of the bold words in the ar-

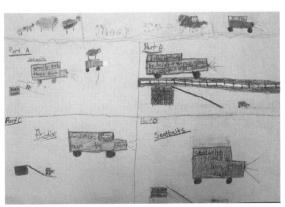

SAMPLE SHEEP IN A JEEP POSTERS

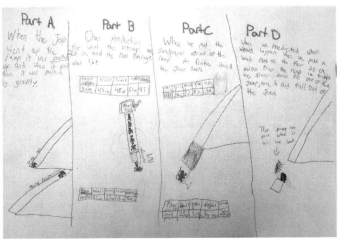

ticle: *force, motion, inertia, gravity,* and *friction*. Students can now make new sentences based upon the information they read in the article.

Ask students to justify their new sentences with evidence from the article as you move around to each team. Possible correct sentences include

- Sheep push jeep.
- Force causes motion.
- Inertia keeps sheep in motion.
- Gravity pulls sheep.
- Gravity pulls jeep.
- Friction slows jeep.

Discuss all the concepts the students have explored in each part of the checkpoint lab using the terminology they learned through the Motion and Forces Article and the word sort. The following explanations of each part of the checkpoint lab are for you; modify as necessary to help students understand and apply the concepts.

Part A: The force that caused the jeep to move up the ramp was the push provided by the student's hand. The force that caused the jeep to move down the ramp was gravity. (Friction between the wheels and the ramp and between the jeep and the air played a part in slowing the motion of the jeep as it traveled down the ramp and when it reached the flat surface.)

Part B: As the jeep rolled down the lower ramp, its speed increased. As the jeep rolled down the higher ramp, its speed increased even more. The jeep rolled a longer distance from the bottom of the ramp when the ramp was raised because it was moving faster when it reached the bottom of the ramp. The faster the jeep was moving when it left the ramp, the more distance it could cover before friction slowed it.

Part C: Friction is a force that slows motion. It is caused by things rubbing against each other. In this case the jeep's wheels rubbed against the tile floor and then the sandpaper. The rough sandpaper caused more friction against the jeep's wheels than the smooth tile floor, so the jeep slowed down faster and thus rolled a shorter distance on the sandpaper.

Part D: As the jeep rolled down the ramp, its speed increased. The sheep had the same speed as the jeep. When the jeep hit the book, the force of impact stopped the jeep, but the unbelted sheep was free to continue moving until some force stopped it. The jeep and the sheep both had inertia, a resistance to a change in motion. Once started, both continued to move until outside forces acted against them, causing them to stop. The book stopped the jeep's motion, and air resistance slowed the sheep's forward motion as gravity pulled it down to the ground. Tell students everyone should always wear a seatbelt because, if your vehicle stops and you are unbelted, your inertia will keep you moving until you hit something—the windshield or the ground!

After this discussion, send students back to their posters to add the following terminology where appropriate: force, motion, inertia, gravity, and friction.

elaborate

Sheep Leap
Pass out the Sheep Leap student pages to each student. Provide materials for students to invent a device that slows the fall of a toy animal. Allow ample time for them to test their inventions.

After students complete the Sheep Leap activity and the student page, use the questions below to help students apply the new labels, definitions, and explanations they learned in

explain

Sheep Leap Diagram

Explain that friction with the air is called *air resistance*. Use the Sheep Leap diagram overhead transparency to explain how the force of gravity pulls all objects toward the center of the Earth and air resistance pushes up against objects in motion.

? In the Sheep Leap, which force was stronger, gravity or air resistance? (gravity)

? What is your evidence? (The sheep fell to the ground.)

Have students add arrows and the words *gravity* and *air resistance* to their drawings on the Sheep Leap student page.

evaluate

Review and Motion Quiz

Use the team posters and the Sheep Leap student page to review the concepts and vocabulary of motion and forces. Then give students the Motion Quiz. Answers follow.

1 A push and a pull (or a person pushing and a person pulling)

2 Gravity

3 Smooth metal

4 Rough sandpaper

5 There is more friction between the car's wheels and the sandpaper than the other surfaces. Friction slows the car's motion.

6 The doll will fly off (or keep moving) when the car stops. The doll is in motion so it tends to stay in motion even though the car stops. (Or the doll's inertia keeps it in motion.)

7 (b) Air resistance slows the paper airplane down, and gravity pulls it to Earth.

TESTING AN INVENTION IN "SHEEP LEAP"

the *Sheep in a Jeep* activities to this new experience. This way, the students are beginning to provide formal definitions and labels to their work after they have constructed their own ideas about motion and forces through their hands-on experiences and class discussions. Ask

? What force pulls the plastic animals to the ground when they "leap"? (gravity)

? In the Sheep in a Jeep activity, we learned that friction (rubbing) slows objects down as they move. Is your plastic animal "rubbing" against anything as it falls? (Yes. The animals are rubbing against the air as they fall.)

? Does rubbing against the air slow an object down? (Yes.)

? How does your invention slow down the falling animal? (Answers will vary, but should include friction with or "rubbing against" the air.)

Inquiry Place

Have students brainstorm "investigatable" questions such as

- Will adding weight make a difference in how far the jeep travels?

- Will the jeep travel farther on rough or fine sandpaper?

- What happens to the distance the jeep travels if you keep increasing the angle of the ramp?

- How does the weight of the load affect the motion of the parachute?

Then have students select a question to investigate as a class, or groups of students can vote on the question they want to investigate as teams. After they make their predictions, they can experiment to test their predictions. Students can present their findings at a poster session.

More Books to Read

Cole, J. 1998. *Magic school bus plays ball: A book about forces.* New York, NY: Scholastic.
Summary: Ms. Frizzle and her class shrink to fit inside a physics book where they enter a page about a baseball field with no friction. The kids learn about how throwing, running, and catching would work in a world without friction.

Frazee, M. 2003. *Roller coaster.* New York, NY: Harcourt, Inc.
Summary: The spare text and dynamic artwork of this picture book capture the anticipation and excitement a young girl experiences on her very first roller coaster ride. This book can be used as a delightful introduction to motion and forces.

Karpelenia, J. 2004. *Motion: Energy works! series.* Logan, IA: Perfection Learning Corporation.
Summary: This informational chapter book on motion and forces includes a glossary, index, and several brief activities for readers to try.

Stille, D. 2004. *Motion: Push and pull, fast and slow.* Minneapolis, MN: Picture Window Books.
Summary: Lively cartoons illustrate this engaging nonfiction picture book about how things move and what makes them stop. Includes simple descriptions of inertia, gravity, friction, and relative motion. Fun facts, experiments, and a glossary are included.

Reference

Gertz, S. E., D. J. Portman, and M. Sarquis. 1996. *Teaching physical science through children's literature: 20 complete lessons for elementary grades.* Middletown, OH: Terrific Science Press. Sheep in a Jeep Checkpoint Lab adapted from "Ramps and Cars" on pages 189-196.

Sheep in a Jeep
Team Task Cards

Reader

Read the directions out loud for your team. Put the green cup on top if your group is working. Put the red cup on top if you have a question or if you are ready for a check mark.

Releaser/Calculator

Wait until you hear the directions from the Reader. Then release the jeep from the top of the ramp without pushing it. Calculate the average distance the jeep rolls in Parts B and C.

Part B Measurer

Use a tape measure to measure the distance the jeep rolls from the end of the ramp in Part B. Measure to the nearest centimeter.

Part C Measurer

Use a tape measure to measure the distance the jeep rolls from the end of the ramp in Part C. Measure to the nearest centimeter.

Name: _____

Sheep in a Jeep
Checkpoint Lab

Follow the directions below. If your team is working, put the green cup on top. If you have a question, put the red cup on top. If you are finished with a part and you are ready for a check from your teacher, put the red cup on top.

Part **A** Motion and Forces

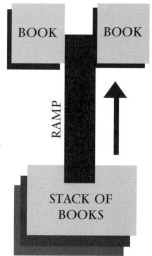

BOOK   BOOK

RAMP

STACK OF BOOKS

- Tape the sheep (or other animal) into the jeep with one piece of tape.
- Stack some books until they are about **5 cm** high.
- Raise one end of the ramp and place it on the books.
- Make a chute with some books at the end of the ramp.
- Push the jeep up the ramp to the top.

1 What force caused the jeep to move *up* the ramp?

_____

- Now let the jeep roll down the ramp without pushing it.

2 What force caused the jeep to move *down* the ramp?

_____

Checkpoint A ☐

NATIONAL SCIENCE TEACHERS ASSOCIATION

Name: _____

Sheep in a Jeep
Checkpoint Lab cont.

Part **B** Changing the Height of the Ramp

- Release the jeep without pushing from the top of the **5-cm**-high ramp.
- Measure in centimeters how far it rolls from the end of the ramp and record under Trial 1 Distance. (If it falls off before reaching the bottom, do over!)
- Repeat for Trial 2 and Trial 3.
- Find the average distance the jeep rolled by adding the three distances and dividing by 3.

Ramp Height	Trial 1 Distance	Trial 2 Distance	Trial 3 Distance	Average Distance
5 cm				

Make a prediction: If you raise the ramp to **10 cm** high, will the jeep roll a longer distance or a shorter distance from the end of the ramp?

_____

- Now raise the ramp to **10 cm** high and release the jeep without pushing.
- Measure in centimeters how far it rolls from the end of the ramp and record under Trial 1 Distance. (If it falls off before reaching the bottom, do it over!)
- Repeat for Trial 2 and Trial 3.
- Find the average distance the jeep rolled by adding the three distances and dividing by 3.

Ramp Height	Trial 1 Distance	Trial 2 Distance	Trial 3 Distance	Average Distance
10 cm				

Name: _____

Sheep in a Jeep
Checkpoint Lab cont.
Part B Questions

1 Were there any trials that your team didn't record? Why or why not?

_____

2 What was the average distance the jeep rolled with a **5-cm**-high ramp?

_____

3 What was the average distance the jeep rolled with a **10-cm**-high ramp?

_____

4 Did the jeep roll a shorter or longer distance when you raised the ramp?

_____

5 Write a conclusion: How does the height of the ramp affect the distance the jeep rolls? What is your evidence?

_____

_____

_____

Checkpoint B ☐

Name: _____

Sheep in a Jeep
Checkpoint Lab cont.
Part C Changing the Surface

- Change the ramp back to **5 cm high**. Release the jeep from the top of the ramp without pushing.
- Measure in centimeters how far it rolls from the end of the ramp and record under "Trial 1 Distance." Repeat for Trial 2 and Trial 3.
- Find the average distance the jeep rolled by adding the three distances and dividing by 3.

Floor Surface	Trial 1 Distance	Trial 2 Distance	Trial 3 Distance	Average Distance
Tile				

Make a prediction: If you cover the tile floor at the end of the ramp with sandpaper, will the jeep roll a longer distance or a shorter distance from the end of the ramp?

_____

- Now cover the floor at the end of the ramp with two sheets of sandpaper taped together and release the jeep without pushing.
- Measure in centimeters how far it rolls from the end of the ramp and record under "Trial 1 Distance." Repeat for Trial 2 and Trial 3.
- Find the average distance the jeep rolled by adding the three distances and dividing by 3.

Floor Surface	Trial 1 Distance	Trial 2 Distance	Trial 3 Distance	Average Distance
Sandpaper				

Name: _____

Sheep in a Jeep
Checkpoint Lab cont.

Part C Questions

1 Did the jeep roll a shorter or longer distance from the end of the ramp when you covered the tile floor with sandpaper?_____

2 Write a conclusion: How does the surface of the floor affect the distance the jeep rolls? What is your evidence?_____

_____

_____

_____

_____

_____

_____

_____

_____

Checkpoint C ☐

Sheep in a Jeep
Checkpoint Lab cont.

Part **D** "Sheep-Belts"

- Remove the tape from the sheep and place the sheep back in the jeep.
- Change the ramp to **10 cm** high.
- Place a book flat on the floor **20 cm** from the end of the ramp.

Make a prediction: What will happen to the sheep when the jeep hits the book?

_____

_____

_____

- Release the jeep from the top of the **10-cm**-high ramp without pushing it. Let it hit the book.

Part **D** Questions

1 What happened to the sheep when the jeep hit the book? Why?

_____

_____

2 Why is it important to always wear a seatbelt in a moving vehicle?

_____

_____

Checkpoint D ☐

Sheep in a Jeep
Checkpoint Lab cont.

Part **E** Poster Session

Make a poster with your team displaying what you learned about forces and motion from the Sheep in a Jeep lab. Label your poster with **Part A, Part B, Part C, and Part D**. Some things to think about for your poster:

- What is the most important information to share from each part of the checkpoint lab activity?

- What data tables or graphs will you include?

- What pictures will you draw?

- Who is going to explain each part of the poster? (Everyone on your team should have a turn!)

Be ready to share your poster with the class and answer any questions they might have.

Checkpoint E ☐

Motion & Forces

Sentence Cards

Directions: Cut out the cards below and make sentences with
them. Then read the article "Motion and Forces" and make new
sentences with them.

force	motion
inertia	friction
gravity	causes
keeps	sheep
in	motion

Motion & Forces

Sentence Cards cont.

jeep	slows
pulls	jeep
push	sheep
jeep	sheep
pulls	gravity

NATIONAL SCIENCE TEACHERS ASSOCIATION

Motion and Forces

What is a force?

A **force** is a push or a pull. In *Sheep in a Jeep*, the sheep push the jeep. The push is a force. The sheep also tug, or pull, on the jeep. The pull is a force.

What is motion?

We consider an object to be in **motion** when it is not standing still. In order for an object to move or to stop moving, a **force** must be applied to it. The sheep apply a force as they push the jeep and the force causes motion. When the jeep hits the tree, the tree applies a force to the jeep and the jeep stops moving.

What is inertia?

Inertia is a resistance to change in motion. For example, when the jeep gets stuck, its inertia keeps it from moving easily. It is at rest and tends to stay at rest. When the jeep full of sheep hits the tree, the inertia of the sheep keeps them in motion. Because the sheep are not wearing seatbelts to stop them, they tend to stay in motion.

What is gravity?

Gravity is a force that we encounter all the time. It is the force that pulls all things toward Earth. When the sheep push the jeep to the top of the hill, gravity pulls the jeep down the hill. Gravity also pulls the sheep down the hill after the jeep.

What is friction?

The jeep's tires rub against the road as it rolls. The rubbing is called **friction**. Friction is a force that slows things down as a result of the rubbing. Friction between the road and the jeep's tires slows the jeep. A rough road causes more friction than a smooth road.

Name: _____

Sheep Leap

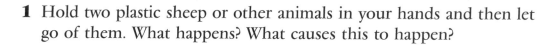

1 Hold two plastic sheep or other animals in your hands and then let go of them. What happens? What causes this to happen?

_____

2 Use any of the following supplies to invent something that will slow the fall of one of your animals. When testing your invention, drop both animals from the same height at the same time to see which one falls more slowly.

String   Tape

Piece of paper   Scissors

Plastic bag   Paper bag

3 Did your invention work? What is your evidence?

_____

_____

_____

4 Draw and label a picture of your invention falling through the air in the box below.

Sheep Leap

Air resistance

Gravity

Name: _____

Motion Quiz

1 Look at the picture above. What two forces are causing the wagon to move?_____ and _____

2 Look at the picture above. What force is causing the ball to roll down the ramp?

_____

Motion Quiz cont.

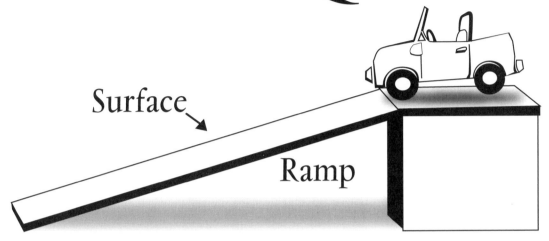

Surface

Ramp

Ramp Surface	Trial 1 Distance	Trial 2 Distance	Trial 3 Distance	Average Distance
Smooth Metal	85 cm	125 cm	90 cm	100 cm
Smooth Wood	90 cm	70 cm	65 cm	75 cm
Rough Sandpaper	18 cm	24 cm	18 cm	20 cm

Jamie is testing to see how the surface will affect the distance a toy car travels. He is using a small car and a long ramp that is 10 centimeters high. Jamie puts different surfaces on the ramp, and then lets the car roll down the ramp. He measures how far the car travels from the bottom of the ramp.

3 On which surface does the car roll the longest distance?

_____

4 On which surface does the car roll the shortest distance?

_____

Name: _____

Motion Quiz cont.

5 What do you think causes the car to roll the shortest distance on that surface?

_____

6 If a doll is sitting on the hood of Jamie's car, and the car hits a brick at the bottom of the ramp, how will the doll's motion be affected? What causes that to happen?

_____

_____

_____

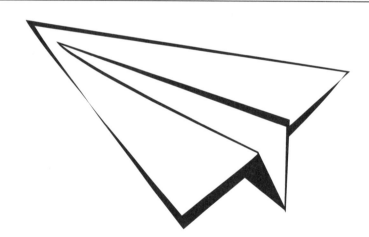

7 Marla throws a paper airplane. The airplane flies for several meters, then slows down and begins to fall to the ground. What two forces cause the airplane to slow down and fall to the ground?

a Friction from Marla's hand makes it slow down, and a magnetic force pulls it to Earth.

b Air resistance slows it down, and gravity pulls it to Earth.

c Gravity makes it slow down, and the pull of the Moon makes it fall to Earth.

NATIONAL SCIENCE TEACHERS ASSOCIATION

Sounds of Science

Description

Learners explore how sound is produced by vibrations. They make a straw instrument and investigate how to vary its pitch. Learners also design and build an instrument that produces a high pitch and a low pitch and explain how it works.

Suggested Grade Levels: 3–4

Lesson Objectives Connecting to the Standards

Content Standard B:
Physical Science

K–4: Understand that sound is produced by vibrating objects. The pitch of the sound can be varied by changing the rate of vibration.

Content Standard E:
Science and Technology

K–4: Use oral, written, and pictorial communication of the design process and product.

Featured Picture Books

Title	*Sound (Energy Works! Series)*
Author	**Jenny Karpelenia**
Publisher	**Perfection Learning**
Year	**2004**
Genre	**Non-narrative Information**
Summary	**Explains that vibrations create sound, how high and low pitches are made, how the ear works, and how musical instruments make sound**

Title	*The Remarkable Farkle McBride*
Author	**John Lithgow**
Illustrator	**C. F. Payne**
Publisher	**Simon & Schuster**
Year	**2000**
Genre	**Story**
Summary	**The musical prodigy Farkle McBride tries a number of instruments before discovering that conducting the orchestra makes him happy.**

Time Needed

This lesson will take several class periods. Suggested scheduling is as follows:

Day 1: **Engage** with straw instrument demonstration, **Explore** with playing straw instruments, and **Explain** with read aloud from *Sound*

Day 2: **Explore** with making high and low sounds, and **Explain** with read aloud from *Sound*

Day 3: **Elaborate** with Making Music and *The Remarkable Farkle McBride*

Day 4: **Evaluate** with Make an Instrument (project due after one week)

Materials

- Straws (nonflexible, plastic, several per student)
- Wooden rulers (1 per team)
- Scissors
- Making Music Answer Key
- Optional: Recordings of various instruments

Student Pages

- Making Music
- Make an Instrument

engage

Straw Instrument Demonstration

In advance, make a straw instrument by cutting one end of a straw into a triangular shape. Insert the cut end into your mouth forming a soft seal in your mouth so that no air leaks out. Blow

into the straw to make the flaps vibrate like reeds, and you will hear a buzzing sound. You may need to chew the flaps to flatten them out a little bit. Then play the straw instrument for your students.

"FLAPS" OF STRAW INSTRUMENT

explore

Playing Straw Instruments

Give students one straw each and have them try to make it sound the same as your straw instrument. Let students try for a few minutes. Have students consider the following questions as they experiment with their straws.

? What is sound?

? What causes sound?

If you have students who are unsuccessful in producing sound after many attempts at playing the straw instrument, you may want to provide them with an instrument that is easier to play, such as a slide whistle or recorder.

explain

Read Aloud

Using Features of Nonfiction

Tell students that you have a nonfiction book, *Sound*, that might be able to help them answer their questions about sound. Model how to use the index of a nonfiction book by looking up the answer to the question, "What is sound?" Flip to the index and demonstrate how to look up a word; point out "sound, definition of, 8"; and turn to that page. Tell

PLAYING STRAW INSTRUMENTS

students that many nonfiction books include an index that can save the reader a lot of time when looking for a specific piece of information. The definition of sound on page 8 is, "Sound is a form of energy caused by vibrations." Write this definition on the board.

 ### Determining Importance

Continue reading pages 8 and 9 ("Sound Energy") in *Sound* and have students listen for any clues that might help them get their straws to make a sound.

? What causes sound? (vibrations)

? What does *vibration* mean? (Vibration is a very fast back and forth motion.)

? How do you think you can get the straw to vibrate? (answers will vary)

Have students try different ways to get their straws to vibrate. Then show them how you cut a triangular shape into the end of the straw that goes in your mouth. Students can now cut the ends of their straws into triangular shapes and try to produce a buzzing sound. They can try chewing on the triangular flaps a little bit if they can't produce a sound. Tell them that when they blow just right, the flaps vibrate. The vibrating plastic causes the air inside the straw to vibrate, making a humming sound. Give students time to explore their straw instruments.

explore

Making High and Low Sounds

After everyone has successfully made a straw instrument, have students brainstorm ideas to make their straw instruments produce a high sound and a low sound. Provide extra straws, and give them time to try their ideas.

After a few minutes of exploration, tell students this next activity will give them a hint about how to make high and low sounds with their straws. Give each team of four students a wooden ruler. Have them hold the ruler flat

on the desk with about 25 cm of the ruler hanging over the edge of the desk. Have them flick the part of the ruler hanging over the edge so that it vibrates against the desk. Students should observe a low-pitched sound. Next, have them pull the ruler back so that only 20 cm of it is hanging over the edge and flick the end again. Students should observe a higher-pitched sound. They can repeat the activity, varying the length of the ruler each time.

? How does the length of the ruler hanging over the edge of the desk affect the pitch? (The longer the part hanging over the edge, the lower the pitch. The shorter the part hanging over the edge, the higher the pitch.)

explain

Read Aloud

Tell students that the scientific term *pitch* is used to describe how high or low a sound is.

 ### Determining Importance

Have students listen for clues on how to make their straw instruments produce high and low pitches as you read about wind instruments on pages 28 and 29 of the book *Sound*.

? What kind of instrument is the straw instrument? (wind instrument)

? How do people who play wind instruments change pitch? (opening and closing holes on the instrument)

? How does the size of a wind instrument affect its pitch? (the larger the instrument, the lower the pitch)

? The pitch of a note depends on the length of the column of vibrating air. How can you change the length of the column of vibrating air on your straw instrument? (cut it off or make holes in it to use as keys)

Using scissors, students can snip three small holes into their straw instruments to be used as keys. They should space the holes so that one of their fingers can cover each hole. They can test how opening and closing the holes can change the pitch. First, have them cover all of the holes with their fingers and blow into the straw. Then, have them uncover one key at a time and notice the change in pitch. Ask

? Why does the pitch sound lower when you cover one of the holes? (A longer column of air is created.)

? Why does the pitch sound higher when you uncover one of the holes? (A shorter column of air is created.)

elaborate

Making Music and *The Remarkable Farkle McBride*

 ### *Determining Importance*

Give students the Making Music student page. Read pages 28 through 32 in *Sound* about how wind, stringed, and percussion instruments create high and low pitches. After each section, have students summarize what you read by filling in the corresponding row on the student page.

 ### *Synthesizing*

Introduce the author and illustrator of *The Remarkable Farkle McBride* and then read the book aloud, having students identify each instrument that Farkle plays as a wind instrument, stringed instrument, or percussion instrument. Discuss how each instrument in the book makes sound and changes pitch.

If you like, ask your school's music teacher for recordings of the instruments played in the book so students can hear what each instrument sounds like. Compare the sizes of the instruments to their pitch. Smaller instruments, such as the flute, produce higher-pitched sounds. Larger instruments, such as the trombone, produce lower-pitched sounds.

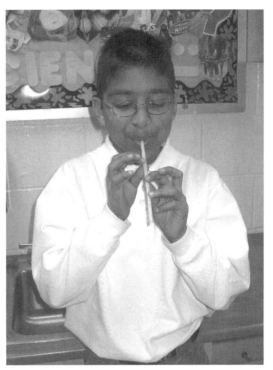

USING THE "KEYS" ON A STRAW INSTRUMENT

evaluate

Make an Instrument

Tell students they are going to be using what they have learned about sound and pitch to make their own instruments. Pass out the Make an Instrument student page, and discuss the requirements for the presentation. Students should include

● the name of the instrument

● the type of instrument (wind, percussion, or stringed)

● an explanation of how they made the instrument

● an explanation and demonstration of how the instrument makes sound

● an explanation and demonstration of how the instrument changes pitch

Tell students that they must get a check mark or stamp from you at the checkpoint before they can begin making their instruments. Make sure they are able to answer the following questions before you give them a check or stamp.

? How will your instrument make sound?

? How will your instrument change pitch?

You can either provide materials for students to make their instruments at school or assign the project as homework.

Use the following rubric to assess student instrument presentations:

Scoring Rubric for Instrument Presentations

4 Point Response	The student states the name of the instrument, identifies the materials used and clearly explains how the instrument was built, correctly identifies the type of instrument, demonstrates and accurately describes how the sound is produced, and demonstrates and accurately describes how the pitch is changed.
3 Point Response	The student demonstrates a flaw in understanding of the concepts and is missing one required element OR demonstrates understanding but is missing two required elements of the presentation.
2 Point Response	The student demonstrates a flaw in understanding of the concepts AND is missing two required elements of the presentation.
1 Point Response	The student demonstrates a flaw in understanding of the concepts AND is missing three or more required elements of the presentation.
0 Point Response	The student does not make an instrument.

Inquiry Place

Have students brainstorm "investigatable" questions such as

? Does sound travel through water?

? Through which solids does sound travel the best?

? What are the best materials for sending sound through a toy "telephone"?

? What materials muffle sound the best?

Then have students select a question to investigate as a class, or groups of students can vote on the question they want to investigate as teams. After they make their predictions, they can design an experiment to test their predictions. Students can present their findings at a poster session.

More Books to Read

Beech, Linda. 1995. *The magic school bus in the haunted museum: A book about sound.* New York, NY: Scholastic.
Summary: On the way to a concert at the Sound Museum, the Magic School Bus breaks down in front of a haunted house. Ms. Frizzle's class hears some weird sounds coming from the spooky house. When they go inside to investigate, they learn about sound and how it is produced.

Hayes, A. 1995. *Meet the orchestra.* New York, NY: Voyager Books.
Summary: This lyrical introduction to the orchestra begins with animal musicians slowly gathering for the evening performance. Each instrument of the orchestra is explained, with clear definitions as well as information on how each one sounds.

Hunter, R. 2001. *Discovering science: Sound.* Austin, TX: Steck-Vaughn.
Summary: Provides information and activities exploring sound. Includes information on sound waves, hearing, volume, musical instruments, and uses of sound.

Moss, L. 1995. *Zin! zin! zin! A violin.* New York, NY: Simon and Schuster Books for Young Readers.
Summary: Written in elegant and rhythmic verse and illustrated with playful and flowing artwork, this unique counting book is the perfect introduction to musical groups.

Pfeffer, W. 1999. *Sounds all around.* New York, NY: Harpercollins.
Summary: Provides simple explanations of sound and hearing for younger readers. Activities listed at the end of the book would be fun for home or school.

Reference

Karpelenia, J. *Sound: Energy works! series.* 2004. Logan, IA: Perfection Learning. Straw instrument adapted from an activity on page 29. Ruler activity adapted from page 17.

Name: _____

Making Music

Fill out the chart below as your teacher reads about each type of instrument.

Type of Instrument	Picture	How the Sound Is Made	How the Pitch Is Changed
Wind	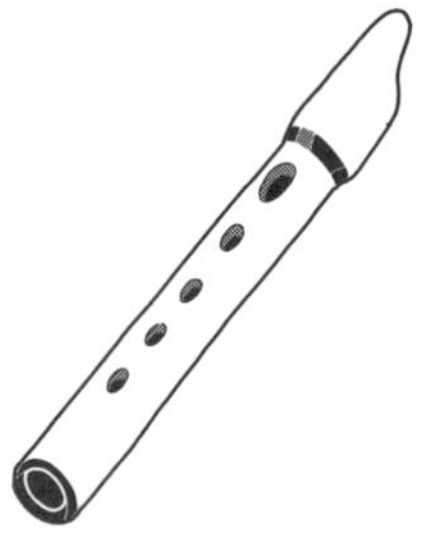		
Stringed			
Percussion			

NATIONAL SCIENCE TEACHERS ASSOCIATION

Making Music
Answer Key

Type of Instrument	Picture	How the Sound Is Made	How the Pitch Is Changed
Wind		Blowing into it makes the wood, plastic, or brass vibrate, causing the air inside the instrument to vibrate.	Pushing keys changes the length of the column of vibrating air, which changes the pitch.
Stringed		Plucking or strumming strings causes them to vibrate. The air inside the instrument vibrates, too.	Placing fingers on the strings creates different string lengths.
Percussion		Hitting or shaking materials causes them to vibrate.	Hitting different sized instruments or different sized parts of the instrument creates different pitches.

Name: _____

Make an Instrument

Design and make an instrument that produces a high and a low pitch. You will be presenting your instrument to the class and playing a high and a low pitch with it.

Include the following in your presentation:

1 The name of your instrument

2 The type of instrument (wind, percussion, or stringed)

3 An explanation of how you made the instrument and what materials you used

4 An explanation and demonstration of how your instrument makes sound

5 An explanation and demonstration of how your instrument changes pitch

Think about how your instrument will make sound and change pitch. Design your instrument in the space below, and label the materials you will use to build it.

Sketch

Checkpoint ☐

NATIONAL SCIENCE TEACHERS ASSOCIATION

Chemical Change Café

Description

Learners explore the differences between chemical and physical changes by observing a variety of changes in matter. Learners observe the chemical change of cooking pancakes and identify new menu items for the Chemical Change Café.

Suggested Grade Levels: 3–6

Lesson Objectives Connecting to the Standards

Content Standard A:
Scientific Inquiry

K–4: Use data (observations) to construct a reasonable explanation.

5–8: Develop descriptions, explanations, and predictions using evidence.

Content Standard B:
Physical Science

K–4: Understand that objects have many observable properties, including size, weight, shape, color, temperature, and the ability to react with other substances.

5–8: Understand that substances react chemically in characteristic ways with other substances to form new substances with different characteristic properties.

Featured Picture Book

Title	***Pancakes, Pancakes!***
Author	**Eric Carle**
Illustrator	**Eric Carle**
Publisher	**Aladdin Picture Books**
Year	**1990**
Genre	**Story**
Summary	**By cutting and grinding the wheat for flour, Jack starts from scratch to help make his breakfast pancake.**

Pancakes, Pancakes!

Time Needed

This lesson will take several class periods. Suggested scheduling is as follows:

Day 1: **Engage** with changing paper, and **Explore** with Observing Changes in Matter lab stations

Day 2: **Explain** with Chemical Changes article, Frayer Model, and *Pancakes, Pancakes!* read aloud

Day 3: **Elaborate** with Chemical Change Café

Day 4: **Evaluate** with New Menu Items

Materials

- Piece of paper
- Glass jar
- Matches (for teacher use only)

For Observing Changes in Matter Activity

SAFETY

Station 1: Before this activity, check with your school nurse to see if any students have latex allergies. Students who are allergic to latex should not do the activity at Station 1.

Station 3: Before this activity, demonstrate for students the safe way to smell any chemical by "wafting."

- A red plastic cup and a green plastic cup with the openings taped together (1 per team)
- Station 1
  + Thumbtacks
  + Balloons
- Station 2
  + Cup of vinegar
  + Cup of baking soda
  + Wax paper
  + Spoon
  + Pipette
- Station 3
  + Cup of fresh milk covered with foil (labeled "fresh")
  + Cup of sour milk covered with foil (labeled "sour")
- Station 4
  + Lump of clay

- Station 5
  + New steel wool
  + Rusted steel wool in water (leave in water for at least 24 hours)
- Station 6
  + Zipper baggies (1 per team)
  + Spoon
  + Graduated cylinder
  + Cup of cream of tartar mixed with an equal amount of baking soda
  + Room temperature water
  + Thermometers (3, labeled "1" "2," and "3.")
- Station 7
  + Graduated cylinder
  + Clear plastic cups
  + Cup of whole milk
  + Cup of vinegar

For Chemical Change Café:

SAFETY

Before using this activity, check your school's policy on eating as part of a science lab activity. Some schools forbid it, and commercial labs can be fined for even the appearance of eating. Make sure your students know they should never taste anything in a lab activity. *Exploring Safely: A Guide for Elementary Teachers* recommends "Nothing should be tasted or eaten as part of science lab work" (Kwan and Texley 2002). Also check with your school nurse to see if any students have dietary restrictions.

- Box of "just add water" pancake mix (1 per group)
- Metric measuring cups for food preparation (1 per group)
- Water
- Wire whisks or spoons (1 per group)
- Mixing bowls (1 per group)
- Hot plate and pancake pan or electric griddle
- Spatula
- Paper plates
- Forks
- Bottles of pancake syrup

Student Pages

- Observing Changes in Matter
- Chemical Changes Article
- Chemical Change Frayer Model
- Chemical Change Café Menu
- New Menu Items

engage

Changing Paper

Show students a piece of blank paper. Ask

? What can I do to change this piece of paper?

Students may suggest folding it, rolling it up, cutting it, tearing it, writing on it, and crumpling it up into a ball. Try all of the students' suggestions, and, after each one, ask

? Is it still paper? (Yes.)

Then ask

? What if I want to change it into something other than paper? What could I do?

Roll up the piece of paper, and put it in a large glass jar. Strike a match, light the paper on fire, and let the students watch it burn. After the paper has finished burning, ask students

? Is it still paper? How do you know? (No. It is a different substance with new properties.)

explore

Observing Changes in Matter Lab Stations

In advance, set up seven separate locations in the room as lab stations. Number each station, and supply all of the necessary materials for the Observing Changes in Matter activity to be done at that station. Put students in groups of two to four, and give each student the Observing Changes in Matter student page. Tell students they will have a red-green cup to signal the teacher. While they are working, they should keep the green side on top. If they need help, or if they are finished and ready to move to the next station, they should put the red side on top.

Each team will begin at a different station and will visit all seven stations during the lab. Students will complete the activities at each station and record their observations on the student page. Each member of the

"WAFTING" FRESH AND SOUR MILK IN THE LAB

SAFETY Demonstrate for students the safe way to smell any chemical by "wafting" (Station 3). Remind students that they should never taste anything during a laboratory activity.

group is responsible for writing responses. When all teams are finished (all red cups are up), students may rotate to the next numbered station.

explain

Chemical Changes Article

 Pairs Read

Pass out the Chemical Changes article. Have students take turns reading aloud from the article. While one person reads a paragraph, the other listens and then summarizes. Students can use the information they learn from this article on the Chemical Change Frayer Model student page.

 Frayer Model

The Frayer Model is a tool to help students develop their vocabulary by studying concepts in a relational manner. Students write a particular word in the middle of a box and proceed to list characteristics, examples, nonexamples, and a definition in other quadrants of the box. They can proceed by using the examples and characteristics to help them

formulate a definition or, conversely, by using the definition to determine examples and nonexamples.

In this case, have students use the preceding article to formulate a definition for "chemical change" in their own words in the top left box of the Chemical Change Frayer Model. Then have students write some characteristics of chemical changes in the top right box. Have students work in pairs to come up with examples and nonexamples from their own lives. As you observe students working, encourage them to use their previous experiences as a basis for their chemical change examples. Students can then present and explain their models to other groups. As they present to each other, informally assess their understanding of the concept and clarify as necessary.

After the reading and the Frayer Model activity, point out that, with a chemical change, the change happens without any external assistance. For example, water can get hot in a physical change if there is an external source of heat. Materials can change color in a physical change if there is an external source of color—paint, for example.

Refer back to the paper you used in the Engage phase. Ask students

Physical and Chemical Changes in *Pancakes, Pancakes!*

Physical Changes	Chemical Changes
Cutting wheat	Burning wood for a fire
Separating grain from chaff	Cooking the pancake
Grinding wheat	
Squirting milk in the pail	
Churning butter	
Melting butter	
Chopping wood	
Breaking an egg	
Stirring the batter	

? Which of the changes that I made to the paper demonstrated a chemical change? Why? (Burning the paper was a chemical change because when the change was complete, there was a new substance formed: black ash.)

With this new information students have learned from the article, have them go back to the Observing Changes in Matter student page they completed in the Explore phase and identify each change as physical or chemical by circling "P" or "C."

Answers:

The physical changes in the "Observing Changes in Matter" exploration were

Station 1: Blowing up and popping a balloon

Station 4: Forming clay into different shapes

The chemical changes in the "Observing Changes in Matter" exploration were

Station 2: Vinegar and baking soda reaction (gas bubbles produced)

Station 3: Souring milk (change in odor)

Station 5: Rusted steel wool (change in color and odor)

Station 6: Cream of tartar, baking soda, and water reaction (change in temperature)

Station 7: Vinegar and milk reaction (precipitate formed)

explain

Pancakes, Pancakes!

Introduce the author and illustrator of *Pancakes, Pancakes!* Ask students if they have read any other books by Eric Carle (information about him can be found at *www.eric-carle.com*). Read *Pancakes, Pancakes!* aloud to students the first time just to enjoy the story.

 Rereading

Tell students you are going to read the story again, but this time, students should listen for examples of chemical and physical changes that occur in the story. Have students signal (raise their hands) when they hear examples. Have them classify the change as chemical or physical and provide justification.

elaborate

Chemical Change Café

The day after reading *Pancakes, Pancakes!*, convert your classroom into the Chemical Change Café. Set up a hot plate and pancake pan or an electric griddle for your use only. Locate the cooking area away from any high traffic areas in your classroom. Provide a box of "just add water" pancake mix, metric measuring cup, spoon or whisk, and container of water for each table of students.

Greet students at the door, divide them into groups, and distribute the menus. All supplies should be on the desks, and students will follow directions on the menu to make the batter. Invite groups to bring their prepared batter to the cooking area, and they will observe changes as you cook the pancakes according to the package direction. On the menus, students will draw a picture of the batter before and after it is cooked and explain why cooking pancakes is a chemical change.

Student Procedure for Chemical Change Café (Making Pancakes):

- Please mix 250 ml of pancake mix with 175 ml of water and stir until smooth.

- Please raise your hand to notify the chef that you are ready to have your batter cooked.

- Watch as the batter is changed into a light and fluffy pancake.

- Add a little syrup.

- Enjoy!

PICTURES FROM THE CHEMICAL CHANGE CAFÉ

Table # 5

evaluate

New Menu Items

As a final evaluation of student understanding of chemical versus physical changes, have students complete the New Menu Items student page.

The following items can be added to the Chemical Change Café menu because they are turned into new substances with new properties:

1 Toast

3 Scrambled eggs

6 Buttermilk biscuits

8 Cottage cheese

10 Toasted marshmallows

The other items cannot be served at the Chemical Change Café because they undergo only physical changes in their preparation.

Inquiry Place

Have students brainstorm "investigatable" questions such as

? How does temperature affect the rate of a chemical change?

? Will steel wool rust faster in water, salt water, or vinegar?

? How can you make a sugar cube undergo a physical change? a chemical change?

Have students select a question to investigate as a class, or groups of students can vote on the question they want to investigate as teams. After they make their predictions, they can design an experiment to test their predictions. Students can present their findings at a poster session.

More Books to Read

Cole, J. 1995. *The magic school bus gets baked in a cake: A book about kitchen chemistry.* New York, NY: Scholastic Books.
Summary: Miss Frizzle's class takes the magic school bus to the local bakery to find out about the chemistry of baking.

References

American Chemical Society. 2001. *Safety in the elementary (K-6) science classroom: Second edition.* Washington, DC: ACS.

Kwan, T., and J. Texley. 2002. *Exploring safely: A guide for elementary teachers.* Arlington, VA: NSTA Press

Name: _____

Observing Changes in Matter

Follow the directions below and record your observations at each station. Use all of your senses, except taste, to make your observations. You will decide whether each change is *physical* (P) or *chemical* (C) later in this lesson.

Station 1   P or C

• Observe a balloon. Record your observations.

_____

_____

• Blow up the balloon.
• Pop it with the thumbtack.
• Observe the balloon again. How has it changed?

_____

_____

Station 2   P or C

• Observe the cup of baking soda and the cup of vinegar, and record your observations.

_____

_____

• Put a small spoonful of baking soda on the wax paper.
• Put 5 drops of vinegar on the baking soda.
• Observe what is on the wax paper. How has it changed?

_____

_____

NATIONAL SCIENCE TEACHERS ASSOCIATION

Observing Changes in Matter cont.

Station 3:   P or C

- Observe the fresh milk.
- Smell the fresh milk by "wafting."

_____

_____

- Take the foil off the sour milk and observe.
- Smell the sour milk by "wafting."
- How has the milk changed?

_____

_____

Station 4:   P or C

- Observe the clay, and record your observations.

_____

_____

- Form the clay into a different shape.
- Observe the clay again. How has it changed?

_____

_____

Name: _____

Observing
Changes in Matter cont

Station 5:   P or C

- Observe the new steel wool, and record your observations.

_____

_____

- Observe the steel wool that has been in water.
- Describe the differences between the new steel wool and the wet steel wool.

_____

_____

Station 6:   P or C

- Put a spoonful of cream of tartar and baking soda in a zipper baggie.
- Observe the cream of tartar and baking soda.
- Record its temperature with thermometer 1.

_____

- Observe the water in the cup.
- Record its temperature with thermometer 2.

_____

- Add 10 ml of water to the cream of tartar and baking soda in the baggie.
- Feel the outside of the baggie.
- Record the temperature of the "stuff" inside the baggie with thermometer 3.

_____

- How have the water and cream of tartar and baking soda changed?

_____

_____

NATIONAL SCIENCE TEACHERS ASSOCIATION

Name: _____

Observing
Changes in Matter cont.

Station 7:   P or C

- Observe the milk, and record your observations.

  _____

  _____

- Observe the vinegar, and record your observations.

  _____

  _____

- Pour 20 ml of milk into a clear plastic cup.
- Pour 10 ml of vinegar into the milk, stir once, and let it sit for 1 minute.
- Observe the "stuff" in the cup. How have the milk and vinegar changed?

  _____

  _____

Name: _____

Chemical Changes

Changing Matter

Every day, we see changes in the matter around us. Sometimes there is a change in the appearance of matter and other times the change results in an entirely new substance.

Chemical Changes

A **chemical change** is a change in matter that produces new substances. For example, when a piece of wood is burned, it is no longer wood. It is changed into an entirely new substance with new properties. The wood changes from a hard solid into various gases, smoke, and a pile of ash. When cake batter is cooked, the ingredients form a new substance with a different smell, color, texture, and taste.

Physical Changes

The opposite of a chemical change is a **physical change**. A physical change is a change in matter that might change the form or appearance of a substance, but does not produce any new substances. For example, when you tear a piece of paper, its appearance changes, but it is not a new

substance. It is still paper. When you put water in the freezer, it turns to ice, but it is still water, just in a different form.

Evidence of a Chemical Change

You can use your senses to detect chemical changes. Here are some characteristics that can help you determine if a chemical change has occurred:

- Gas produced (bubbles)
- Change in temperature
- Change in odor
- Change in color
- A solid formed when combining two liquids (precipitate)
- Light emitted

Any one of these characteristics is evidence that a chemical change has occurred. But sometimes a physical change can have similar results. The key characteristic of a chemical change is the presence of a new substance or substances that are entirely different than the starting substances.

Chemical Changes

Frayer Model

Definition	Characteristics

Chemical Change

Examples	Nonexamples

Chemical Change Café

Menu

Is cooking pancakes a physical or chemical change? What is your evidence?

_____
_____
_____
_____
_____
_____
_____
_____
_____
_____
_____
_____
_____
_____

Draw the pancakes before cooking.

Draw the pancakes after cooking.

Today's Special

Pancakes

- Please mix **250 ml of pancake mix** with **175 ml of water** and stir until smooth.
- Please raise your hand to notify the chef that you are ready to have your batter cooked.
- Watch as the batter is changed into a light and fluffy pancake.
- Add a little syrup.
- Enjoy!

Name: _____

New
Menu Items

The Chemical Change Café would like to add some new items to the menu. Only food that has been prepared through a chemical change can be featured on our menu. Put a check mark next to each item that can be added to the menu at the Chemical Change Café.

❏ **1** Toast

We begin with a plain white piece of bread and heat it until it turns brown and produces a delightful smell.

Is making toast a chemical change? Why or why not?

_____

_____

❏ **2** Orange Juice

Lovely fresh oranges are hand squeezed until the delicious juice drips into your glass.

Is making orange juice a chemical change? Why or why not?

_____

_____

❏ **3** Scrambled Eggs

Grade A eggs are cooked until they are light, fluffy, and yellow.

Is making scrambled eggs a chemical change? Why or why not?

_____

_____

New Menu Items

cont.

❏ **4** Strawberry Smoothie

We begin with strawberries, ice, sugar, and milk. We blend them together to make a thick, delicious drink.

Is making a strawberry smoothie a chemical change? Why or why not?

_____

_____

❏ **5** Trail Mix

We mix together the finest fresh nuts and dried fruits to create this tasty blend.

Is making trail mix a chemical change? Why or why not?

_____

_____

❏ **6** Buttermilk Biscuits

Creamy buttermilk, baking powder, flour, butter, and salt are mixed together and baked until gas bubbles cause them to rise. The batter turns into flaky, golden brown biscuits. The aroma of the baked biscuits is delightful.

Is making buttermilk biscuits a chemical change? Why or why not?

_____

_____

Name: _____

New Menu Items

cont.

❏ **7** Orange-sicles

We freeze our finest fresh orange juice until the orange liquid becomes a tasty, frozen solid.

Is making orange-sicles a chemical change? Why or why not?

_____

_____

❏ **8** Cottage Cheese

Fresh milk is combined with special enzymes until the milk becomes thick and clumpy with a completely new taste and smell.

Is making cottage cheese a chemical change? Why or why not?

_____

_____

❏ **9** Fruit Salad

Fresh pineapple, strawberries, kiwi, and blueberries are sliced and mixed together to make this sweet treat.

Is making fruit salad a chemical change? Why or why not?

_____

_____

❏ **10** Toasted Marshmallows

Fluffy white marshmallows are toasted over an open flame until they begin to turn golden brown and smell heavenly.

Is making toasted marshmallows a chemical change? Why or why not?

_____

_____

The Changing Moon

Description

Learners make observations of the Moon each night for a month, model how the Moon changes shape, and illustrate a picture book with scientifically accurate moon phases.

Suggested Grade Levels: 3–6

Lesson Objectives Connecting to the Standards

Content Standard A:
Science as Inquiry

K–4: Ask a question about objects, organisms, and events in the environment.

K–4: Use data to construct a reasonable explanation.

5–8: Develop descriptions, explanations, predictions, and models using evidence.

Content Standard D:
Earth and Space Sciences

K–4: Understand that objects in the sky have patterns of movement. The moon moves across the sky, and its observable shape changes on a daily basis in a cycle that lasts about a month.

5–8: Understand that most objects in the solar system are in regular and predictable motion. Those motions explain such phenomena as the day, the year, phases of the moon, and eclipses.

Featured Picture Books

Title	***Rise the Moon***
Author	**Eileen Spinelli**
Illustrator	**Raul Colon**
Publisher	**Dial Books for Young Readers**
Year	**2003**
Genre	**Story**
Summary	**A variety of people and animals are touched by an enchanting moonlit night.**

Title	***The Moon Book***
Author	**Gail Gibbons**
Illustrator	**Gail Gibbons**
Publisher	**Holiday House**
Year	**1998**
Genre	**Nonnarrative Information**

Summary	**Describes the movement, phases, and exploration of the Moon**

Title	***Papa, Please Get the Moon for Me***
Author	**Eric Carle**
Illustrator	**Eric Carle**
Publisher	**Simon and Schuster Books for Young Readers**
Year	**1986**
Genre	**Story**
Summary	**Monica's father gets the moon for her after it is small enough to carry, but it continues to change in size.**

Time Needed

This lesson will take several class periods. Suggested scheduling:

One month before Day 1: **Engage** with read aloud of *Rise the Moon* and **Explore** with Moon Journals

Day 1: **Explain** with Moon Survey, moon modeling, and read aloud of *The Moon Book*

Day 3: **Elaborate** and **Evaluate** with *Papa, Please Get the Moon for Me* retelling

Day 4: **Evaluate** with Moon Phases Quiz

Materials

- White foam balls (1 per student) Opaque foam balls work best, but they can be difficult to find. Plain foam balls can be rolled in white latex paint to make them more opaque.
- Pencils (1 per student)
- Lamp (lampshade removed so light is given off in all directions)
- Optional: CD of night animal sounds

Student Pages

- Moon Journal
- Moon Survey
- The Moon Book Extended Anticipation Guide
- Phases of the Moon
- *Papa, Please Get the Moon for Me* Retelling Book
- Moon Phases Quiz

engage

Read Aloud

Introduce the author and illustrator of *Rise the Moon* to the students. If you like, set the mood for this poetic book by turning down the lights and playing a CD of night animal sounds. Then read the book aloud.

Questioning

After one time reading through the book, turn back to some pages that interest you and model the questioning skills of a good reader. You can demonstrate how to interact with the text by placing sticky notes on the corresponding pages with these questions (or just large question marks) on them:

? Does the Moon really pull the ocean?

? Where does the Moon's light come from?

? Is the Moon only visible at night?

? I wonder what makes the Moon look different sometimes?

explore

Moon Journal

Invite students to tell you what they are wondering about the Moon. Ask students how they might find the answers to some of their questions. Discuss that scientists find answers by means such as making careful observations of things, doing experiments over and over, and communicating with other scientists.

Tell students that they are going to find out more about the Moon by observing it every evening for a month. Give each student a copy of the Moon Journal. Ask them to look at the Moon each night and draw what it looks like (if it can be seen). You can also keep a daily bulletin board of the moon phases for that month. Check *www.stardate.org* for monthly moon calendars. *moon calculator*

Students often have the misconception that the Moon gets larger and smaller. Empty circles on the Moon Journal student page are provided so that students can darken the areas of the Moon that are not lighted. This method of recording moon phases takes into account that the entire Moon is present, even if some of its surface cannot be seen.

Discuss students' observations throughout the month using some of the questions that follow.

? Was the Moon the same shape each time you saw it?

? Was the Moon the same color each time you saw it?

? Did you see the Moon every time you looked for it?

? Was the Moon in the same place in the sky each time you saw it?

? On a cloudy night, how can you tell if the Moon is still there?

? What did the Moon look like on the first night of your journal? What did the Moon look like on the last night of your journal?

? When you look at your journal, do you see any patterns?

explain

Moon Survey, Moon Modeling, and Read Aloud

The day before this activity, assign the Moon Survey student page to students as homework. In this assignment, they record the responses of three people to the question: What causes the Moon to look different each night?

Have students take out their completed Moon Survey student page and discuss the results of their surveys before they begin the next activity. Ask the following questions as you discuss the surveys:

MODELING THE MOON PHASES

? How did people feel about answering the question on the survey?

? What are some of the answers you received?

? Are there any answers that you think are wrong? Why?

? What do you think is the correct answer to the question on the survey?

Moon Modeling

Now that students have heard a lot of different ideas people have about why the Moon looks different from night to night, tell them that they can find the answer to the question using a model.

Darken the room—the darker, the better. Give each student a pencil and a foam ball. Explain that the foam ball, stuck on the end of a pencil, is a model of the Moon; the lamp is a model of the Sun; and their heads represent Earth. Before the guided activity below, give students time to explore the model and test different ideas about what causes moon phases.

Next, guide students through the following activity to model how the Moon changes shape.

1 With their faces toward the lamp, students hold the balls slightly above their heads so that they have to look up a little to see them. In this position, students cannot see the lighted side of the ball. This is called a *new moon.*

2   Tell students to turn their bodies slightly to the left while still looking at the ball and holding it a little above their heads. They should turn until they see a *crescent moon.*

Ask

?   Where does the Moon's light come from? (The light is coming from the Sun and is reflected off the Moon.)

?   Some people think that the moon phases are caused by the Earth's shadow. How does this model disprove that theory? (The shadow of my head, which represents the Earth, is nowhere near the Moon in this position. It is behind me.)

?   Instruct the students to keep turning to the left and soon they will see more of the lighted half of the ball. This is called a *quarter moon.*

?   Have them turn a little more and almost all of the ball will be lit. This is called a *gibbous moon.*

?   Students can keep turning until they see all the lighted half of the ball. This is a *full moon.*

?   As students continue to turn in the same direction, they will see less and less of the lighted part of the ball. First they will see a gibbous moon, then a quarter moon, then a thin crescent moon, and finally they will be back to the new moon.

?   Tell students that the shapes they have observed in this activity are called the *moon phases.*

?   Have students go through the rotation several times. Ask them to chorally respond with the name of each phase as it is modeled.

?   Point out that no matter where they are in the Moon's orbit, half of the Moon is always lighted by the Sun. Sometimes we see the whole lighted half from Earth (full moon), sometimes we see almost all of the lighted half (gibbous moon), sometimes we see half of the lighted half (quarter moon), sometimes we see only see a tiny sliver of the lighted side (crescent moon), and sometimes we can't see any of the lighted half (new moon). The portion we see from Earth depends on where the Moon is in its orbit around the Earth.

You may want to challenge students to use the foam ball and lamp model to develop an explanation for how lunar and solar eclipses occur.

After the activity, ask students these questions.

?   How does the pattern of the phases you observed in your Moon Journal compare to the pattern of the phases you observed in the model? (The patterns observed in one month with the journal are the same as the pattern observed in one orbit of the Moon in the model.)

Tell students that scientists often use their observations in combination with models to develop explanations of scientific events. Ask

?   What explanations can we develop from our month of moon observations and the moon modeling activity we just did? (The moon phases occur in a regular pattern. The orbit of the Moon around the Earth causes the phases.)

Next, have students go back to their Moon Survey to see if anyone they surveyed had the correct explanation for the cause of moon phases. Encourage them to use the moon phases model to show the people they surveyed how the Moon appears to change shape.

 Determining Importance

Have students complete the "Agree/Disagree" section of the Moon Book Extended Anticipation Guide. Then take students to a reading

corner (or have them put their papers away). Tell them that you will be reading a nonfiction book, *The Moon Book,* to find the answers to the questions on the anticipation guide. Have students signal (raise their hands) when they hear an answer to one of the questions from the anticipation guide. After you read, they can fill in the "Explanations from the Reading" section of the anticipation guide and write their explanations of whether their choices were right or wrong. When students finish, go over each question and ask students to share their answers.

Give students the Phases of the Moon student page. Have them use the information they learned from the moon phases model and *The Moon Book* to label and order the moon pictures. The correct sequence for moon phases is as follows: new moon, crescent moon, quarter moon, gibbous moon, full moon.

Elaborate & Evaluate

Papa, Please Get the Moon for Me Retelling

Determining Importance

Introduce the author and illustrator of *Papa, Please Get the Moon for Me,* and read it once just for fun. Then tell the students that you are going to read it again for a different purpose. Explain that this book was not written as a science book, but you would like them to listen for anything that might be scientifically incorrect. Ask them to think back to the things they have learned about the Moon, and if they see a picture or hear something in the book

they think is incorrect, they should raise their hands and explain their reasoning. Responses might include:

- A ladder could not reach the Moon.
- The Moon cannot talk.
- The moon phases don't change the way they are pictured in the book.
- The Moon is too big to carry.

Tell students that Eric Carle didn't write *Papa, Please Get the Moon for Me* as a science book, so it's all right if isn't scientifically accurate. Tell students they are going to use his ideas as a basis for a book that *is* scientifically accurate. Pass out copies of the *Papa, Please Get the Moon for Me* Retelling Book and have students illustrate the story and label the correct moon phases in their drawings. When students are finished illustrating and labeling, they should cut out each page separately and staple the pages together in order.

Evaluate

Moon Phases Quiz

Give students the Moon Phases Quiz. The answers follow.

1. A. Sun

    B. Moon

    C. Earth

2. c. The Moon revolves around the Earth.

3. e. gibbous moon

4. a.

5. b. new moon, crescent moon, first quarter moon, gibbous moon, full moon

Inquiry Place

See "Teaching Science Through Inquiry," Chapter 3, for an example of how one teacher chose to use this Inquiry Place in her classroom.

Choose one of the following questions to investigate or have students brainstorm "investigatable" questions about the Moon:

? Does the speed of a meteorite affect the size of the crater it makes?

? Does the size of a meteorite affect the size of the crater it makes?

? Does the weight of a meteorite affect the size of the crater it makes?

? Does the shape of the meteorite affect the shape of the crater it makes?

You can choose one of these questions for a whole-class investigation, students can select a question to investigate as a class, or groups of students can vote on the question they want to investigate as teams. After they make their predictions, they can design an experiment to test their predictions. Students can present their findings at a poster session.

More Books to Read

Branley, F. M. 1987. *The Moon seems to change.* New York, NY: HarperTrophy,
Summary: Easy-to-read text and simple diagrams explain how the Moon seems to change, and includes how to model the changing moon phases using a pencil, an orange, and a flashlight.

Branley, F. M. 2000. *What the Moon is like.* New York, NY: HarperTrophy.
Summary: Photos and information gathered by the Apollo space missions are used to describe how the Moon's composition, terrain, and atmosphere differ from Earth's. Apollo landing sites are identified and operation of a future moon colony is depicted.

Pollock, P. 2001. *When the Moon is full: A lunar year.* New York, NY: Little, Brown, and Company.
Summary: This lunar guide describes the 12 moons according to Native American tradition in short verse and beautifully detailed hand-colored wood cuts. A question-and-answer section includes information about the Moon's surface, an explanation of a lunar eclipse, and the true meaning of a blue moon.

Simon, S. 2003. *The Moon.* New York, NY: Simon & Schuster.
Summary: From Apollo 11's first landing to the mystery of moonquakes and the genesis of craters, this introduction to our nearest neighbor in space describes the Moon and its relationship to Earth. Includes full-color photography and an informative text.

CHAPTER 17

Name: _____

Moon Journal

Dates of Observation _____

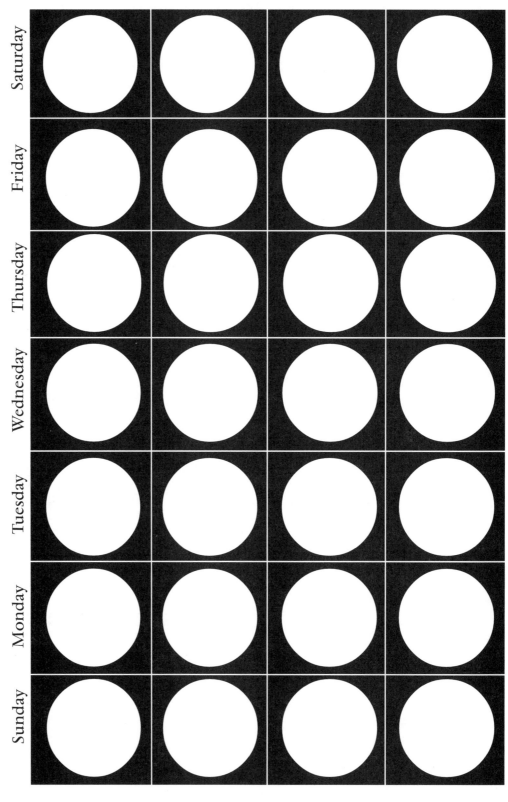

Moon  Survey

Ask three people the following question and record their answers on the lines below.

What causes the Moon to look different each night?

1st Person

_____
_____
_____
_____
_____

2nd Person

_____
_____
_____
_____
_____

3rd Person

_____
_____
_____
_____
_____

Name: _____

The Moon Book
Extended Anticipation Guide

	Agree	Disagree

1 The Moon produces light.　　　□　　　□

2 The Moon takes about one year to travel around Earth.　　　□　　　□

3 The same side of the Moon is always facing Earth.　　　□　　　□

4 The Moon's pull on the oceans is strong enough to cause tides.　　　□　　　□

Explanations from the reading:

1 _____
_____

2 _____
_____

3 _____
_____

4 _____
_____

CHAPTER
17

The Moon Book
Extended Anticipation Guide Answer Key

	Agree	Disagree
	(answers will vary)	

1 The Moon produces light. ☐ ☐

2 The Moon takes about one year to travel around Earth. ☐ ☐

3 The same side of the Moon is always facing Earth. ☐ ☐

4 The Moon's pull on the oceans is strong enough to cause tides. ☐ ☐

Explanations from the reading:

1 The Moon reflects light from the Sun.

2 The Moon takes about one month to travel around Earth.

3 The Moon rotates once in its revolution, which results in the same side always facing Earth.

4 The Moon's pull is strong enough to cause tides.

Name: _____

Phases of the Moon

Directions: Write the name of each moon phase on the line. Then cut out the cards and put the moon phases in order. Start with the new moon.

New Moon
Quarter Moon
Full Moon
Gibbous Moon
Crescent Moon

Moon Phase:

_____

Moon Phase:

_____

Moon Phase:

_____

Moon Phase:

_____

Moon Phase:

_____

NATIONAL SCIENCE TEACHERS ASSOCIATION

Name: _____

Papa, Please Get the Moon for Me Retelling Book

By Eric Carle

Retold by

_____

1

Before Monica went to bed she looked out of her window and saw the full moon. The moon looked so near. "I wish I could play with the moon," said Monica to her Papa. But no matter how much she stretched, she could not touch the moon.

2

"The moon is much too big and too far away to play with," said her Papa. "But you can play in the light reflected off the moon." So every night before she went to bed Monica jumped and danced in the moonlight.

3

But the moon seemed to get smaller and smaller each night, until finally it disappeared altogether.

Papa, Please Get the Moon for Me

Retelling
Book cont.

4

Then, one night, Monica saw a thin sliver of the moon reappear.

5

Each night the moon seemed to grow ...

6

and grow ...

7

... until it was full again.

Name: _____

Moon Phases Quiz

1 Look at the picture below. Label each object using the words Earth, Moon, or Sun. (Picture is not to scale.)

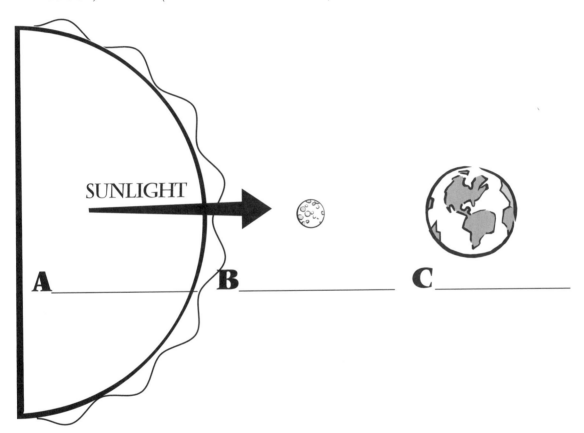

SUNLIGHT

A_____ B_____ C_____

2 The phases of the Moon occur because:

a Clouds cover part of the Moon.

b The Earth's shadow falls upon the Moon.

c The Moon revolves around the Earth.

Name: _____

Moon Phases Quiz cont.

3 Vonda keeps a journal of the moon phases she sees each night. Tonight she observes a gibbous moon. What moon phase can Vonda expect to see in about one month?

   a full moon

   b crescent moon

   c gibbous moon

4 The pictures above show phases of the Moon, taken four nights apart. Which of the pictures below shows the Moon four nights later?

      a   **b**   **c**

5 Which of the following states the correct order of the moon phases?

   a new moon, first quarter moon, gibbous moon, crescent moon, full moon

   b new moon, crescent moon, first quarter moon, gibbous moon, full moon

   c new moon, full moon, first quarter moon, crescent moon, gibbous moon

NATIONAL SCIENCE TEACHERS ASSOCIATION

Day and Night

Description

Using a model, learners explore time zones and what causes day and night and how time zones change. Learners observe the position of the Sun in the sky at different times of day and relate those positions to the rotation of the Earth.

Suggested Grade Levels: 4–6

Lesson Objectives Connecting to the Standards

**Content Standard A:
Science as Inquiry**

K–4: Ask a question about objects, organisms, and events in the environment.

K–4: Use data (observations) to construct a reasonable explanation.

5–8: Develop descriptions, explanations, predictions, and models using evidence.

**Content Standard D:
Earth and Space Science**

K–4: Understand that objects in the sky have patterns of movement. The sun appears to move across the sky in the same way every day, but its path changes slowly over the seasons.

5–8: Understand that most objects in the solar system are in regular and predictable motion. Those motions explain such phenomena as the day, the year, phases of the moon, and eclipses.

Featured Picture Book

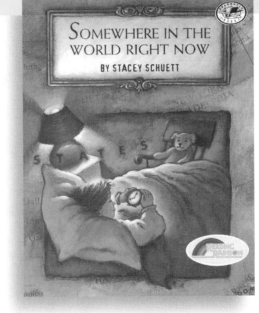

Title	***Somewhere in the World Right Now***
Author	**Stacey Schuett**
Illustrator	**Stacey Schuett**
Publisher	**Dragonfly Books**
Year	**1997**
Genre	**Story**
Summary	**Describes what is happening in different places around the world at a particular time**

Time Needed

This lesson will take several class periods. Suggested scheduling is as follows:

Day 1:   **Engage** with read aloud of *Somewhere in the World Right Now*

Day 2:   **Explore** and **Explain** with modeling with lamps and globes

Days 3–5: **Elaborate** with Where Is the Sun?

Day 6:   **Evaluate** with Make a Picture Book

Materials

- Several clocks set at different times labeled with city and country
- Globes (1 per group)
- Lamps (1 per group)

Student Pages

- Somewhere in the World Right Now
- Where Is the Sun?
- Make a Picture Book

engage

Before class, bring in several clocks set at different times around the world and label them with the city and country. You can find times of many cities around the world at *www.timeanddate.com/worldclock*.

 Questioning

Introduce the author and illustrator of *Somewhere in the World Right Now*. Skip "A Note to the Reader" in the front of the book (this section will be used later to provide the scientific explanation for the students), and read the book aloud to students. Model the questioning skills of a good reader by asking the following types of questions as you read.

? Is it true that somewhere in the world it is already tomorrow?

? How can the Sun be rising and setting at the same time?

? How can all of these things be happening in the world right now?

 Making Connections:

Text-to-Self

Ask students

? Do you know someone who lives in a different part of the country or world where it is a different time than it is here?

? Have you ever been to a place where you had to set your watch differently?

Have students examine the clocks set for different times for different places in the world. Determine students' prior knowledge and misconceptions about Earth-Sun relationships by asking them to share ideas about how it can be so many different times at the same moment.

explore & explain

Modeling with Lamps and Globes

Provide each group of students with a lamp and a globe. Tell them they are going to use the lamp as a model of the Sun and the globe as a model of the Earth.

Before they begin the activity, ask students

? How does the Earth move? (It rotates on its axis and revolves around the Sun.)

? What do the movements of the Earth have to do with how we keep time? (One rotation is one day and one revolution is one year.)

? Which movement do you think causes day and night? (Earth's rotation)

Then give students a few minutes to explore the following question with the model:

? How can it be different times in different places on the Earth?

After students have had time to explore the model, pass out the Somewhere in the World Right Now student pages. Tell students to use the lamp and globe to answer the questions on the student pages.

Discuss the student responses on the Somewhere in the World Right Now student pages. Have students share any observations, answers, and questions.

STUDENTS MODELING DAY AND NIGHT WITH LAMPS AND GLOBES

The correct answers for the student pages follow.

1   List three locations that are experiencing night when it is daytime in your city. (Answers will vary but should be locations on the opposite side of the globe.)

2   Can the Sun be rising and setting at the same time? Explain. (Yes. It is always rising somewhere on the Earth and setting on the opposite side of the Earth at the same time.)

3   Where on the globe is the international date line? (It runs through the middle of the Pacific Ocean in a north-south direction.)

4   Why do you think the international community agreed to place the international date line in that location? (To have a date change in the middle of a country would cause too many problems for people living there. There aren't very many people living in the middle of the Pacific Ocean, so few people are affected by the change of date there.)

5   Which locations are first to begin the new day? (Places west of the international date line move into the new date first. Those locations include New Zealand, Russia, and Japan.)

6   Which locations are last to see the sunrise on that day? (Locations just east of the international date line are last to see the sunrise on a particular day. Those locations include Hawaii, Marquesas, and the Aleutian Islands.)

7   Which part of the United States is the first to see the sunrise, the East Coast or the West Coast? (the East Coast)

8 Think back to the book *Somewhere in the World Right Now.* On the lines below, explain how all of the events in the book could be taking place in the same moment. (All of those events were happening at the same moment because different places have different times based on location. Somewhere right now it is day and somewhere else right now it is night because the Sun lights up half of Earth at all times. As Earth rotates, different locations enter the sunlight at different times.)

 Determining
Importance

Tell students you will be reading an informational page titled "A Note to the Reader" from the front of *Somewhere in the World Right Now.* Have students listen for answers to any questions they might still have about time zones, the international date line, and Earth's rotation.

elaborate

Where Is the Sun?

Distribute the Where is the Sun? student pages. Have students choose a location where they can face south and observe the Sun in the morning, at noon, and in the afternoon. Students will record the position of the Sun rela-

 SAFETY Never look directly at the Sun! Looking at the Sun can damage your eyes!

LOOKING FOR THE LOCATION OF THE SUN IN THE SKY

tive to a landmark at each of these times for three days.

After the third day, students can answer the questions on the Where Is the Sun? student pages. Have them revisit the lamp and globe model to reinforce their understanding of the abstract concepts they are learning with a concrete representation. Then discuss the questions from the student pages together.

1 Did you notice any patterns in where you saw the Sun in the sky each day? (Students should notice that the Sun is always lowest in the eastern sky in the morning, highest in the sky at noon, and lowest in the western sky in the afternoon.)

2 At what time of day did the Sun seem highest in the sky? (noon)

3 Think back to the globe and lamp you used to model day and night. Does the

Sun really move across the sky during the day? Explain. (No, in our model, the Sun stayed in the same place and the globe was rotating.)

4 How does the rotation of the Earth affect the appearance of the Sun in the sky in the morning, at noon, and in the afternoon? (In the morning, my location is turning toward the Sun. It appears in the east because of the direction the Earth turns. At noon, my location is turned all the way toward the Sun, so it appears to be right above me. In the afternoon, my location is turning away from the Sun. It appears in the west because of the direction the Earth turns.)

evaluate

Make a Picture Book

Pass out the Make a Picture Book student page. Tell students they will be writing and illustrating a children's picture book that can be used to explain what causes day and night, and what causes the Sun to appear to move across the sky each day. Their finished products should include simple text, colorful illustrations, and clearly labeled diagrams.

Have available some picture books about astronomy written for young children, such as *The Sun is My Favorite Star* by Frank Asch and *The Moon Book* by Gail Gibbons. Share some examples of simple text, colorful illustrations, and clearly labeled diagrams.

Scoring Rubric for Make a Picture Book

4 Point Response	The picture book includes an accurate explanation of what causes day and night, a clearly labeled diagram showing what causes day and night, an accurate explanation of what causes the Sun to appear to move across the sky each day, a clearly labeled diagram of what causes the Sun to appear to move across the sky each day, simple text, and colorful, scientifically accurate illustrations.
3 Point Response	The student demonstrates a flaw in understanding of the concepts OR the book is missing one or two required elements.
2 Point Response	The student demonstrates a flaw in understanding of the concepts AND the book is missing one or two required elements; OR the student demonstrates understanding, but the book is missing three required elements.
1 Point Response	The student demonstrates a flaw in understanding of the concepts AND the book is missing three or more required elements; OR the student demonstrates understanding, but the book is missing four or more required elements.
0 Point Response	The book shows no understanding of the concepts AND is missing all required elements; OR the student did not make a book.

Inquiry Place

Have students brainstorm "investigatable" questions such as

? How does the length of daylight in summer compare to the length of daylight in winter where you live?

? How does the length of daylight in summer compare to the length of daylight in winter at the North Pole? How can you use a model to explain this difference?

? How do the direction and length of your shadow in the morning compare to its direction and length at noon or in late afternoon?

Students can select a question to investigate as a class, or groups of students can vote on the question they want to investigate as teams. Students can present their findings at a poster session.

More Books to Read

Branley, F. M. 1986. *What makes day and night?* New York, NY: HarperTrophy.
Summary: A simple explanation of how the rotation of the Earth causes day and night.

Dolan, G. 2001. *The Greenwich guide to day and night.* Chicago, IL: Heinemann Library.
Summary: Photographs, diagrams, and clear text answer questions such as: How long does it take for the Sun's light to reach Earth? How can shadows help us tell time? What is a solar eclipse?

Dolan, G. 2001. *The Greenwich guide to measuring time.* Chicago, IL: Heinemann Library.
Summary: Photographs, diagrams, and clear text answer questions such as What do we call the length of time for the Earth to go around the Sun? How do astronomers use stars to tell the time? Why do we have leap years?

Fletcher, R. 1997. *Twilight comes twice.* Boston, MA: Houghton Mifflin.
Summary: Free-verse text describes the transition from day to night and from night to day, revealing the magic in these everyday moments.

Web Sites

Virtual Globe: Areas of Sunlight and Darkness Updated Every Five Minutes
www.anutime.com/globe/3Den.html

World Clock
www.timeanddate.com/worldclock

References

Asch, F. 2000. *The Sun is my favorite star.* New York, NY: Harcourt.

Gibbons, G. 1997. *The Moon book.* New York, NY: Holiday House.

Name: _____

Somewhere in the World Right Now

Place your lamp and globe about 50 cm apart with the lamp shining toward the globe. Use the lamp to represent the Sun and the globe to represent Earth.

● Find the arrow near the equator that shows the direction the Earth turns. Be sure to always turn your globe in that direction.

● Model daytime in your city.

1 List three locations that are experiencing night when it is daytime in your city.

_____

● Model sunrise in your city by turning the globe so that your city is just entering the lamp's light.

2 Can the Sun be rising and setting at the same time? Explain.

_____

_____

● Find the international date line on your globe. This is where one day changes to the next.

3 Where on the globe is the international date line?

_____

4 Why do you think the international community agreed to place the international date line in that location?

_____

_____

_____

Somewhere  in the World Right Now cont.

- Turn your globe so that the international date line is just entering the lamp's light (sunrise).

5 Which locations are first to begin the new day?

_____

- Slowly turn your globe and notice each location turning toward the lamp.

6 Which locations are last to see the sunrise on that day?

_____

- Model sunrise in the United States. Be sure you are turning the globe in the direction the Earth turns.

7 Which part of the United States is the first to see the sunrise, the East Coast or the West Coast?

_____

8 Think back to the book *Somewhere in the World Right Now.* On the lines below, explain how all of the events in the book could be taking place at the same moment.

_____

_____

_____

_____

_____

Name: _____

Where Is the Sun?

1 Choose a spot to observe the position of the Sun and face south.

2 Locate a landmark (tree, flagpole, building, etc.) and draw it in each box. Be sure to use the same landmark all three days.

3 Draw the position of the Sun relative to the landmark in the morning, at noon, and in the afternoon for three days. Be sure to stand in the **exact same location**, facing south each time.

4 Write the time of day inside each picture of the Sun.

SAFETY

Never look directly at the Sun!

Looking at the Sun can damage your eyes!

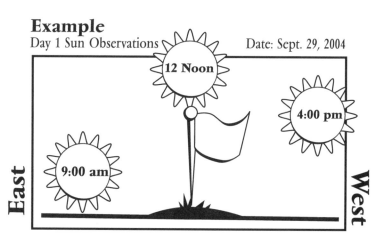

Example
Day 1 Sun Observations   Date: Sept. 29, 2004

Day 1 Sun Observations   Date: _____

East   West

Where Is the Sun? cont.

Day 2 Sun Observations
Date: _____

East

West

Day 3 Sun Observations
Date: _____

East

West

Name: _____

Where Is the Sun? cont.

Questions:

1 Did you notice any patterns in where you saw the Sun in the sky each day?

_____

_____

2 At what time of day did the Sun seem highest in the sky?

_____

_____

3 Think back to the globe and lamp you used to model day and night. Does the Sun really move across the sky during the day? Explain.

_____

_____

_____

4 How does the rotation of the Earth affect the appearance of the Sun in the sky in the morning, at noon, and in the afternoon?

_____

_____

_____

_____

NATIONAL SCIENCE TEACHERS ASSOCIATION

Make a Picture Book

Write and illustrate a children's picture book that can be used to explain what causes day and night, and to explain what causes the Sun to *appear* to move across the sky each day.

Books should include:

1 An accurate explanation and clearly labeled diagram showing what causes day and night.

2 An accurate explanation and clearly labeled diagram of what causes the Sun to *appear* to move across the sky each day.

3 Simple text a young child could understand.

4 Colorful, scientifically accurate illustrations.

Be creative! Have fun!

Grand Canyon

Description

Learners explore through a checkpoint lab simulation how weathering and erosion have contributed to the formation of the Grand Canyon. They will create a travel brochure for the Grand Canyon demonstrating their understandings about weathering and erosion.

Suggested Grade Levels: 3–6

Lesson Objectives Connecting to the Standards

**Content Standard A:
Science as Inquiry**

K–4: Use data to construct a reasonable explanation.

K–4: Communicate investigations and explanations.

5–8: Develop descriptions, explanations, predictions, and models using evidence.

5–8: Communicate scientific procedures and explanations.

**Content Standard D:
Earth and Space Science**

K–4: Understand that the surface of the Earth changes. Some changes are due to slow processes, such as erosion and weathering.

5–8: Land forms are the result of a combination of constructive forces (e.g., crustal deformation, volcanic eruption, and deposition of sediment) and destructive forces (e.g., weathering and erosion).

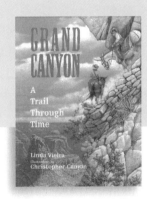

Featured Picture Books

Title	**Erosion: The Weather Report Series**	Title	**Grand Canyon: A Trail Through Time**
Author	**Virginia Castleman**	Author	**Linda Vieira**
Publisher	**Perfection Learning**	Illustrator	**Christopher Canyon**
Year	**2004**	Publisher	**Walker and Company**
Genre	**Non-narrative Information**	Year	**1997**
Summary	**Tells how water, wind, and ice change the surface of the Earth through erosion**	Genre	**Narrative Information**
		Summary	**Describes the deep trench known as the Grand Canyon and activities of visitors to the national park**

Time Needed

This lesson will take several class periods. Suggested scheduling is as follows:

Day 1: **Engage** with thinking about the Grand Canyon, and **Explore** with Wind and Water Checkpoint Lab

Day 2: **Explain** with reading and relating to the Checkpoint Lab

Day 3: **Elaborate** and **Evaluate** with Grand Canyon Brochure

Materials

- Optional: Pictures of the Grand Canyon (photos, prints, books, etc.)

For the Wind and Water Checkpoint Lab:

- A red plastic cup and a green plastic cup with the openings taped together (1 per team)
- Bucket of large unwashed gravel
- Bucket of small unwashed gravel
- Bucket of soil
- Small unwashed rocks (1 cup per team)
- Plastic jar or wide-mouthed jug (1 per team)
- Large plastic or aluminum pans (2 per team)
- Water
- Plastic or wire strainer (1 per team)
- Paper coffee filters (1 per team)
- Safety goggles (1 per person)
- Bucket of sand
- Lids from copy paper boxes or other large, shallow box lids (1 per team)
- Measuring cup (1 per team)

Student Pages

- Grand Canyon
- New Vocabulary List
- Wind and Water Checkpoint Lab
- Grand Canyon Brochure

engage

Thinking about the Grand Canyon

Pass out the Grand Canyon student page and have students make inferences from the picture. Providing students with additional color photographs of the canyon before they answer the following questions would be helpful.

? How do you think the Grand Canyon formed?

? Why do you think it has gotten wider and deeper over time?

? How long do you think it took for the Grand Canyon to form?

explore

Wind and Water Checkpoint Lab

In advance, prepare all of the materials necessary for the Wind and Water Checkpoint Lab. See "Teaching Science Through Inquiry," Chapter 3, for tips on managing a checkpoint lab.

 ## Using Features of Nonfiction

Tell students you have a nonfiction book that might help them find out how the Grand Canyon formed. Show them the cover of *Erosion*. Tell students that a unique feature of nonfiction is that the reader can enter the text at any point to get information. Turn to page 15, and read the inset about the Grand Canyon.

Tell students that they will be doing activities in a checkpoint lab to help them understand how wind and water can cause changes on the surface of the Earth.

Checkpoint Lab

Distribute the Wind and Water Checkpoint Lab student pages. Tell students to take turns being the reader for their team. The reader's job involves reading the directions out loud for the team, putting the green cup on top if the team is working, and putting the red cup on top if the team has a question or if it is ready for a check mark. Each member of the group is responsible for recording data and writing responses.

SHAKING THE JAR OF ROCKS
IN THE CHECKPOINT LAB

Have the students complete the checkpoint lab, working at their own paces. While they are working, observe and listen to them interact. Before you give a team a check mark or stamp so they can move ahead in the lab, informally evaluate them by asking probing questions of each member of the team, such as

? How do you know?

? What is your evidence?

? Are you surprised by the results? Why or why not?

? What do you think will happen next?

explain

Reading and Relating to the Checkpoint Lab

 ### New Vocabulary List

Ask students if they have ever heard the words *weathering* and *erosion*, and discuss their prior knowledge of the terms. Pass out the New Vocabulary List student page. A new vocabulary list is a "guess and check" type of visual representation. Students develop vocabulary as they draw and write predictions about a new word's meaning, read the word in context, and then draw and write their new definitions of the word. Have students write the words *weathering* and *erosion* in the top two boxes of the first column. Then have them draw and write what they think each word means in the next column. Tell students they will use this sheet to keep track of new words as they learn about the Grand Canyon. Let them know that they will get to find out if their predictions about the meanings of the words *weathering* and *erosion* are correct by comparing their observations from the checkpoint lab to the information in *Erosion*.

Read pages 5 through 7 in *Erosion* about weathering. (Skip the inset "Know Your Rocks" about the three types of rocks.) Then ask the students

? What is weathering? (Weathering is the natural breakdown of rocks into particles.)

? In which part of the checkpoint lab did you observe weathering? (Part B, in which we shook up the jar of rocks and water and observed that some particles broke off.)

Provide time for students to fill in the "What It Means" column of the New Vocabulary List student page.

Read page 11 about erosion, including the captions in *Erosion*. Then ask the students

? What is erosion? (Erosion is the process by which weathered rock and soil on Earth's surface are picked up in one location and moved to another.)

? In which part of the checkpoint lab did you observe erosion? (Part D in which we observed small particles being carried to the bottom of the pan by water.)

Provide time for students to complete the "What It Means" column of the New Vocabulary List student page.

Ask students to add the words *water erosion* and *wind erosion* to the "Word" column of the New Vocabulary List student page. Provide time for them to fill in the second column, "What I Think It Means," based on what they have learned so far. Then, read pages 12 through 14 about water erosion in *Erosion*.

? What is water erosion? (Water erosion occurs when water flows over the ground and takes other loose weathered material with it.)

? In which part of the checkpoint lab did you observe water erosion? (Part D in which we observed small particles being carried to the bottom of the pan by water.)

Provide time for students to complete the "What It Means" column of the New Vocabulary List student page.

Then, read pages 21 and 22 in *Erosion* about wind erosion, including the inset about the dust bowl. (See *Children of the Dust Days* in the "More Books to Read" section for more information.) Then ask students

? What is wind erosion? (Wind erosion is the movement of very small particles by wind.)

? In which part of the checkpoint lab did you observe wind erosion? (Part C in which wind [or breath] carried some of the sand, and we felt it hitting our hands.)

Provide time for students to complete the "What It Means" column of the New Vocabulary List student page.

Then ask

? Are weathering and erosion constructive forces (that build things up) or destructive forces (that wear things away)? (They are destructive forces.)

Determining Importance

Go back to the original questions asked on the Grand Canyon student page:

? How do you think the Grand Canyon formed?

? How do you think it has gotten wider and deeper over time?

? How long do you think it took for the Grand Canyon to form?

Introduce the author and the illustrator of the book *Grand Canyon: A Trail Through Time*. Tell students they can find out if their inferences about the Grand Canyon were correct by listening as you read the book. Have students signal (raise their hands) if they hear any clues from the reading and invite discussion on them.

? How do you think the Grand Canyon formed? (The Grand Canyon was formed by weathering and erosion. The Colorado River flowed through it over a long period of time and weathered away the rock, and the rock was carried away by the water, page 11.)

? How do you think it has gotten wider and deeper over time? It has gotten wider and deeper as the rushing Colorado River continues to flow through it, deepening the canyon by eroding away rocks and soil. Blustering wind and pounding rain continue to weather away the rocky sides of the canyon, page 28.)

? How long do you think it took for the Grand Canyon to form? (The Colorado River took almost six million years to carve the canyon, page 11.)

Elaborate & Evaluate

Grand Canyon Brochure

Pass out the Grand Canyon Brochure assignment. Use the following rubric to assess student work.

Scoring Rubric for Grand Canyon Brochure

4 Point Response	The brochure includes a creative slogan, a drawing or photograph of the Grand Canyon, a map showing the correct location of the Grand Canyon, complete definitions of weathering and erosion with clear descriptions of how each contributed to the formation of the canyon, an accurate explanation of the changes still occurring at the Grand Canyon, and three reasons tourists should visit the Grand Canyon.
3 Point Response	The student demonstrates a flaw in understanding of the concepts of weathering and erosion OR the brochure is missing one or two required elements.
2 Point Response	The student demonstrates a flaw in understanding of the concepts of weathering and erosion AND the brochure is missing one or two required elements; OR the student demonstrates understanding, but the brochure is missing three required elements.
1 Point Response	The student demonstrates a flaw in understanding of the concepts of weathering and erosion AND the brochure is missing three or more required elements; OR the student demonstrates understanding, but the brochure is missing four or more required elements.
0 Point Response	The brochure shows no understanding of the concepts of weathering and erosion AND is missing all required elements.

Inquiry Place

Have students brainstorm "investigatable" questions such as

? How will a mound of dirt in the school yard change in width and height over a one-week period? Two weeks? Four weeks? Twelve weeks?

? Which type of rock will react the most to chemical weathering (acid): limestone, sandstone, or granite?

Have students select a question to investigate as a class, or groups of students can vote on the question they want to investigate as teams. After they make their predictions, they can design an experiment to test their predictions. Students can present their findings at a poster session.

More Books to Read

Anderson, P. 1997. *A Grand Canyon journey: Tracing time in stone.* Danbury, CT: Franklin Watts.
Summary: Color photographs and informative text take readers on a guided tour from the rim of the Grand Canyon down to the valley floor, describing the geological history that created the canyon along the way.

Coombs, K. M. 2000. *Children of the dust days.* Minneapolis, MN: Carolrhoda Books.
Summary: This informative book brings the dust days of the 1930s to life through simple, straightforward text and period photographs. Explains how poor farming techniques and drought led to massive erosion.

Minor, W. 2000. *Grand Canyon: Exploring a natural wonder.* New York, NY: Blue Sky Press.
Summary: Retraces the steps of nineteenth century artist-explorer Thomas Moran, whose paintings helped convince Congress to preserve the Grand Canyon as a national park. Lyrical text and stunning watercolors describe both the scenery of the Grand Canyon and the emotions it stirs in the visitor.

Stewart, M. 2002. *Sedimentary rocks.* Chicago, IL: Heinemann Library.
Summary: This informational book answers questions about the three kinds of rock, how sedimentary rock forms, how rocks are changed by erosion and weathering, how the Grand Canyon formed, and how the Great Sphinx lost its nose. Includes full-color photographs, diagrams, bold-print vocabulary words, table of contents, glossary, and index.

Reference

Castleman, V. *Erosion: The weather report series.* 2004. Logan, IA: Perfection Learning. "How can water cause changes in rocks?" activity adapted from the activity on page 10. "How can wind cause changes in rocks?" adapted from the activity on page 23.

Name: _____

Grand Canyon

Look carefully at the photograph of the Grand Canyon.

U.S. NATIONAL PARK SERVICE

1 How do you think the Grand Canyon formed?

_____
_____
_____
_____
_____
_____
_____
_____
_____
_____

2 How do you think it has gotten wider and deeper over time?

_____
_____
_____
_____

3 How long do you think it took for the Grand Canyon to form?

_____
_____
_____
_____

Name: _____

New Vocabulary List

Word	What I Think It Means (Draw and Write)	What It Means (Draw and Write)

Name: _____

Wind and Water
Checkpoint Lab

Follow the directions below. If your team is working, put the green cup on top. If you have a question, put the red cup on top. If you are finished with a part and you are ready for a check from your teacher, put the red cup on top.

Part A How does water carry rocks and soil?

- Fill a large plastic jar halfway with large and small gravel, sand, and soil.
- Add water to fill up the jar.
- Close the jar, and then take turns shaking the jar for a total of one minute.
- Set the jar aside for at least 20 minutes (you will observe it in Part D).

Part B How can water cause changes in rocks?

- Divide a cup of rocks into two equal piles.
- Put one pile of rocks into a plastic jar, and fill the bottle halfway with clear water.
- Close the lid, and take turns shaking the jar for a total of 10 minutes.
- Pour the mixture through a strainer into another container.

1 How do the rocks that were shaken in the water compare to the other pile of rocks?

_____

2 Examine the water. Is it still clear? _____

3 *Very slowly* pour the water through a coffee filter into a pan.

4 Examine the coffee filter. What do you see on it?

_____

Checkpoints A and B ☐

Wind and Water
Checkpoint Lab cont.

Part **C** How can wind cause changes in rocks?

- All team members must have safety goggles covering their eyes before continuing!
- Open a sheet of newspaper in the center of your table.
- Place a paper box lid in the center of the newspaper.
- Pour a cup of sand into one end of the lid.
- Have one student put his or her hand inside the other end of the box, open palm facing the pile of sand.
- Have someone blow *gently* on the sand, and then blow harder until the sand hits the other student's hand.
- Repeat until all team members have felt the sand hitting their hands.

1 How did the sand feel blowing against your hand?

_____

- Observe the sand that was blown to the other end of the box and rub it between your fingers.
- Do the same to the sand left in the original pile.

2 How are the textures of the sand different? Why do you think this is so?

_____

Checkpoint C ☐

Name: _____

Wind and Water
Checkpoint Lab cont.

Part D How does water carry rocks and soil?

1 In the box below, sketch and label materials in the jar from Part A.

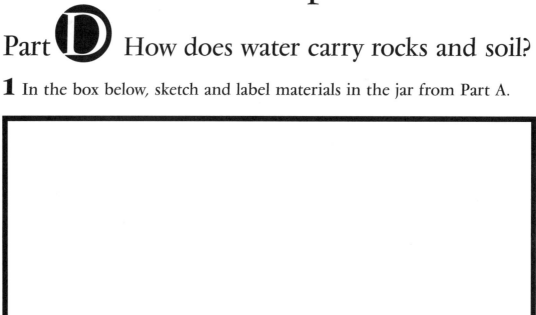

- Now imagine that the water in the jar is flowing down a river.

2 Which type of material would be carried for the longest distance?

_____

3 Which type of material would settle to the bottom of the river?

_____

- Prop up an empty pan by placing one end on a book.
- *Very, very slowly* pour the contents of the jar into the high end of the tilted pan and observe.

4 What happened to each of the materials in the jar when you poured them out into the pan? Which materials were carried with the water?

_____

Checkpoint D ☐

Name: _____

Grand Canyon
Brochure

Create a travel brochure advertising the Grand Canyon to tourists.
Include the following in your brochure:

1 A catchy slogan to grab the attention of the reader.

2 A drawing or photograph of the Grand Canyon.

3 A map showing the location of the Grand Canyon.

4 A definition of weathering, and a description of how weathering contributed to the formation of the Grand Canyon.

5 A definition of erosion, and a description of how erosion contributed to the formation of the Grand Canyon.

6 An explanation of the changes that still occur every day in the Grand Canyon as a result of weathering and erosion.

7 Three reasons tourists should visit the Grand Canyon.

Be creative! Have fun!

Brainstorms:
From Idea to Invention

Description
Learners explore the design process by improving an existing invention; designing and building a drink holder for an airplane seat and communicating their design process; and designing an investigation to evaluate Scotchgard.

Suggested Grade Levels: 5–6

Lesson Objectives Connecting to the Standards

Content Standard A: Science as Inquiry	Content Standard E: Science and Technology	Content Standard F: Science in Personal and Social Perspectives	Content Standard G: History and Nature of Science
5–8: Design and conduct a scientific investigation.	**5–8:** Design a solution or product, considering constraints—such as cost, time, trade-offs, and materials needed—and communicate ideas with drawings and simple models.	**5–8:** Understand that social needs, attitudes, and values influence the direction of technological development.	**5–8:** Understand that women and men of various social and ethnic backgrounds—and with diverse talents, qualities, and motivations—engage in the activities of science, engineering, and related fields.
5–8: Use appropriate tools and techniques to gather, analyze, and interpret data.	**5–8:** Implement a proposed design.	**5–8:** Understand that science and technology have advanced through contributions of many different people, in different cultures, at different times in history.	
5–8: Communicate scientific procedures and explanations.	**5–8:** Evaluate completed technological designs or products.		
	5–8: Communicate the process of technological design.		

Featured Picture Books

Title	***Imaginative Inventions***	Title	***Girls Think of Everything: Stories of Ingenious Inventions by Women***
Author	**Charise Mericle Harper**	Author	**Catherine Thimmesh**
Illustrator	**Charise Mericle Harper**	Illustrator	**Melissa Sweet**
Publisher	**Little, Brown**	Publisher	**Houghton Mifflin**
Year	**2001**	Year	**2002**
Genre	**Dual Purpose**	Genre	**Narrative Information**
Summary	**The who, what, when, where, and why of roller skates, potato chips, marbles, and pie told in whimsical verse**	Summary	**How women throughout the ages have responded to situations by inventing various items**

Time Needed

This lesson will take several class periods. Suggested scheduling is as follows:

Day 1: **Engage** with Draw an Inventor and read aloud of *Girls Think of Everything*

Day 2: **Explore** and **Explain** with *Imaginative Inventions* read aloud and Improve an Invention

Day 3: **Explore** and **Explain** with Design Your Product

Day 4: **Elaborate** and **Evaluate** with Evaluate an Invention Checkpoint Lab, and **Evaluate** with Draw an Inventor

Materials

- Optional: Chocolate chip cookies (1 per student)
- Optional: Examples of Inventions from *Imaginative Inventions*
- Colored pencils
- "Think pads" (sticky notes)

For the Design of Your Product Activity:

- Bags or trays with the following supplies (1 per pair):
  - 1 meter of masking tape
  - 40 plastic straws (not the flexible kind)
  - scissors
  - full can of soda
  - small styrofoam or plastic bowl
- Timer or clock

For the Evaluate an Invention Checkpoint Lab:

- 1 can Scotchgard Fabric Protector (It takes 24 hours for Scotchgard to dry.)
- A red plastic cup and a green plastic cup with the openings taped together (1 per pair)
- Fabric pretreated by teacher with Scotchgard (5 swatches per pair)
- Fabric not pretreated with Scotchgard (5 swatches per pair)
- Various substances for staining fabric such as
  - mustard
  - spaghetti sauce
  - grape juice
  - tomato juice
- Pipette and cup for each staining substance

Student Pages

- Draw an Inventor (2 copies per student)
- Imaginative Inventions
- Improve an Invention
- Letter from Straighten Up and Fly Right Airline
- Design Your Product
- Questions about Your Product Design
- Evaluate an Invention Checkpoint Lab

engage

Draw an Inventor

To determine student preconceptions of gender, social and ethnic backgrounds, talents, and qualities of inventors, ask students to draw what they think an inventor looks like and describe some characteristics of the inventor on the Draw an Inventor student page. Provide colored pencils.

engage

Read Aloud

 Inferring

Show the cover of *Girls Think of Everything,* and introduce the author and illustrator. Ask students to predict what the book is about by looking at the cover. Read pages 8 through 10 of *Girls Think of Everything* about inventor Ruth Wakefield, but instead of the words "chocolate chip cookie," say "this invention." Have students use clues from the reading to guess the name of the invention. Students can write down their inferences on sticky-note "think pads" while you are reading. Pause periodically to allow students time to write and revise their inferences as they get more clues from the reading.

Then read pages 19 through 22 in *Girls Think of Everything* about Bette Nesmith Graham, but instead of the words *Liquid Paper correction fluid* and *white-out,* say "this invention." Have students use clues from the text to guess the name of this invention. Again, pause periodically to allow students time to write and revise their inferences as they get more clues from the reading.

Finally, read pages 27 through 30 in *Girls Think of Everything* about Ann Moore, leaving out the name of her invention (the Snugli baby pouch). Have students use clues from the text to guess the name of this invention. Again, pause periodically to allow students time to

write and revise their inferences as they get more clues from the reading.

Discuss the following questions.

? What do all of these inventors have in common? (They are all women, creative people, problem-solvers, etc.)

? Who are some other inventors?

? Have you ever had an idea for an invention?

? What qualities do you think are necessary for a person to be an inventor?

? Do you think inventing a new product would be an easy process? Why or why not?

explore & explain

Imaginative Inventions and Improve an Invention

 Determining Importance

Introduce the author and illustrator of *Imaginative Inventions.* Tell students to listen for the problem, solution, and name of invention for each story. Pass out the Imaginative Inventions student page to students, and have them complete it as you read aloud the book to the class. Pause periodically to give them time to complete the student page as you read.

Next, pass out the Improve an Invention student page to each student. Explain that, instead of coming up with completely new inventions, inventors often think of ways to make an old one better. Have pairs of students choose an invention from the book that they would like to improve upon. Then have them complete the Improve an Invention student page. If you like, have samples of some of the inventions in the book—such as a Frisbee, eyeglasses, or a paper bag—available for students to look at while they are completing the student page. Then have students present their advertisements for their improved inventions, explain their improvement process, and tell why the improvement would make the invention more useful and/or fun.

explore & explain

Design Your Product

Tell students you have been contacted by the CEO of a major airline. She would like the students to design a device to help solve a problem for the airline. Give each team of students a copy of the letter from Straighten Up and Fly Right Airline, and read it aloud to the class.

Each team will now be asked to design and build an imaginary product—a drink holder—given three constraints—time, materials, and size. Tell them they will have only 40 minutes

to design and build the product. Pass out the Design Your Product student page and the following materials to each pair, but don't let them begin yet.

- 1 meter of masking tape
- 40 plastic straws (not the flexible kind)
- scissors
- full can of soda
- small styrofoam or plastic bowl

Tell students that they must complete the Design Your Product student page before they can begin building. As soon as everyone has the student page and materials, set the timer for 40 minutes and announce that it is time to begin. Circulate as teams work, asking questions and informally assessing their progress toward the goal.

When the 40 minutes are up, instruct students to stop building and fill out the Questions About Your Product Design student page. Discuss the following questions from the student page.

? Was your product effective? How do you know?

? What challenges did you face during the design process?

? What improvements would you make if you had more time and more materials?

Explain to students that perfectly designed solutions do not exist. All technological solutions have trade-offs, such as safety, cost, efficiency, and appearance. Inventors almost always have

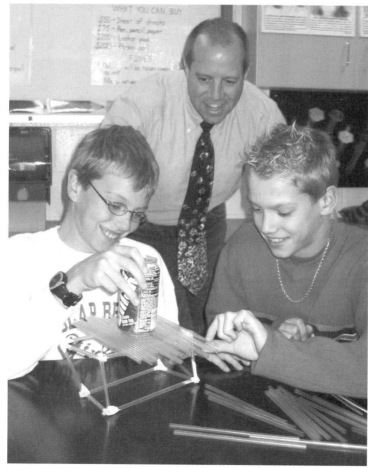

STUDENTS IN MR. WINTZ'S CLASS BUILD A DRINK HOLDER FOR AN AIRLINE TRAY

constraints. Constraints limit choices in technological design, for example, cost, time, trade-offs, and materials needed. Ask

? What were the trade-offs you were forced to make while designing the drink holder? (The materials were cheap, but the trade-off was a weak and unattractive product. We worked quickly, but the trade-off was a shoddy product.)

? What were the constraints you dealt with while designing the drink holder? (Forty minute time limit, size requirements, and limited materials.)

elaborate & evaluate

Evaluate an Invention Checkpoint Lab

In advance, prepare all of the materials necessary for the Evaluate an Invention Checkpoint Lab. See "Teaching Science Through Inquiry," Chapter 3, for a list of tips for managing a checkpoint lab.

 ### *Determining Importance*

Ask students to listen for the constraints that inventor Patsy O. Sherman faced when developing Scotchgard as you read pages 23 through 26 in *Girls Think of Everything*.

? What constraints did Patsy O. Sherman have to deal with when inventing Scotchgard? (She was not allowed in the textile mills because she was a woman. She had to figure out a way to make it economical so people would be willing to pay for it. She had to come up with a protector for new permanent press fabrics, some-

thing that would repel stains *and* release them when they are washed.)

Tell students they are going to have a chance to try out Patsy O. Sherman's invention and evaluate it. Pass out the Evaluate an Invention Checkpoint Lab. Have students work in pairs. They put the green cup on top if their team is working. They put the red cup on top if their team has a question or if they are ready for a check mark. Both members of the group are responsible for recording data and writing responses.

Have the students complete the checkpoint lab, working at their own paces. While they are working, observe and listen to them interact. Before you give a team a check mark or stamp so that they can move ahead in the lab, evaluate their work by asking probing questions of both members of the team. As a final evaluation, you can assess each student's checkpoint lab.

evaluate

Draw an Inventor

To determine whether student preconceptions of gender, talents, qualities, and social and ethnic backgrounds of inventors have changed, ask students to again draw what they think an inventor looks like. Have them describe some characteristics of the inventor on another Draw an Inventor student page. Provide colored pencils.

Engage students in a discussion of how their first drawing compares to the second drawing. Survey students to find out how many drew women, men, or minorities. (See *Brainstorm!* in the "More Books to Read" section at the end of this lesson for more stories about child inventors of many backgrounds.)

Inquiry Place

Have students keep an Inventor's Journal for one week. They should keep their journals with them at all times to record any ideas and designs that come to them during the week. Remind students that every time they write in their journals, they should initial, date, and have a witness sign it. A witness can be a parent, or a friend. Tell students the witness's signature provides proof that their ideas are original. Guide students with the following questions:

? What problems do you observe other people having around their homes, jobs, or neighborhoods that could be solved by an invention?

? If you could invent something to make your life easier, what would you invent?

? What are your constraints?

Students can present their new product ideas and designs at a poster session. Some other inquiries for students to try include

? Which brand of paper towel is the strongest? The most absorbent?

? Which brand of diaper holds the most liquid?

? Which detergent cleans stains the best?

Have students select a question to investigate as a class, or groups of students can vote on the question they want to investigate as teams. After they make their predictions, they can design an experiment to test their predictions. Students can present their findings at a poster session.

More Books to Read

Foltz Jones, C. 1994. *Mistakes that worked.* New York, NY: Doubleday.
Summary: Cartoons illustrate the stories behind serendipitous inventions such as Silly Putty, Coca Cola, Popsicles, penicillin, and bricks.

Perry, A. 2003. *Here's what you do when you can't find your shoe (Ingenius inventions for pesky problems).* New York, NY: Atheneum.
Summary: This collection of clever poems introduces imaginary inventions to make life easier, such as "The Sure-Footed Shoe Finder," a device with a "powerful Foot-Odor-Sensitive Vent" that "tracks down your sneaker by matching its scent." Humorous pen-and-ink cartoons accompany each selection.

Tucker, T. 1998. *Brainstorm! The stories of twenty American kid inventors.* New York, NY: Sunburst.
Summary: This inspiring book features young inventors from colonial to modern times. Black-and-white photographs and pen-and-ink drawings accompany the stories describing the invention of earmuffs, the Popsicle, the resealable cereal box, and many more.

Draw an Inventor

Draw what you think an inventor looks like in the box below:

Describe some characteristics of the inventor:

_____

_____

_____

Name: _____

Imaginative Inventions

Problem or Need	Solution	Name of Invention
Fried potatoes too thick	Cut fries up super thin	Potato chips

NATIONAL SCIENCE TEACHERS ASSOCIATION

Name: _____

Improve an Invention

Part A Questions to Consider

1 Choose an invention from the book *Imaginative Inventions* that you would like to improve upon.

_____

2 What was the original purpose for this invention?

_____

3 What could you do to make this invention more useful or more fun?

_____

_____

4 What parts of the original invention will you keep?

_____

_____

5 How could you test the product to make sure it works?

_____

_____

6 What will you call your new product?

_____

Part B Advertise Your Idea

Create an advertisement for your new product. Be sure to include a drawing of it and how it will be more useful and/or more fun than the original.

Straighten Up and Fly Right Airline

Dear Inventors,

We really need your help. Straighten Up and Fly Right Airline is downsizing the cabin areas on its airplanes. We are trying to accommodate four passengers in a row instead of two. This will result in a size reduction of the pull-down serving trays fastened to seat backs. The reduced tray size has become problematic because passengers will no longer have space for the signature in-flight meal, Sloppy Joe Soup and 7-Upchuck Cola. To solve this problem, Straighten Up and Fly Right Airline would like to provide passengers with a drink holder to go on each serving tray.

These are the product specifications:

1 The device must support a full 12 ounce can of soda above a 30 cm by 30 cm tray.

2 A soup bowl must be able to fit underneath the drink holder.

3 The device must be assembled by your design team in 40 minutes or less.

We have enclosed the supplies you can use to create your version of the drink holder. Please use only these supplies. We cannot afford any additional supplies at this time. Send your drink holder invention to us as soon as possible. Please also send the "Design Your Product" sheet and the "Questions about Your Product Design" along with your finished drink holder.

Sincerely,

Ms. Penny Pincher

Ms. Penny Pincher, CEO

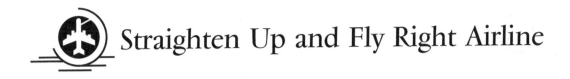 Straighten Up and Fly Right Airline

Design Your Product

Names of Inventors:

_____

Name of Product:

_____

Diagram of the Product: (Please label with dimensions in centimeters and identify where the soda can will fit.)

Straighten Up and Fly Right Airline

Questions about Your Product Design

Names of Inventors: _____

_____

Name of Product: _____

_____

1 Was your product effective? How do you know? _____

_____

2 What challenges did you face during the design process? _____

_____

_____

_____

_____

_____

3 What improvements would you make if you had more time and more
materials?_____

_____

_____

_____

_____

_____

NATIONAL SCIENCE TEACHERS ASSOCIATION

Name: _____

Evaluate an Invention
Checkpoint Lab

You just heard about
how Patsy Sherman invented Scotchgard.
Let's find out if it works!

Part **A** Prepare the Product for Testing

1 Get five index cards and label each one with "No Scotchgard" on one half and "Scotchgard" on the other half.

2 Ask your teacher for five swatches of fabric *not* treated with Scotchgard. Staple one piece of untreated fabric onto the "No Scotchgard" half of each index card.

3 Ask your teacher for five swatches of fabric treated with Scotchgard. Staple one piece of treated fabric onto the "Scotchgard" half of each index card.

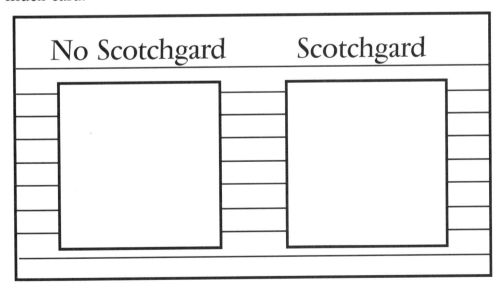

No Scotchgard   Scotchgard

Now you are ready to design your experiment!

Checkpoint A ☐

Name: _____

Evaluate an Invention
Checkpoint Lab cont.

Part B Design a Procedure

1 How will you keep the test fair? (What things will you need to keep the same?)

_____

_____

2 What procedure will you use to determine if Scotchgard is an effective product? List the steps of your procedure below.

_____

_____

_____

_____

3 Draw a data table below to help you organize your observations.

Checkpoint B ☐

Name: _____

Evaluate an Invention
Checkpoint Lab cont.

Part C Evaluate the Invention

When evaluating the overall effectiveness of an invention, there are many things to consider. Write a summary of your product test, and give your evaluation of Scotchgard. Continue on the back of this page if you need more room to write. Use the following questions to guide you:

- How did you keep the test "fair"?
- How well did the product work? How do you know? (Use the data from your experiment to answer this one.)
- How does it fulfill a consumer's needs or desires?
- What is the price? Is it affordable?
- Is it safe for the consumer and the environment? (Read the label.)
- What would you do differently if you were going to repeat your experiment? Why?

_____

_____

_____

_____

_____

_____

_____

_____

_____

_____

Checkpoint C ☐

Glossary

Note: All definitions attributed to (Colburn 2003) are verbatim from the book referenced at the end of the glossary.

Anticipation guides—Sets of questions that serve as a pre- or post-reading activity for a text, anticipation guides can activate and assess prior knowledge, determine misconceptions, focus thinking on the reading, and motivate reluctant readers by stimulating interest in the topic.

Assessment—"Assessment, broadly defined, means information gathering. Grading (or evaluating) students is certainly one type of assessment. Tests, portfolios, and lab practicals are all assessment devices. However, teachers assess students in other ways. When teachers check for understanding, to determine whether or not to continue teaching about a particular idea and where to go next with instruction, they are also assessing their students. Ungraded pretests and self-tests likewise represent assessment. Any information that helps the teacher make instructional decisions is assessment.

"Assessment is valuable to students as well as teachers (not to mention parents and other education stakeholders) because it helps students figure out what they do and don't understand and where they need to place their efforts to maximize learning. Assessment is also used to sort or rank students, letting them know how their performance compares to others, both for placement purposes and as a way to ensure minimum competencies in those who have passed particular tests." (Colburn 2003, p. 37)

Checkpoint labs—One way to manage a guided inquiry is to use a checkpoint lab. This type of lab is divided into written sections, with a small box located at the end of each section for a teacher check mark or stamp. Students work in teams, each one proceeding at its own pace. Teams use a red cup and a green cup taped together at their openings to signal the teacher—green on top when a team is working and red on top when a team has a question or reaches a checkpoint at which it needs the teacher's approval to continue.

Chunking—Chunking, just like it sounds, is dividing the text into manageable sections and reading only a section at any one time.

Constructivism—"Constructivism has multiple meanings, and it's important that when people discuss the concept they be sure they're talking about the same thing! Much of the confusion stems from the fact that constructivism refers to both an explanation (theory) about how people learn and a philosophical position related to the nature of learning (see Matthews 1994, 137–39). Increasingly, people are also using the term to refer to teaching techniques designed to build on what students already know, for example, open-ended, hands-on inquiry (Brooks and Brooks 1993).

"I'd like to focus on constructivism as an explanation about learning; that's probably what is most relevant to readers. In this context, "constructivism" refers to the concept that learners always bring with them to the classroom (or any other place where learning takes place) ideas about how the world works—including ideas related to whatever may be in today's lesson. Most of the time learners are unaware they even have these ideas! The ideas come from life experiences combined with what people have learned elsewhere.

"According to constructivist learning theory, learners test new ideas against that which they already believe to be true. If the new ideas seem to fit in with their pictures of the world, they have little difficulty learning the ideas. There's no guarantee, though, that they will fit the ideas into their pictures of how the world works with the kind of meaning the teacher intends. . . .

"On the other hand, if the new ideas don't seem to fit the learner's picture of reality then they won't seem to make sense. Learners may dismiss them, learn them well enough to please the teacher (but never fully accept the ideas), or eventually accommodate the new ideas and change the way they understand the world. As you might guess, this third outcome is most difficult to achieve, although it's what teachers most often desire in students.

"Seen this way, teaching is a process of trying to get people to change their minds—difficult enough as is, but made even more difficult by the fact that learners may not even know they hold an opinion about the idea in question! People who study learning and cognition often contrast constructivism with the more classical idea that students in our classes are "blank slates" who know nothing about the topics they are being taught. From this perspective, the teacher "transmits" new information to students, who mentally store it away. In contrast, constructivist learning theory says that students are not blank slates; learning is sometimes a process whereby new ideas help students to "rewrite" the misconceptions already on their slates." (Colburn 2003, pp. 58–59)

Dual-purpose books—Intended to serve two purposes, present a story and provide facts, dual-purpose books employ a format that allows readers to use the book as a storybook or as a non-narrative information book. Some-times information can be found in the running text but more frequently appears in insets and diagrams. Readers can enter on any page to access specific facts or read the book through as a story.

Elaborate—See 5E model of instruction.

Engage—See 5E model of instruction.

Evaluate—See 5E model of instruction.

Explain—See 5E model of instruction.

Explore—See 5E model of instruction.

Features of nonfiction—Many nonfiction books include a table of contents, index, glossary, bold-print words, picture captions, diagrams, and charts that provide valuable information. Modeling how to interpret the information is important because children often skip over these features.

5E model of instruction—"The 5E model of instruction is a variation on the learning cycle model, pioneered by the Biological Sciences Curriculum Study (BSCS 1993). The five Es of the model are *engage, explore, explain, elaborate,* and *evaluate. Engage* refers to beginning instruction with something that both catches students' attention and helps them relate what is to come with what they already know. *Explore* is virtually identical with the exploration phase of the learning cycle, as *explain* is the concept- or term-introduction phase and *elaborate* is the application phase. *Evaluation* is both formative and summative since it helps determine whether instruction should continue or whether students need more time and teaching to learn the unit's key points." (Colburn 2003, p. 23)

Frayer model—A Frayer model is one of several organizers that can help learners activate prior knowledge, organize thinking, understand the essential characteristics of concepts, and see relationships among concepts. It can be used for prereading, for assessment, or for summarizing or reviewing material. See also *K-W-L chart, O-W-L chart, T-chart, semantic map,* and *personal vocabulary list.* See Chapters 6 and 16 for examples.

Genre—Picture books are a genre in themselves, but in this text, genre refers to types of picture books: storybooks, non-narrative information book, narrative information books, and dual-purpose books.

Guided inquiry activity—"In a guided inquiry activity, the teacher gives students only the problem to investigate (and the materials to use for the investigation). Students must figure out how to answer the investigation's question and then generalize from the data collected." (Colburn 2003, pp. 20–21)

Inquiry—"Historically, discussions of inquiry generally have fallen within two broad classes. Sometimes people talk about inquiry as describing what scientists do and sometimes as a teaching and learning process. Authors of the *National Science Education Standards* (NRC 1996) seemed to recognize this dichotomy:

Scientific inquiry refers to the diverse ways in which scientists study the natural world and propose explanations based on the evidence derived from their work. Inquiry also refers to the activities of students in which they develop knowledge and understanding of scientific ideas, as well as an understanding of how scientists study the natural world. [emphasis added] (23)

"To make this distinction less confusing, people also sometimes use the phrase 'inquiry-based instruction.' This term refers to the creation of a classroom where students are engaged in (essentially) open-ended, student-centered, hands-on activities. This means that students must make at least some decisions about what they are doing and what their work means—thinking along the way.

"While most people in the science education community would probably think of inquiry as hands-on, it's also true that many educators would 'count' as inquiry any activity where students are analyzing real-life data—even if the information were simply given to students on paper, without any hands-on activity on their part.

"As readers can begin to see, inquiry and inquiry-based instruction represent ideas with broad definitions and occasional disagreements about their meaning. Two people advocating inquiry-based instruction may not be advocating for the same methods! Some define 'inquiry' (instruction) in terms of open-ended, hands-on instruction; others define the term in terms of formally teaching students inquiry skills (trying to teach students how to observe or make hypotheses, for example); and some define inquiry so broadly as to represent any hands-on activity." (Colburn 2003, pp. 19–20)

K-W-L chart—A K-W-L chart ("What I <u>K</u>now, What I <u>W</u>ant to Know, What I <u>L</u>earned") is one of several organizers that can help learners activate prior knowledge, organize their thinking, understand the essential characteristics of concepts, and see relationships among concepts. It can be used for prereading, for assessment, or for summarizing or reviewing material. See also *O-W-L chart, Frayer model, T-chart, semantic map,* and *personal vocabulary list.* See Chapter 9 for an example.

Learning cycle—"Different versions of the learning cycle exist today. However, the general pattern is to begin instruction with students engaged in an activity designed to provide experience with a new idea. The idea behind this exploratory phase of the cycle is that learning of new ideas is maximized when students have had relevant, concrete experience with an idea before being formally introduced to it (Barman and Kotar 1989).

"This exploratory phase is ideally followed by a concept- or term-introduction phase. That phase generally begins with class discussion about student findings and thoughts following the previous part of the cycle. Sometimes the teacher can then go on to simply provide names for ideas that students previously discovered or experienced.

"Finally, students expand on the idea in an application phase of instruction in which they use the new idea(s) in a different context. Using a new idea in a new context is an important part of maximizing learning. In addition, some students don't begin to truly understand an idea until they've had the time to work with it for a while, in different ways. The learning cycle model provides these students with time and opportunities that help them learn.

"Ideally, the application phase of the cycle also introduces students to a new idea. In this sense, the application phase of one learning cycle is also the exploratory phase of another learning cycle—hence the 'cycle' part of 'learning cycle.' (Notice that the previous sentence began with the word 'ideally'; sometimes it's difficult for an application phase activity to also encourage students to explore other ideas.)" (Colburn 2003, p. 22)

Misconceptions—"[L]earners always bring preconceived ideas with them to the classroom about how the world works. Misconceptions, in the field of science education, are preconceived ideas that differ from those currently accepted by the scientific community. Educators use a variety of phrases synonymously with 'misconceptions,' including 'naive conceptions,' 'prior conceptions,' 'alternate conceptions,' and 'preconceptions.' Many people have interviewed students to discover commonly held scientific ideas (Driver, Guesne, and Tiberghien 1985; Osborne and Freyberg 1985)." (Colburn 2003, p. 59)

Narrative information books—Narrative information books communicate a se-quence of factual events over time and sometimes recount the events of a specific case to generalize to all cases. Teachers should establish a purpose for reading so students focus on the science content rather than the storyline. Teachers may want to read the book through one time for the aesthetic components and a second time for specific science content.

National Science Education Standards—"The National Science Education Standards were published in 1996, after a lengthy commentary period from many interested citizens and groups . . .

"The Standards were designed to be achievable by all students, no matter their background or characteristics. . . .

"Beside standards for science content and for science teaching, the *National Science Education Standards* includes standards for professional development for science teachers, science education programs, and even science education systems. Finally, the document also addresses what some consider the bottom line for educational reform—standards for assessment in science education.

"Although the information in the *National Science Education Standards* is often written in a rather general manner, the resulting document provides a far-reaching and generally agreed upon comprehensive starting place for people interested in changing the U.S. science educational system." (Colburn 2003, pp. 81–82)

Non-narrative information books—Factual texts that introduce a topic, describe the attributes of the topic, or describe typical events that occur. The focus is on the subject matter, not specific characters. The vocabulary is typically technical, and readers can enter the text at any point in the book.

Open inquiry activity—"Open inquiry, in many ways, is analogous to doing science. Problem-based learning and science fair activities are often open inquiry experiences for students.

Basically, in an open inquiry activity students must figure out pretty much everything. They determine questions to investigate, procedures to address their questions, data to generate, and what the data mean." (Colburn 2003, p. 21)

O-W-L chart—An O-W-L chart ("Observations, Wonderings, Learnings") is one of several organizers that can help learners activate prior knowledge, organize their thinking, understand the essential characteristics of concepts, and see relationships among concepts. It can be used for prereading, for assessment, or for summarizing or reviewing material. See also *K-W-L chart, Frayer model, T-chart, semantic map*, and *personal vocabulary list*. See Chapters 10 and 11 for examples.

Pairs read—In a pairs read, one learner reads aloud, while the other listens and then summarizes the main idea. Benefits include increased reader involvement, attention, and collaboration and students who become more independent learners.

Personal vocabulary list—A personal vocabulary list is one of several organizers that can help learners activate prior knowledge, organize their thinking, understand the essential characteristics of concepts, and see relationships among concepts. It can be used for prereading, for assessment, or for summarizing or reviewing material. See also *K-W-L chart, O-W-L chart, Frayer model, T-chart*, and *semantic map*. See Chapter 19 for a variation of a personal vocabulary list.

Reading aloud—Being read to builds knowledge for success in reading and increases interest in reading and literature and in overall academic achievement. See Chapter 2 for more on reading aloud, including 10 tips on how to do it.

Reading comprehension strategies—The six key reading comprehension strategies featured in *Strategies That Work* (Harvey and Goudvis 2000) are *making connections, question-*ing, visualizing, inferring, determining importance, and synthesizing. See Chapter 2 for fuller explanations.

Rereading—Nonfiction text is often full of unfamiliar ideas and difficult vocabulary. Rereading content for clarification is an essential skill of proficient readers, and you should model this frequently. Rereading for a different purpose can aid comprehension. For example, a teacher might read aloud for enjoyment and then revisit the text to focus on science content.

Semantic map—A semantic map is one of several organizers that can help learners activate prior knowledge, organize their thinking, understand the essential characteristics of concepts, and see relationships among concepts. It can be used for prereading, for assessment, or for summarizing or reviewing material. See also *K-W-L chart, O-W-L chart, Frayer model, T-chart*, and *personal vocabulary list*. See Chapter 8 for an example.

Sketch to stretch—Learners pause briefly to reflect on the text and do a comprehension self-assessment by drawing on paper the images they visualize in their heads during reading. Teachers should have students use pencils so they understand the focus should be on collecting their thoughts rather than creating a piece of art. You may want to use a timer.

Stop and jot—Learners stop and think about the reading and then jot down a thought. If they use sticky notes, the notes can be added to a whole-class chart to connect past and future learning.

Storybooks—Storybooks center on specific characters who work to resolve a conflict or problem. The major purpose of stories is to entertain. The vocabulary is typically commonsense, everyday language. A storybook can spark interest in a science topic and move students toward informational texts to answer questions inspired by the story.

Structured inquiry activity—"In a structured inquiry activity, the teacher gives students a (usually) hands-on problem they are to investigate, and the methods and materials to use for the investigation, but not expected outcomes. Students are to discover a relationship and generalize from data collected.

"The main difference between a structured inquiry activity and verification lab (or 'cookbook activity') lies in what students do with the data they generate. In structured inquiry activities, students are largely responsible for figuring out what the data might mean—that is, they analyze and interpret the data. Students may ultimately interpret the data differently; different students may come to somewhat different conclusions. In a verification lab, on the other hand, all students are expected to arrive at the same conclusion—there's a definite right answer that students are supposed to be finding during the lab activity." (Colburn 2003, p. 20)

T-chart—A T-chart is one of several organizers that can help learners activate prior knowledge, organize their thinking, understand the essential characteristics of concepts, and see relationships among concepts. It can be used for prereading, for assessment, or for summarizing or reviewing material. See also *K-W-L chart, O-W-L chart, Frayer model, semantic map,* and *personal vocabulary list.* See Chapters 6, 12, and 14 for examples.

Think-pair-share—Learners pair up with a partner to share ideas, explain concepts in their own words, or tell about a connection they have to the book. This method allows each child to be involved as either a talker or a listener.

Word sorts—Word sorts help learners understand the relationships among key concepts and help teach classification. Used as a prereading activity, they can reveal misconceptions. In an *open sort,* learners sort the words into categories of their own making. In a *closed sort,* the teacher gives learners the categories for sorting.

References

Barman, C. R., and M. Kotar. 1989. The learning cycle. *Science and Children* (April): 30–32.

Biological Sciences Curriculum Study (BSCS). 1993. *Developing biological literacy.* Dubuque, IA: Kendall/Hunt.

Brooks, J. G., and M. G. Brooks, 1993. *In search of understanding: The case for constructivist classrooms.* Alexandria, VA: Association for Supervision and Curriculum Development.

Colburn, A. 2003. *The lingo of learning: 88 education terms every science teacher should know.* Arlington, VA: NSTA Press.

Driver, R., E. Guesne and A. Tiberghien. 1985. *Children's ideas in science.* Buckingham, England: Open University Press.

Harvey, S., and A. Goudvis. 2000. *Strategies that work: Teaching comprehension to enhance understanding.* York, ME: Stenhouse Publishers

Matthews, M. R. 1994. *Science teaching: The role of history and philosophy of science.* New York: Routledge.

National Research Council (NRC). 1996. *National science education standards.* Washington, DC: National Academy Press. Available online at *http://books.nap.edu/html/nsts/html/index.html.*

Osborne, R., and P. Freyberg. 1985. *Learning in science.* Portsmouth, NH: Heinemann.

Index

*Page numbers in **boldface** type refer to tables or illustrations.*